The Essentials of
PROJECT
MANAGEMENT

The Business Literacy for HR Professionals Series

The Business Literacy for HR Professionals series educates human resource professionals in the principles, practices, and processes of business and management. Developed in conjunction with the Society for Human Resource Management, these books provide a comprehensive overview of the concepts, skills, and tools HR professionals need to be influential partners in developing and executing organizational strategy. Drawing on rich content from Harvard Business School Publishing and the Society for Human Resource Management, each volume is closely reviewed by a content expert as well as by senior HR professionals. Whether you are aspiring to the executive level in your organization or already in a leadership position, these authoritative books provide the basic business knowledge you need to play a strategic role.

Other books in the series:

The Essentials of Corporate Communications and Public Relations
The Essentials of Finance and Budgeting
The Essentials of Managing Change and Transition
The Essentials of Negotiation
The Essentials of Power, Influence, and Persuasion
The Essentials of Strategy

BUSINESS LITERACY FOR HR PROFESSIONALS

The Essentials of PROJECT MANAGEMENT

Harvard Business School Press
Boston, Massachusetts
and
the Society for Human Resource Management
Alexandria, Virginia

10 09 08 07 06   5 4 3 2 1

ISBN-13: 978-1-59139-924-7

Library of Congress Cataloging-in-Publication Data forthcoming

Contents

Introduction

Project management is an important tool of modern HR management, particularly for big projects, unique ones, and projects that require many skills and players. But what is project management, exactly? We define *project management* as the allocation, tracking, and utilization of resources to achieve a particular objective within a specified period of time. This form of management focuses on the characteristic activities of a *project*—namely, a set of activities that (1) aims to produce a unique deliverable and (2) has clear beginning and ending points. The act of designing a new performance management system, for example, fits this definition of a project. Its deliverable may be defined as a unique set of performance metrics and processes for establishing targets and comparing actual performance against those targets. Once those metrics and processes have been defined, the project ends; responsibility for using the new system is handed over to department or business unit leaders with guidance from the human resource department.

Why has it become more important than ever for HR professionals to master the art of project management? Thanks to rapid change and the pressures of intense competition, more and more organizational work has become project work. Changes in technology and in customer preferences have made work less routine and less repeatable—presenting new challenges to business departments geared to daily routines. At the same time, competitive pressures have forced enterprises to do their work more quickly.

Naturally, getting a project to deliver on time, within budget, and in line with quality standards requires savvy management. And the bigger the project, the more challenging good management becomes. A project manager in any function—whether HR, marketing, operations, or another part of the company—is expected to transform a vague concept into a measurable outcome by channeling a broad array of knowledge, skills, and resources toward a critical organizational goal. Thus, talented project managers help organizations get big, important jobs done. By strengthening your project management skills, you can generate valuable benefits for your organization, including the following:

- **Achieving crucial results.** You ensure that results meet team, department, and strategic business objectives.

- **Getting things done on time, within budget, and according to quality standards.** Thus, you add predictability to the business.

- **Minimizing development time.** By finding ways to deliver on objectives within reasonable planning horizons, you help your company avoid business-cycle risk.

- **Using resources effectively.** Sound project management saves money and makes the best possible use of valuable employees' time.

Given these benefits, it's not surprising that project management techniques are being applied to a wide array of efforts—everything from major HR initiatives, construction jobs, and the development of military and commercial aircraft to e-commerce site construction, motion pictures, and charity drives. Even political campaign managers use project management techniques to boost their clients' chances of getting into office.

Origins

The goal setting, organizing, planning, and managing that lie at the heart of project management are nothing new. They were surely practiced in one form or another in the distant past. Indeed, the grand constructions of the ancient world—Egypt's pyramids, Rome's monumental buildings and road and water systems—have most of the hallmarks characterizing modern-day projects. None of these efforts would have been completed without substantial engineering, financing, human labor, and, yes, management. Likewise, the late nineteenth century saw waves of projects of unprecedented complexity and scope: the first skyscrapers, continent-spanning railroads, and the construction of massive steam-powered ships.

But despite the long history of project management, only relatively recently have people sought to document the process. By the early twentieth century, innovators in the field of civil engineering began to think more systematically about their work. They started listening to advocates of scientific management, and by the 1930s, some techniques applied by contemporary professional project managers came into use. For example, Hoover Dam, built between 1931 and 1935, made extensive use of a graphic planning tool developed by Henry Laurence Gantt—the now familiar Gantt chart. And during World War II, the Manhattan Project developed the first nuclear weapon using project management techniques. In the late 1950s, DuPont, aided by the computing technology of Remington Rand Univac, applied the now familiar critical-path methodology to the job of coordinating complex plant operation and maintenance. At roughly the same time, the consulting firm of Booz Allen Hamilton was working with the U.S. Navy to create Program Evaluation and Review Technique (PERT). The charts and schedules associated with PERT played an integral role in the Navy's development of the enormously complex Polaris nuclear submarine program.

Since those formative years, project management techniques have diffused from their origins in civil engineering, construction, and the defense industry to many other fields—including HR and other vital business functions. Perhaps your company has created a project to install enterprise resource planning software, to develop an e-commerce site, or to create an employee orientation or mentoring program. Some companies, in fact, structure themselves around sets of major projects. Instead of organizing their activities based on conventional departments (finance, marketing, etc.), these companies subsume those functions within the handful of key projects that define their businesses. Microsoft is one such company. Although it has traditional departments, Microsoft's project organizations (Office, Windows, etc.) drive the company's success and define how it operates much more than its traditional departments do.

Growing Professionalism

As HR professionals have played an increasingly central role in generating strategic value for their organizations, their project management skills have likewise grown more essential than ever. In many companies, the HR group manages a wide range of major projects that contribute directly to the organization's success. These include setting up an HR department, conducting legal compliance audits, developing employee handbooks and orientation and mentoring programs, implementing human resource information systems, and outsourcing HR activities. Additional examples of project-related work in HR include assisting with mergers and acquisitions, managing a reduction in force or restructuring, facilitating companywide cultural transformation, and developing a crisis management or disaster recovery plan. All of these efforts qualify as projects—and they must be managed skillfully if they are to succeed.

Given the diffusion of project management techniques among companies in a wide range of industries, it is not surprising that HR and other business leaders are getting better and better at planning and structuring work. Those techniques have also become the focus of numerous training courses, consulting services, and certification programs.

This increasing professionalism of project management can be seen in the growth of its supporting organizations. The Netherlands-based International Project Management Association (www.ipma.ch), for example, has chapters located throughout western Europe and Russia and in a number of developing countries. The organization provides training, holds conferences on project management issues, and sponsors technical publications. Meanwhile, the Project Management Institute (www.pmi.org), headquartered in the United States near Philadelphia, boasts more than a hundred thousand members in 125 countries around the world. The institute sponsors research and publications and maintains a rigorous examination-based certification program to advance the project management profession. It supports research aimed at expanding the body of knowledge on project management and provides training through periodic seminars and online courses.

The only dark side to increased professionalism and consensus on how projects should be managed is this: it is very hard to spell out everything about a project in advance. The future unfolds in surprising ways as a project team moves forward. That is particularly true in fast-moving industries. Every book on this subject will tell you that project managers must prepare themselves for surprises and that they need to design plans that are sufficiently flexible to accommodate those surprises. Thus, project managers must pay careful attention to risk management—the part of project management that attempts to anticipate and plan for what can go wrong. What if a training program prototype fails? What if your internal customers' requirements change before you finish that information system project? Effective project managers develop contingency plans to deal with such risks.

Unfortunately, no one can anticipate all the things that might go wrong on a project. Nor can we foresee all the opportunities we will encounter along our journey—opportunities we should take advantage of by scrapping our old plan and adopting a new one. The thing is, once a project team agrees on plans and schedules and sets them down in planning documents, those plans and schedules often become untouchable. People who deviate from the plans or fail to deliver on time and within budget risk losing favor with other team members and with managers and executives overseeing the project.

In making plans and schedules untouchable, business leaders sometimes unwittingly foster dysfunctional behavior in which project team members sweep problems under the rug and ignore or cast out individuals who sound the alarm that trouble's brewing. This is not unusual. Everyone with substantial experience in business can point to one or another project that, on the surface, appeared to be on track—only to fail in the final stretch because people feared revealing known problems. Such problems invariably come home to roost in the project's final weeks or months, when it's too late to do anything about them. We'll address this behavioral problem at two points in this book, where we discuss the need to balance planning and adaptation. Project managers must learn to fulfill expectations formed at the beginning of a project *and* make midcourse adjustments as needed.

What You'll Find in This Book

Like other books in the Business Literacy for HR Professionals series, this one is not designed to make you an expert, nor will it lead you through lengthy academic research. Instead, it provides the action-oriented advice you need to quickly become more effective in your role as an HR practitioner. It addresses the two essential aspects of the subject: (1) the techniques of project management (design, planning, execution, etc.) and (2) the many team-specific issues that are crucial for success. The team component of project management is of critical importance, yet many books overlook it.

Chapter 1 sets the stage by explaining the benefits of honing your project management skills, introducing the world of HR project management, and identifying key challenges unique to managing HR projects. The chapter concludes with a list of the defining characteristics of effective HR project managers.

Chapter 2 introduces you to the big picture, briefly describing the four processes involved in project work: defining and organizing the project, planning, managing project execution, and closing down the project once the job is done. Subsequent chapters describe those processes in much greater detail.

Chapter 3 reveals the cast of characters typically involved in project work: the sponsor, project manager, team leaders, and team members. Each player has roles and responsibilities, and they are spelled out here.

The next chapter, chapter 4, takes a leaf from the operating manual for team-based work. Like every team, a project needs a charter that states what it will do, the time frame in which it will operate, the resources at its disposal, and the deliverables expected by the sponsor and other key stakeholders. In the absence of a signed charter, the project team cannot be certain of its objectives or the expectation of stakeholders. Worse, at the end of the road, the sponsor might say, "That's not what I meant!" It happens.

Once it has its charter, a project is ready to roll. But not so fast. Internal operating issues must be addressed and agreed to. These include how decisions will be made, a method of keeping track of unresolved questions, a plan for communicating with project members and stakeholders, and so forth. Such internal issues are covered in chapter 5.

Chapter 6 introduces one of the foundational techniques of project management: work breakdown structure (WBS). You cannot plan a project if you don't have a firm grasp on this technique. WBS decomposes a project into a set of manageable, bite-sized tasks, with an estimate of the time and money needed to complete each.

If you take care to think of everything that must be done to meet your objective, you will be ready for chapter 7, on scheduling the work. Scheduling begins with understanding the dependencies that exist between the tasks defined through WBS. Dependencies matter. For example, when you get ready for work in the morning, it's best to take a shower *before* getting dressed. Wouldn't you agree? And when you do get dressed, it's wise to put on your socks before you put on your shoes. Handling those tasks in the wrong order would create quite a mess. It's the same with project tasks; some must wait until others are completed—or partially completed. Others can be done in parallel. You'll learn about task dependencies in chapter 7, and you'll also read about how you can use that knowledge to schedule tasks using project tools such as Gantt and PERT charts. The important issue of the critical path is also explained.

Work breakdown structure and scheduling often uncover discrepancies between what is possible and what is specified in the charter or expected by the stakeholders. You may, for example, have a boss who insists on project completion within four months with a budget of $200,000. If satisfactory completion under the existing terms is impossible, trade-offs and adjustments—the subject of chapter 8—will have to be made.

Chapter 9 is about managing risk. Project planning involves the future, which is bound to contain surprises and setbacks. What are the major risks facing your project? Will the scientific staff fail to produce a working prototype on schedule? What would happen if a key supplier went out of business or delivered substandard materials? This chapter will show you how to identify your risks, take actions to avoid or minimize their impact, and develop contingency plans.

The subject of risk is continued in chapter 10, but here the focus is on the risks that you cannot reasonably identify or anticipate. This chapter proposes an adaptive project management approach as a solution. That approach emphasizes small incremental steps followed by evaluation and adjustment, fast cycles, early value delivery, and rapid learning by project team members.

Chapter 11 is about two preparatory details that must be tended to: the all-important project launch and team-based work. The launch section explains the why and how of project launch meetings. This meeting must signal the beginning of an important endeavor—one that is aligned with the organization's highest goals and from which all participants will benefit. It should also provide clear evidence that top management supports the project and its people. The next section of chapter 11 is a primer on the basics of team-based work. It explains how project leadership must establish norms of behavior, such as meeting attendance, how to give and receive feedback, the importance of confidentiality, and so forth. Unless people understand how to work as a team, success is unlikely.

Chapter 12 tells project managers and team leaders how they can maintain control and keep people's work on track. When resources are finite and deadlines are fixed, they cannot allow individuals and work teams to operate willy-nilly and without coordination. Everyone must work toward the same goals. Some of the means of maintaining project control offered in this chapter include pacing spending through budgets, turning time-wasting conflict to collaboration, communicating effectively, and clearing away problems

Chapter 13 addresses the fourth and final phase of project management: the closedown. Closedown is almost as important as the project launch. It is the point at which the team delivers its results to the sponsor and stakeholders, thanks people for their contributions, celebrates, documents its work, and then attempts to learn from the experience. Of these steps, learning may be the most important. People must answer the question, If we could start over again tomorrow, what would we change? They will take that answer—and its lessons—to their next projects. And make no mistake, there will be future projects.

In chapter 14, we examine the unique challenges in managing a wide variety of HR projects that you'll most likely champion and lead directly. These projects include starting an HR department, conducting a legal compliance audit, developing an employee handbook, designing an employee orientation and mentoring program, implementing a human resource information system, creating an employee expatriation program, and outsourcing HR processes. You'll also find suggestions for winning other executives' support for an HR project you're proposing.

Chapter 15 shifts focus to high-level projects that have significant HR implications—and in which you must play a strong supporting role. Such projects include developing a crisis management and recovery plan, assisting with mergers and acquisitions, managing a downsizing initiative, facilitating cultural change in your organization, and realigning your company's performance appraisal system.

The book closes with chapter 16—which summarizes key principles and practices in HR project management, explains how you can extract lessons from every HR project and apply them to subsequent projects, and offers ideas for further enhancing your project management expertise.

The back matter of this book contains four items you may find useful. The first, in appendix A, is a set of project management worksheets. The second item, in appendix B, is "A Guide to Effective Meetings." Projects generally require lots of meetings. Most conscientious people dislike meetings, and rightly so, since many meetings are time wasters. But meetings are essential, and effectively run meetings get things done. They aren't time wasters. This short guide will help you prepare for meetings, run them effectively, and follow up for better results.

Another helpful item is a glossary of terms. Every discipline has its special vocabulary, and project management is no exception. When you see a word italicized in the text, that's your cue that the word is defined in the glossary.

Finally, "For Further Reading" identifies books, articles, and on-line tools that can tell you more about topics covered in this book. If you want to dig deeper into any aspects of project management, these supplemental sources are readily available.

The content of this book draws heavily on a number of books, articles, and online publications of the Society for Human Resource Management (SHRM) and Harvard Business School Publishing—in particular, the project management and leading teams modules of Harvard ManageMentor, an online service (http://elearning.hbsp .org). All other sources are noted with standard endnote citations.

The Essentials of
PROJECT
MANAGEMENT

CHAPTER ONE

Project Management and the HR Professional

A Key Competency

Key Topics Covered in This Chapter

- *Why developing your project management skills is more important than ever*

- *A tour through the world of HR project management*

- *Typical challenges you may face while managing projects*

- *Hallmarks of an effective HR project manager*

CONGRATULATIONS! By deciding to read this book, you've taken an important step in strengthening your HR project management skills. An HR professional who masters the art of project management generates enormous benefits for his or her organization and career—something you'll learn more about in this chapter. But to create those benefits, you need to familiarize yourself with the wide world of HR project management and the typical obstacles human resource practitioners often face while managing key projects. You'll find sections in this chapter that explore the many types of HR projects you may encounter during your career, as well as descriptions of the major challenges you can expect to face. You'll also discover the hallmarks of an effective HR project manager—and a self-assessment that helps you gauge how you measure up. Finally, the chapter provides a multiple-choice questionnaire that lets you test your current knowledge about HR project management, complete with an answer key and pointers to specific book chapters of interest for each question.

With this preview in mind, let's get started!

Why Develop Your Project Management Skills?

Developing strong project management skills goes hand in hand with several other fundamental HR competencies you must possess in order to support your company's goals. When you know how to manage projects skillfully, you strengthen the following four core competencies:

1. **Strategic contribution.** Making a strategic contribution means helping position your company ahead of its rivals and meet its

stakeholders' demands. It also means providing your organization with a sustainable competitive advantage, as well as ensuring that the various parts of the company are all pulling in the
same direction defined by the executive team. (For more information on the HR practitioners' strategic role, see *The Essentials of Strategy,* another volume in this series.)

Often, skillful management of culture-related projects can
enable an HR professional to make these vital strategic contributions. For example, perhaps you've determined that in order to
carry out its corporate strategy, your company needs an organizational culture marked by qualities such as innovative thinking,
a willingness to take risks, an ability to work well in teams, and a
genuine passion for serving customers. Such attitudes, abilities,
values, and work habits all determine a company's culture.

To make a strategic contribution through culture management, you may initiate and orchestrate any number of projects.
For example, you might set out to diagnose your company's
current overall culture or a particular department's or unit's
culture. Or perhaps you would design an initiative to communicate the corporate strategy throughout your organization and
convey the work habits and attitudes necessary for people to
succeed. Other culture-related projects might include setting up
processes that enable employees to have more direct and meaningful contact with customers, establishing a performance management program that rewards new types of behaviors and
assigns consequences to poor performance, and training managers to help their employees feel more comfortable taking risks
and adopting a more entrepreneurial spirit. Of all the activities
that define your role, culture management may well exert the
greatest impact on your firm's overall business performance.

2. **Personal credibility.** Establishing your personal credibility constitutes another key HR competency that you can strengthen through
successful project management. When you build your personal
credibility, you are seen as competent, trustworthy, and valuable in
the eyes of your fellow executives and the line managers and other
internal customers you serve. The higher others' perceptions of

your credibility, the more invitations and opportunities you receive to participate in important strategy-related decisions and debates.

So how does good project management help you improve your personal credibility? Put simply, it enables you to achieve results. When you successfully manage important projects, you build a track record of generating valued results for your company. People conclude that you can be relied on to meet your commitments, perform accurate work, and demonstrate high integrity. And—not surprisingly—they'll eagerly look forward to collaborating with you on future efforts.

3. **HR delivery.** As an HR professional, it's vital that you effectively carry out a specific set of activities to serve your internal customers. These activities include managing staffing; developing executives', managers', and employees' skills; and designing needed organizational structures (such as cross-functional teams and new reporting relationships). Additional, equally important activities include measuring the business value generated by your HR activities, ensuring that your organization complies with local and national laws, and creating effective performance management systems.

   For each of these HR deliverables, you can initiate and manage numerous projects. Consider staffing. Projects related to staffing might include an analysis of the gap between your company's staffing needs and current staffing, an initiative designed to improve recruiting or reduce turnover, and management of a reduction in force or the blending of two workforces during a merger. Meanwhile, projects supporting your legal compliance duties might include a compliance audit. And projects corresponding to development might include a new-employee orientation or mentoring program, an executive education curriculum, and a training program designed to help employees master a new technology platform.

   Every time you successfully carry out a project related to any of these core HR deliverables, you further enhance the operational and strategic value you provide your company.

4. **HR technology.** Technology is playing an increasingly prominent role in today's workplace and has become an important

vehicle through which you and other HR professionals deliver value. When you know how to leverage technology, you not only provide faster service to your internal clients on a global scale; you also reduce the costs associated with HR transactions. And you free up time to focus further on making a strategic contribution rather than investing energy in administrative activities.

A wide range of technology-related projects, properly managed, can help you seize advantage of the benefits that technology has to offer. Such projects may include any of the following: establishing a Web site through which job candidates can review and apply for available positions; automating the tracking of individuals through the employment cycle; creating a system that enables employees to enroll in benefits programs and modify their benefits preferences through online self-service; and adopting a software application that facilitates 360-degree online evaluations or that enables employees to fill out surveys online and you to tabulate their responses quickly and easily.

As with establishing personal credibility and improving your HR delivery, managing technology-related projects effectively can help you make important strategic contributions in your organization.[1]

Of course, honing your project management skills not only benefits your company; it also benefits you. How? As one expert pointed out, successfully managed projects often become stepping-stones to promotions.[2] Handling projects deftly also gives many people a profound and satisfying sense of accomplishment. In addition, it lends variety to your workday—because no two projects are completely identical. Finally, when you skillfully guide a key project to its completion, you sweeten the odds of effecting important change across your entire organization—further deepening your sense of personal achievement.

With these benefits in mind, let's now take a tour through the world of HR project management—that vast landscape featuring projects of every size and shape. We'll take a closer look at several particularly core HR projects later in this book. But at this point in your reading, you may find it helpful to gain an overall sense of the range of HR projects you will likely encounter during your career.

The World of HR Project Management

The types of projects you need to manage as an HR professional are
hugely varied. Moreover, in addition to managing HR-specific projects (such as developing a human resource information system), you
may often need to manage or play a key role in projects initiated by
non-HR leaders (such as handling HR issues during a merger or
acquisition). In other words, while you'll be leading your own HR-
related projects, you can also expect to play an important supporting
part in non-HR business initiatives as well.

Common HR Project Management Opportunities

Below are brief descriptions of common HR-specific projects:

- **Starting an HR department.** Do you work for a small, growing company? Are you employed by a large corporation that is
  decentralizing HR throughout its divisions? In either case, you
  may find yourself needing to establish an HR department—
  either for your company overall or for your division. To successfully carry out this project, you'll want to establish a mission
  for your new HR department that supports the company's
  mission, to decide whether the department will play more of an
  administrative or strategic role, and to orchestrate numerous
  additional details.

- **Conducting a legal compliance audit.** In an environment
  that's becoming ever more complex in terms of legal and regulatory compliance, it's no surprise that the HR legal compliance
  audit has taken on increasing value. While handling this project,
  you'll want to review all aspects of human resources—including
  recruitment and selection, compensation, labor agreements, record keeping, and many others—to ensure that your company is
  adhering to government regulations and its own policies.

- **Developing an employee handbook.** A well-prepared employee handbook enables you to clearly communicate important
  information to employees about company products, customers,

values, mutual responsibilities, and policies and procedures. In creating an employee handbook, you'll need to make decisions about what level of detail to include, which terminology to use, and how you'll distribute the handbook. You'll also want to pull together information on standard topics included in such documents—such as legal issues (drug screening, employer and employee rights, etc.), benefits, career development, organizational philosophy, and matters concerning the organizational environment (such as rules about solicitation and emergency procedures).

- **Developing an employee orientation or mentoring program.** A well-designed employee orientation or mentoring program can strongly influence how quickly new hires get familiar with the company's culture and mission, master their job responsibilities, and form productive relationships with colleagues. Related project tasks might include preparing content to deliver during an employee orientation session, scheduling regular orientation sessions, assigning mentors to new hires, and establishing a system for ensuring that mentor-protégé relationships are working as planned.

- **Implementing a human resource information system (HRIS).** As you might imagine, implementing an HRIS can be a complex, daunting project. You'll need to identify and document the objectives of the new system, decide which components are "must have" versus "nice to have," seek the advice of other professionals who have carried out major implementations, select team members who will execute the work, decide how to provide end-user training on the new system, and manage numerous other activities.

- **Developing an employee expatriation program.** With increasing globalization of business, more and more companies are sending employees and their families to other countries for short- or long-term assignments. Developing a program for employee expatriation (and repatriation after an assignee returns to the home office) entails managing several important activities. These include determining the personal and professional qualities ⁿᵒww

---

overseas assignees must demonstrate, providing assignees with mentors, managing the risks (cultural misunderstandings, financial problems) inherent in the assignment, preparing assignees and their families for the transition, evaluating the success of the assignment when expats return, and so forth.

- **Outsourcing HR activities.** Many companies outsource some, most, or even all HR activities to support their competitive strategies. A skillfully managed outsourcing project can provide long-term efficiencies and cost savings. It can also help in-house HR leaders focus on their core strategic competencies rather than on benefits administration and other activities that can be done less expensively and more efficiently by a service provider. To manage an outsourcing project, you'll need to identify HR areas that could benefit from third-party assistance, assess potential savings and efficiencies of outsourcing, solicit and evaluate bids and project proposals from service providers, help managers and employees make the transition from the old to the new system, and orchestrate many other tasks.

Other Projects Where HR May Play a Key Role

Clearly, HR-specific projects take a wide variety of forms. Non-HR projects in which you play a major supporting or leading role also show immense variety. Here are brief descriptions of some of the more common projects you may get involved in:

- **Assisting with a merger or acquisition.** Many companies use mergers or acquisitions to spur their growth and obtain the expertise and assets they need to carry out their strategy. As an HR professional, you may be called on to manage or support projects related to a merger or acquisition. Such projects may include integrating HR departments from two merged companies into one entity, preparing an assessment of your company's human capital to increase the perceived value of your organization in the eyes of a potential acquirer, integrating new employees from a company your firm has merged with or acquired, and helping current workers maintain their productivity and morale during the stress and uncertainty of a merger or acquisition.

- **Managing a downsizing initiative, reduction in force, or restructuring.** During a downsizing initiative, reduction in force, or corporate restructuring, you'll need to draw heavily on your project management skills to ensure that the initiative delivers the promised benefits. Leading or supporting such a project often entails numerous activities—such as communicating the goals of the change to the workforce in ways that maintain morale and productivity, helping managers identify candidates for termination, providing job search services and counseling for laid-off workers, deciding which employees can be redeployed versus terminated, and so forth.

- **Facilitating organization-wide cultural change.** Helping your company transform its culture is no simple task. But by making savvy use of your project management abilities, you can make a major contribution to this important effort. Your project activities may include designing a survey instrument to diagnose the company's current culture, defining the cultural changes needed to support your organization's mission and strategy, revising incentive programs to encourage new behaviors and work habits, creating communication programs that help managers and employees understand and embrace the need for cultural change, and many other tasks.

- **Creating a crisis management or disaster recovery plan.** Today, the threat of terrorism has joined natural disasters, cyber-crime, product tampering, and other perils that drive many organizations to create plans for dealing with disaster should it strike. As an HR professional, you may be called on to either create such plans or support others who are doing so. Activities associated with such a project include brainstorming what might go wrong, identifying what crises or disasters would wreak the most damage on your company, determining which systems and processes your firm must put in place in order to prepare itself to respond quickly and effectively should a crisis occur, and designing practice routines and drills to enable managers and employees to implement the plan promptly when needed.

- **Developing a strategy-related organizational performance appraisal system.** When a company defines a new strategy, it often must reexamine its workforce's skills and knowledge to determine whether any changes are necessary. Whether you've helped formulate the new corporate strategy or not, you'll need to develop a plan for ensuring that your company's workforce delivers the performance needed to support the strategy. This project will likely entail determining the new skills and knowledge required by the strategy (such as technical expertise, product development skills, insights into customer preferences, etc.). You'll also need to decide how to acquire the needed skills and knowledge—whether through recruiting, training, or some other approach. And you may need to redesign your company's current incentive systems to reward the levels of performance required to carry out the high-level strategy.

Despite the range of variety in projects you may handle during your career, all projects—whether they're directly or indirectly related to HR—present certain challenges. We'll examine these management challenges next.

Typical Challenges in Managing HR Projects

Most project managers—regardless of the nature of their projects—encounter typical challenges. For example, perhaps you've been asked to take responsibility for an important project—but you don't have formal authority over the individuals whose cooperation you need to successfully carry out the effort. Or maybe you've been presented with an unrealistic deadline for completing the project, or you've been asked to take on a project or two in addition to your usual job responsibilities. Table 1-1 lists and defines typical challenges and offers strategies for surmounting them.

TABLE 1-1

Surmounting project management challenges

Challenge	Description	Strategies
Responsibility-versus-authority trap	The responsibility you've been given isn't commensurate with the formal authority you need to accomplish the mission.	Draw on your expertise, knowledge, and track record to influence and persuade others to support your efforts.*
Unrealistic targets	Your boss insists on a project deadline that you know is unrealistic and impossible to achieve.	Resist the temptation to develop your project schedule by starting with the imposed unrealistic finish date and working your way backward to the current date. Also, assemble evidence showing why the deadline is unrealistic. Present the situation as concisely as possible to your boss.
Territorial team members	Cross-functional project team members show more allegiance to their function than to the project.	Foster a strong sense of team identity by holding a kickoff meeting for the project, as well as communicating shared objectives and benefits of a successful project.
Serving multiple bosses	Someone other than your boss asks you to lead a project that falls outside your usual job duties. You report to the project leader and your boss.	Negotiate conflicting demands coming from both bosses. For example, "Help me here: I'm not sure what level priority this is in my current lineup of projects," or "I'd really like to meet that date, but it wouldn't be in our best interest, since the XYZ deadline takes precedence."
Juggling multiple projects	You're managing several important projects at once.	Create separate work areas and filing systems for each project so you can focus on one at a time while working on each.
Uncertainty	You have limited information on the details, available resources, and requirements of a project.	Use ranges of values instead of single figures when providing estimates on project costs and schedule.

Sources: Gary R. Heerkens, *Project Management* (New York: McGraw-Hill, 2002), 32–36; Jeff Davidson, *10 Minute Guide to Project Management* (Indianapolis: Alpha Books, 2000), Chap. 12.

*See *The Essentials of Power, Influence, and Persuasion* in this series for detailed information and recommendations.

Hallmarks of an Effective HR Project Manager

In addition to the strategies for handling typical challenges suggested in table 1-1, you'll need a diverse range of skills and knowledge to effectively manage HR projects. Some experts categorize these as follows:

- **Project management process skills.** You'll need to be familiar with and know how to use project management tools, techniques, and process technologies to create project schedules, plans, and budgets and to maintain control while the project is being executed. Maintaining control includes balancing deadlines, budgets, and quality of the work, as well as regularly monitoring progress as the project implementation unfolds.

- **Interpersonal skills.** Because managing projects requires you to get things done through other people, you need to know how to lead and motivate teams and individuals (including building team spirit); how to communicate clearly and convincingly through one-on-one conversations and meetings; and how to negotiate, influence, and delegate. You may also have to serve as a coach and mentor for some project team members.

- **Technology management skills.** Many projects have embedded technologies—processes or technologies inherent to the project. A software development project is an apt example, as is the creation of an HRIS. With such projects, you'll have to demonstrate proficiency in the embedded technology as well as supporting technologies. You'll also need to know how to prepare and interpret technical specifications, understand technical designs, and manage intellectual property.

- **Personal qualities.** To successfully manage a project, you must be able to think like a generalist—that is, to always keep the project's big picture in mind. The big picture includes the original purpose of the project, the diverse array of individuals who are contributing to and affected by the effort, and the ultimate desired outcome. In addition, you'll need a high tolerance for ambiguity, complexity, and uncertainty, as well as unassailable honesty and integrity and a willingness to be a doer, not a bystander. You should also know how to manage your time and organize your work effectively.[3]

The best project managers synthesize all of those various skills—knowing when and where to apply them while planning and executing a project. How do you measure up to these project management skills? See assessment tool 1-1 to find out. Then move on to assessment tool 1-2—which helps you take stock of your familiarity with the concepts covered in this book and points you to specific chapters of interest.

Assessment Tool 1-1
How Good a Project Manager Are You?

For each statement below, circle whether you agree or disagree. Then interpret your score using the instructions that follow.

When I'm managing a project, I . . .

1. Develop comprehensive, realistic, and clear plans, estimates, and budgets

   Agree   Disagree

2. Obtain formal approvals of project parameters (cost, schedule, etc.) as needed

   Agree   Disagree

3. Monitor progress and manage problems regularly and effectively

   Agree   Disagree

4. Anticipate problems and develop contingency plans for handling them

   Agree   Disagree

continued

5. Ensure that all relevant technical disciplines are adequately represented on the project team

   Agree   Disagree

6. Effectively communicate technical information to a wide variety of people

   Agree   Disagree

7. Ensure a rational process for selecting any required technology

   Agree   Disagree

8. Constantly assess whether use of a particular technology will help my company achieve defined business results

   Agree   Disagree

9. Seek input on project strategies and plans from multiple sources

   Agree   Disagree

10. Know how to interpret both quantitative and qualitative data

    Agree   Disagree

11. Foster a sense of shared mission and collaboration among everyone who's working on the project

    Agree   Disagree

12. Clearly define roles, responsibilities, performance expectations, and priorities

    Agree   Disagree

13. Leverage diversity among project team members

    Agree   Disagree

14. Promote the project team's visibility to upper
    management

    Agree   Disagree

15. Negotiate project parameters and solutions to problems
    fairly and effectively

    Agree   Disagree

16. Manage conflict productively

    Agree   Disagree

17. Influence and persuade others over whom I have no
    formal authority

    Agree   Disagree

18. Maintain focus and control in the face of ambiguity,
    uncertainty, and complexity

    Agree   Disagree

19. Actively seek learning opportunities that I can apply to
    future projects

    Agree   Disagree

20. Delegate tasks based on project team members' individ-
    ual skills, values, and interests

    Agree   Disagree

21. Empower team members to handle their project
    responsibilities

    Agree   Disagree

22. Provide team members with support, training, instruc-
    tions, and close guidance when needed

    Agree   Disagree

continued

23. Give team members ongoing feedback on the project's progress and invite ongoing feedback from them on my performance as project leader

   Agree   Disagree

24. Clearly identify all of the project's "customers"—the individuals who will benefit from or be affected by the effort—and clarify their needs and expectations

   Agree   Disagree

25. Get the right people involved at the right time at every stage of the project

   Agree   Disagree

26. Use formal and informal networks to move the project forward

   Agree   Disagree

27. Help project team members use their experience on the project to further their professional development

   Agree   Disagree

28. Use an open, informal, and comfortable communication style to get the information I need to keep the project on track

   Agree   Disagree

29. Improvise when unanticipated problems crop up— whether that means adjusting a portion of the project plan, getting needed resources from somewhere else, or revising my assumptions

   Agree   Disagree

30. Invest adequate time and careful thought at the outset of the project to ensure success during the implementation stage

   Agree   Disagree

Totals: Agree _____ Disagree _____

Interpreting your score:

If the total number of your "Agree" responses is:

25–30: You demonstrate many hallmarks of an effective project manager and are probably well positioned to skillfully handle your next big project.

10–24: You possess some skills required to be an effective project manager, but you could probably benefit from acquiring or strengthening additional skills. Look more closely at the statements to which you answered "Disagree." What steps might you take to strengthen those skills?

1–9: You need to strengthen your overall skills considerably in order to serve as an effective project manager. This book will help you. Consider obtaining additional help as well—whether it's a workshop on project management, additional books, or conversations with colleagues whom you know to be good project managers.

SOURCE: Adapted from Gary R. Heerkens, *Project Management* (New York: McGraw-Hill, 2002), 41–46.

Assessment Tool 1-2
Test Your Understanding of Project Management

To gauge your understanding of the concepts in this book, take the following multiple-choice test. Then review the answer key that follows, which points you to particular chapters for more information on specific aspects of HR project management.

1. **What are the main phases of managing a project?**
   A. Preparing your project budget, identifying potential risks, developing contingency plans, and executing the project.

continued

   B. Defining and organizing the project, planning the project, managing project execution, and closing down the project.

   C. Winning executive support for the project, defining roles and responsibilities, implementing the project plan, and extracting lessons learned.

   D. Clarifying desired outcomes, identifying needed resources, allocating the resources, and measuring results.

2. **Which of the following should *not* be a key criterion for membership on a project team?**
   A. Opportunity to develop professional skills.
   B. Technical skill.
   C. Problem-solving ability.
   D. Interpersonal and organizational savvy.

3. **What is the primary information provided in a project charter?**
   A. Names and contact information for all members of the project team.
   B. Roles and responsibilities of the project sponsor and each member of the project team.
   C. Project scope, the value the project should deliver to stakeholders, time frame, and available resources.
   D. A breakdown of the tasks that need to be carried out in order to deliver the project's value.

4. **You're managing a project in which time is of the essence. Which decision-making approach would best suit your project team?**
   A. Participants present and discuss ideas, and then vote. Decisions that receive more than 50 percent of the votes are adopted.
   B. Members reach agreement collectively on issues most important to them, while the team leader makes remaining decisions.

    C. Team members work toward consensus, developing and exploring new alternatives if necessary.

    D. A group of individuals with relevant experience and skills makes decisions.

5. **Which of the following questions does a work breakdown structure help you answer?**

    A. What must your project team do in order to achieve its goals?

    B. How long will the project take to complete?

    C. What will the project cost?

    D. All of the above.

6. **Which of the following project scheduling tools indicates all important task relationships and project milestones?**

    A. Gantt chart.

    B. PERT chart.

    C. Critical path.

    D. Bottleneck diagram.

7. **You realize that your project can't be realistically completed within the time frame or budget the sponsor and key stakeholders originally conceived. Which of the following would be the *best* way to resolve the dilemma?**

    A. Revisit your earlier project planning work—including reevaluating task assignments, reallocating resources, and streamlining tasks.

    B. Consider altering the project's intended deliverables.

    C. Reexamine assumptions about deadline and available resources.

    D. All of the above.

8. **You're quantifying the risk inherent in a project you're managing. What are the two factors you must consider?**

    A. Risk to your project's financial resources and risk to its human resources.

continued

B. Possible difficulties with obtaining key information or materials needed for your project and possible low quality of those supplies.

C. Potential negative impact of a possible risk and probability of the risk's occurrence.

D. Constraints on contingency plans and the financial impact of a project setback.

9. You've decided to use the adaptive management approach to handle a project that has extensive unanticipated risk. Which of the following is an adaptive management technique?

A. Strive to deliver as much value as possible at the project's conclusion.

B. Staff the project with technical experts who can gauge the ramifications of technology changes.

C. Rely heavily on decision-making tools such as return on investment and net present value.

D. Engage in small incremental tasks conducted over fast cycles.

10. You're preparing to hold a launch meeting for a project you're managing. Which of the following principles would you apply?

A. Invite all members of the project team, the project sponsor, key stakeholders, and the highest-ranking official in your organization.

B. Introduce only the core members of the project team by name.

C. Reiterate the project charter and its contents.

D. Ask project team members to explain why the project's work is important to larger organizational objectives.

11. Which of the following is *not* a mechanism for monitoring and controlling your project?

A. The project budget.

B. Quality checks.

C. Mission creep.

D. Milestones.

12. **You're closing down an HR project, and you want to evaluate the project's performance. What do you do?**

A. Assess whether the documentation that you've maintained during execution of the project is sufficiently thorough, accurate, and useful for subsequent projects.

B. Ask whether the project met its objectives, whether it was completed on time, and what it cost.

C. Invite project team members to describe what went well during execution of the project and what didn't go well.

D. Evaluate the quality of your team members' collaboration during the course of planning and implementing the project.

13. **You've decided that your company needs to implement a human resource information system (HRIS). Which of the following actions would *not* be the most effective way to win support for the project from other executives?**

A. Bring in a high-level sales representative from an HRIS software vendor to deliver a presentation on his or her company's products.

B. Cite statistics showing that more companies plan to increase spending on HR technology in the coming years.

C. Explain how implementing an HRIS would support your company's efforts to reduce costs and improve efficiencies.

D. Present market research showing the link between human capital investments and measurable business performance.

14. **As an HR professional, you may frequently need to play a role in supporting critical high-level projects.**

continued

Which of the following statements is true about such projects?

A. You will usually serve as the project sponsor on such initiatives.

B. In assisting during an acquisition, you make the most valuable contribution to the project when you're working in the company that's being acquired.

C. To help facilitate cultural change in your organization, you must first understand the defining characteristics of a positive workplace culture.

D. If your company wants to realign its performance appraisal system, it most likely intends to adopt a quality-improvement system—such as Six Sigma or the Malcolm Baldrige Award.

15. Which of the following statements about learning from your project management experiences do you consider most accurate?

A. The more complex and challenging a project is, the more lessons it offers you to apply to future projects.

B. The most versatile skill you can acquire in managing an HR project is how to use leading-edge technology, such as project management software.

C. To ensure the success of future projects, it's more valuable to cultivate relationships with past project's stakeholders (such as sponsors and internal customers) than with project resources (such as vendors and consultants).

D. Managing projects reveals important weaknesses in your skill set that you should address.

Answers to the questions

1. B. Defining and organizing the project, planning the project, managing project execution, and closing down the project.

   Chapter 2: Project Management as a Process: Four Phases

2. A. Opportunity to develop professional skills.
Chapter 3: The Cast of Characters: Who's Who in Project Management

3. C. Project scope, the value the project should deliver to stakeholders, time frame, and available resources.
Chapter 4: A Written Charter: Your Marching Orders

4. B. Members reach agreement collectively on issues most important to them, while the team leader makes remaining decisions.
Chapter 5: A Framework for Action: Important First Steps

5. D. All of the above.
Chapter 6: Work Breakdown: From Huge Job to Manageable Tasks

6. B. PERT chart.
Chapter 7: Scheduling the Work: Put the Horse Before the Cart

7. D. All of the above.
Chapter 8: Adjustments and Trade-Offs: More Fine Tuning

8. C. Potential negative impact of a possible risk, and probability of the risk's occurrence.
Chapter 9: Managing Risk: Scanning the Hazy Horizon

9. D. Engage in small incremental tasks conducted over fast cycles.
Chapter 10: Project Adaptation: Dealing with What You Cannot Anticipate

10. A. Invite all members of the project team, the project sponsor, key stakeholders, and the highest-ranking official in your organization.
Chapter 11: Getting Off on the Right Foot: Project Needs to Keep in Mind

11. C. Mission creep.
Chapter 12: Keeping on Track: Maintaining Control

continued

12. B. Whether the project met its objectives, whether it was completed on time, and what it cost.
Chapter 13: The Closedown Phase: Wrapping It Up

13. A. Bring in a high-level sales representative from an HRIS software vendor to deliver a presentation on his or her company's products.
Chapter 14: Managing Various HR Projects: Achieving Your Desired Results

14. C. To help facilitate cultural change in your organization, you must first understand the defining characteristics of a positive workplace culture.
Chapter 15: Supporting Critical High-Level Projects: HR's Vital Role

15. D. Managing projects reveals important weaknesses in your skill set that you should address.
Chapter 16: Next Steps: Honing Your Project Management Skills

Summing Up

In this chapter, you learned about the following aspects of project management as a key HR competency:

- The benefits of effective project management include helping your company achieve valuable business results and making effective use of resources, as well as building professional and personal credibility and opening new career opportunities for yourself.

- The world of HR project management includes projects specific to HR (such as setting up an HR department or establishing an HRIS) as well as projects initiated by other executives in which you'll play a supporting or leading role (such as handling aspects of a merger or acquisition).

- Typical challenges in managing any project include reporting to multiple bosses, being asked to agree to unrealistic deadlines and other project parameters, difficulties fostering a strong sense of unity and loyalty in a cross-functional project team, and other challenges.

- The hallmarks of an effective HR project manager include familiarity with project management tools and processes, interpersonal and leadership skills, knowledge of technology, and personal qualities such as the ability to tolerate ambiguity and to remain focused.

Leveraging Chapter Insights: Critical Questions

- How is the competency of project management viewed in your company? Are effective project managers valued and rewarded? If not, how might you convey the message to other executives and managers that project management constitutes a vital business skill?

- What projects do you typically manage? What is the ratio of HR-specific to non-HR-specific projects? Do you believe that ratio should be different—that is, you feel you should be handling more HR-specific projects? If so, how might you go about adjusting the ratio?

- Of the typical project management challenges described in this chapter, which do you most frequently encounter? What strategies have you used so far to surmount these challenges? What, if anything, might you do differently to handle these challenges more skillfully?

- Based on your responses in assessment tool 1-1, what is your overall level of skill as a project manager? What steps might you take to strengthen any weak areas?

CHAPTER TWO

Project Management as a Process

Four Phases

Key Topics Covered in This Chapter

- *An overview of the four phases of project management*
- *Uncovering the core issues of your project*
- *Identifying your project's stakeholders*

A S WE'VE SEEN, HR projects come in all types and
sizes. Yet the essential elements of project management
remain the same, regardless of the specific nature of the
project. You can expect to handle those elements using a four-phase
process:

1. Defining and organizing the project

2. Planning the project

3. Managing project execution

4. Closing down the project

This chapter provides an overview of that process.

Figure 2-1 represents the four phases as an integrated model. In
one sense, this model is linear: first, we define and organize the project, then we plan the work in detail, and so forth. But the reality of
project management is never that tidy. Many aspects of the project
cannot be anticipated. Some such surprises are negative—for example, a key consultant you've hired to help handle a legal compliance
audit turns out to be unavailable at the last minute, owing to a scheduling mix-up, or the printing costs associated with the employee
handbook you're developing skyrocket unexpectedly because of a
spike in paper prices.

Other surprises are positive. For instance, in the course of adopting a new HRIS, you learn of a valuable new application that has
just become available. In order to explore and possibly exploit the

FIGURE 2-1

The project management model

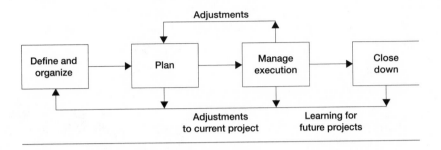

opportunity this development presents, you'll probably need to build time into your HRIS project schedule to evaluate the new application. And you may need to increase the project budget if the new application proves to be so superior to the others you've been evaluating that you decide to adopt it.

Since the project management model is not entirely linear, you need to create feedback loops and opportunities for readjustment between the four phases. Even the final phase of the model, closing down the project, has a feedback loop that informs the next project start-up. That feedback can help you learn from your experience and improve your management of future projects.

In the pages that follow, we briefly describe the four phases of project management, with details on each phase provided in subsequent chapters.

Defining and Organizing the Project

This phase has two purposes:

1. To clearly define the project's objectives as thoroughly as possible

2. To organize the right people and all necessary resources around those objectives

Defining the Objective

In Lewis Carroll's *Through the Looking-Glass,* Alice asked the Cheshire Cat, "Would you tell me, please, which way I ought to go from here?" The cat answered that the right way depended on where she wanted to go. "I don't much care where," said Alice, "as long as I get somewhere." The cat replied, "Oh, you're sure to do that, if only you walk long enough."

Obviously, you don't want to be like Alice, wandering endlessly and randomly until, by chance, you arrive at a suitable "somewhere." The best way to get where you are going is to first identify your destination. This commonsense advice seems obvious, but it's not always observed in practice. What problem is your project expected to solve? What deliverable does the rest of the executive team expect from your project team? You may have clear answers to those questions, but not everyone may agree with you. Other project team members, the stakeholders who will use the project's output, and the senior managers who will judge the success or failure of your work may have slightly different expectations. So before you begin to plan the work, make sure that everyone is singing from the same page in the hymn book. Identify the project's objective or objectives in the clearest possible terms. (In chapter 4, we'll see how a project charter serves this purpose.)

Sometimes project stakeholders find it easy to agree on objectives for the project. This is especially true when the desired outcome follows clearly from the motivation for the project—for example, when everyone says in unison, "The problem is _____." Harvard professors Lynda Applegate, Robert Austin, and Warren McFarlan refer to these situations as "highly structured projects." In describing corporate information technology projects, they say, "High structure implies that the nature of the task defines its outputs, the possibility of users changing their minds about the desired outputs is practically nonexistent, and significant change management issues are not present." [1] Unfortunately, few project situations are highly structured. Stakeholders don't always have the same objectives in mind. Even the definition of the problem that the project is supposed to solve may remain unresolved. Consider this example:

*Senior management has enlisted Sam, manager of the company's IT
department, to develop a new database and data-entry system—and
he's prepared to start work tomorrow. In fact, he has been waiting all
year for the go-ahead to upgrade those parts of the company's IT
system. But will his response really address the problem? "I know what
the problem is," he answers. "Everyone is complaining that they can't
get data out the system fast enough. And then they have to sift through
many reports to compile the customer information they need to make
decisions."*

The complaints cited by Sam may be genuine, but they are only
symptoms of a problem and don't clearly express user needs. What
are those needs? No one knows for certain. People in marketing may
cite some data needs, but employees in manufacturing and finance
may cite others. Nor is there any indication of *when* the fix is needed,
or how much the company is willing to spend to fix the perceived
problems.

Here's another example: "Develop an internal Web site capable
of providing employees with fast, easy, cost-effective benefits self-
service." As a project objective, this contains some problems that may
prevent stakeholders from agreeing on the project's purpose and
goals. For instance, what exactly does "fast" mean? How should
"easy" be defined? And to what degree must the site be cost effective? All of these objectives should be specific and measurable. If they
are not, the project team will have no way of knowing whether the
project's objectives have been met.

One way to achieve clarity on a project's objective is to conduct
a dialogue designed to encourage stakeholders to arrive at agreement on two things: (1) what problem or opportunity is motivating
the project and (2) what the project team's output should look like.
Dialogue participants should also define a time frame within which
the agreed-upon objectives will be achieved.

Project managers who fail to ensure that stakeholders have clarified and agreed on objectives at the effort's outset can run into
major difficulties. For example, Sam, the IT manager, risks wasting
time by designing a system that is either too simple or too complicated—or one that doesn't respond to the fundamental concerns of

stakeholders. His employer risks wasting large sums of money and the energy of many key personnel.

Dialogue is one technique for clarifying project objectives. Another, as suggested by Robert Austin, is to develop a prototype of the project's outcome.[2] For example, for a software project, many managers use a simple working prototype to demonstrate key features and functions. Prototype development takes time and money, but having a tangible, working version of the final output in hand can elicit valuable feedback from stakeholders. Feedback informed by experience with a prototype—such as, "I like the way this works overall, but I'd make it easier to use"—will be more informed and specific than responses to a paper document that describes what a hypothetical piece of software might do. Such feedback also provides some assurance that you will not get to the end of a long project and hear a stakeholder say, "No, this isn't at all what I had in mind."

What are the real issues at the core of your project? Asking these questions can help you uncover them:

- What is the perceived need the project is meant to fulfill?

- Why do people see this need as a problem that must be solved?

- Who has a stake in the project's outcome? (See "Who Are the Stakeholders?")

- How do the various stakeholders' goals differ?

- What criteria will stakeholders use to judge success or failure of the project?

Have those questions answered correctly—and by the stakeholders—and you will increase the likelihood of your project's success.

Organizing the Effort

Once you are satisfied that the project has a clear, unambiguous objective, the next chore is to organize the effort. The moving force behind this step should be you—if you're the executive who proposed and authorized the project or the individual appointed as

Who Are the Stakeholders?

A *stakeholder* is anyone with a vested interest in a project's outcome. Likewise, a stakeholder is anyone who will judge a project's success or failure. Project team members, internal and external customers, and senior management are all likely stakeholders. To identify the stakeholders in your project, pay attention to the following:

- The functions of individuals who will be affected by your project's activities or outcomes

- The contributors of project resources, including personnel, space, time, tools, and money

- The users and/or beneficiaries of the project's output

Each is a stakeholder in your project.

project manager. In either case, you must create a team that's capable of achieving the project's objective.

At this early stage, consider the objective and make a rough-cut determination of which people and resources you'll need to get the job done. In his book *Strategic Benchmarking,* Gregory Watson provides a glimpse of how Ford Motor Company successfully did this in its development of the original Taurus automobile model back in the late 1970s. Ford's senior management literally bet the company on the Taurus project, which represented a major break in design from the company's existing vehicles. But it was a bet that paid off hugely for Ford. And project team organization played a major part in that success.

As described by Watson, completion of the project required the involvement of every functional group in the company. The groups participated through a cross-functional team headed by a senior project manager named Lew Veraldi. According to Watson, Veraldi had broad discretion in selecting team members, which he accomplished

by mapping all areas of technical and market expertise needed to produce and launch a new car model. Team membership was represented
through two levels: an inner circle of key people numbering fewer
than ten, and a larger set of players numbering more than four hundred. It would take that many to get the job done. Only a fraction of
these would dedicate 100 percent of their time to Team Taurus work.
However, each team member would bring along all the know-how
and resources of his or her functional department.[3]

As described here, the mapping exercise identified the people
and resources needed to accomplish the mission. Among these was a
small core group of influential people who formed a kind of executive counsel for the much larger project team. This core group had
organizational clout and the authority to allocate resources. While
hundreds of others were represented within the project team and its
work, this executive council was small enough to make decisions
and had the power to make its decisions stick. (The leader and core
team are *heavyweights*. Steven Wheelwright and Kim Clark, who
developed that term, define *heavyweights* as individuals who have
both high technical expertise and organizational clout. They bring
various strengths and weaknesses to every project effort.)[4] Most HR
projects are unlikely to be as large and complex as the Taurus project. Nevertheless, you should follow a similar approach to organize
the effort—namely, identifying and enlisting all the expertise, resources, and people needed to complete the job. In later chapters,
we'll go into the details of assessing needed skills and resources.

Planning the Project

Planning is the second phase of the project management process. It is
a necessary prelude to action. Project planning generally begins with
the objective and works backward, in effect asking, "Given our
objective of _____, what set of tasks must we complete to
achieve that objective?" More accurately, planners must also decide
in what order and within what time frame they must complete those

tasks. For example, if the objective is to design a new employee mentoring program within five months, a rough-cut plan, or feasibility study, might be useful. The planner would take the stated goal and break it down into a set of key tasks (such as identifying individuals who would be interested in serving as mentors, developing criteria for matching employees with mentors, and delivering a presentation on the new program to various groups in the organization). Just as important, the planner would create time frames within which each task must be completed for the overall objective to be achieved on schedule.

In the project-planning phase, each task and subtask is assigned a reasonable time for completion. When you put tasks and subtasks into a master schedule (with some done in series and others in parallel), you can determine (1) whether some individuals are overloaded while others are not being asked to do enough and (2) the end-to-end time required for the project. If that time is greater than the time frame specified in the project charter, you'll need to adjust the scope of the project, the schedule, and/or the resources committed by the charter.

You and appropriate team members must then analyze the tasks to determine whether all are necessary and whether some can be redesigned to make them faster and less costly to complete.

Managing Project Execution

Once your project is up and running, it must be managed. An unmanaged project will very likely fail. Efforts will prove uncoordinated—wasting time and money—or the project's energy will veer off course, producing deliverables that fail to match those stipulated by the sponsor and stakeholders.

Project execution requires all the traditional skills of sound management: keeping people motivated and focused on goals, mediating between the people above and the people below, making decisions, allocating scarce resources to their highest uses, reallocating resources to deal with emerging problems, and so forth. You must also monitor and control adherence to the schedule, budget, and quality standards. And as we will see later, you want to give particular attention to the kinds of issues that go hand in hand with team-based work: interpersonal conflict, collaboration, and communication.

Closing the Project

Closedown is the final phase of project management. By definition, every project has an end point—the time at which the objectives are achieved and deliverables are handed over to stakeholders. At this point, the project team must fold its tents, and its members return to their regular assignments.

Learning is the most important activity of this phase. Though most participants will be eager to go back to their traditional duties, they should take time to reflect on their experience. What went well, and what went badly? What could have been improved? Using the benefits of hindsight, how (if at all) should the project have been planned and executed differently? Record the lessons learned through reflection and incorporate them in future projects to put your next project team on a strong footing.

The four phases described in this chapter are time tested and highly suitable for most projects. The details of each phase will unfold in the chapters that follow. But as we will learn later, this logical, essentially linear approach is less suitable for projects characterized by high levels of uncertainty.

Summing Up

In this chapter, you discovered:

- Projects have four basic phases: defining and organizing, planning, managing execution, and closing down.

- Though it's easy to assume that the four phases should be handled one after another in a linear fashion, the reality of project work is seldom that tidy.

- The tasks involved in the first phase are to clearly define project objectives and to organize the right people and resources around them.

- The moving force behind organizing the effort is either the executive who proposed and authorized the project or the individual appointed as project manager.

- The second project phase, planning, generally begins with the objective and works backward, identifying the many tasks that must be completed, estimating the time needed to finish them, and scheduling them in the right order.

- The managing execution phase requires all the traditional skills of effective management as well as careful monitoring. Together, they assure adherence to the schedule, budget, and quality standards.

- One unique feature of a project is that it has a limited life. It ends when its objectives are achieved and deliverables are given to stakeholders. The project then terminates, but only after the team wraps up loose ends and reflects on and documents the lessons learned.

Leveraging Chapter Insights: Critical Questions

- Think about the various projects you've handled so far in your career as an HR practitioner. Has your management of these projects followed the four phases described in this chapter? Did you go through those phases in relatively linear order, or did you need to revisit some phases to make adjustments? What changes might you make to more successfully shepherd projects through these four phases?

- Of the four project management phases, which (if any) do you find most difficult or frustrating? What steps might you take to address those difficulties?

- While managing projects, do you find yourself skimping on one or more of the four phases because of time pressure or some other difficulty? If so, how might you ensure adequate attention to each phase?

CHAPTER THREE

The Cast of Characters

Who's Who in Project Management

Key Topics Covered in This Chapter

* *Understanding the roles of the project sponsor, project manager, project team leaders, and team members*

* *Choosing leaders*

* *Selecting team members*

* *The six characteristics of effective teams*

THE SUCCESS OF HR project work depends extensively on the people who participate. Yes, a sound organizational structure matters; so does good project management. But neither of these will produce a satisfactory outcome if the right people are not on board with your project—or if those people aren't clear about their roles. This chapter identifies the key project players and their roles and responsibilities. Furthermore, it describes the characteristics of effective project managers and project teams and explains how to select team members.

Project Sponsor

Whether a project is formed by a manager or by a group of staff members, it must have a *sponsor*. The sponsor (sometimes a steering committee rather than an individual—see "The Project Steering Committee") authorizes the project. He or she should be a manager or executive with a real stake in the outcome and with accountability for the project's performance. The sponsor should also have the authority to define the scope of the work, provide it with necessary resources, and approve or reject the final output. In other words, the sponsor should be a person with real clout—someone who's capable of:

- Championing the project at the highest level

- Clearing away organizational obstructions

- Providing the resources required for success

The Project Steering Committee

Some projects have a level of oversight called the *project steering committee*. In figure 3-1, on page 44, this steering committee occupies the box otherwise occupied by the sponsor. In fact, in projects with steering committees, the sponsor is a member of the committee, along with all other key stakeholders. The role of the committee is to do the following:

- Approve the project charter

- Secure resources

- Adjudicate all requests to change key project elements, including deliverables, schedule, and budget

The project steering committee has the ultimate authority on those matters. A steering committee is a good idea when a number of different partnering companies, units, or individuals have a strong stake in the project. A steering committee represents these different interests. As such, it is well positioned to sort out complicated, interfirm, or interdepartment project problems. Likewise, steering committees are valuable when many change requests—concerning deliverables, schedule, and budget—are anticipated.

The downside of having a steering committee is that it involves another level of oversight and that its meetings take up the time of some of the company's most expensive employees. So don't have a steering committee if you don't need one.

- Communicating effectively with the CEO and key stakeholders

You might serve as a project sponsor in many types of situations. For example, perhaps you've authorized your benefits administration manager to create a project designed to monitor and evaluate the performance of the companies your firm has hired to manage employees' retirement funds. Or maybe you've approved a project whose objective is to change the way your company attracts, evaluates, and recruits new hires. No matter what the project, as its sponsor, you'll have final authority—and you'll share accountability—for the effort's outcome.

In their book *Radical Innovation*, Richard Leifer and his colleagues made an important observation about each of the ten cases they studied. That observation is relevant here. They found that in each case a highly placed sponsor, or patron, was instrumental in providing critical services.[1] These sponsors kept their projects alive by providing funding—sometimes through normal channels, and sometimes under the table. They deflected attempts to terminate innovative projects, and they promoted the value of project goals to higher management. Without the protection and support of these patrons, each of the ten projects would have died or limped along, starving for funds and lacking a clear conclusion.

The sponsor must protect the project from high-level enemies who see its objective as a threat to their personal turf. This is particularly critical when a project team is working to develop products or technologies that, if successful, will cannibalize the sales of current products or render them obsolete. In these instances, powerful executives who represent the current product lines are likely to be hostile to the project's goals and may use their power to withhold funding or disrupt the team's work. Here it is wise to recall Machiavelli's warning in *The Prince* to all who attempt to alter the status quo: "There is nothing more difficult to carry out, or more doubtful of success, nor more dangerous to handle, than to initiate a new order of things. For the reformer has enemies in all those who profit from the old order."

Does your project have an influential sponsor—in yourself or another executive? If you're the sponsor, are you acting as a true champion by providing resources and fending off internal enemies? Are you sufficiently wise to differentiate between unwarranted negativism or territoriality and criticism that identifies real problems?

If you are putting someone else forward to serve as the sponsor for a project, think about the individual you're recommending. Is he or she really committed to the project's success? Does the person act as a champion, or is he or she simply going through the motions? Have you arranged things so that the recommended sponsor has a

Project Sponsor's To-Do List

A project sponsor has important work to do for the project team. He or she must:

- Ensure that the project's progress is communicated to the rest of the organization and to leadership in particular.

- Ensure that senior management supports the project team's decisions and direction.

- Be alert to any change in company objectives that may affect the project's objectives. Project objectives must be aligned with company objectives.

- Remember that some managers will not want their subordinates splitting their time between project duties and their regular assignments. Work with these managers to smooth over difficulties.

personal stake—such as a bonus—in the project team's success or failure? This last point merits special attention. Project sponsors should have "skin in the game." If they have nothing to lose (and perhaps something to gain) from the project's failure, their usefulness is questionable. See "Project Sponsor's To-Do List" for more details about this role.

Project Manager

Every project has a single manager, as shown in figure 3-1. The *project manager* is the individual charged with planning and scheduling project tasks and orchestrating the day-to-day management of the project's execution. He or she is also the person with the greatest accountability for the endeavor's success. This person receives authority from the sponsor and plays a central role in each phase of the

FIGURE 3-1

Sponsors, project managers, project team leaders, and members

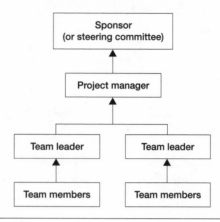

project's life cycle, from design and organization to project close-down and evaluation—and everything in between.

For example, perhaps your CEO has charged you with serving as project manager for an initiative designed to communicate the benefits and processes of your company's new performance management system throughout the organization. Or maybe you head the HR office at a division of your company, and the corporate HR team has asked you to lead a project whose objective is to identify and address the causes of unusually high turnover throughout your division.

In many respects, the project manager's responsibilities resemble those of a manager in any other function. Both must obtain results through people and other resources. And like the traditional manager, the project manager must also:

- Recruit effective participants

- Provide a framework for the project's activities

- Keep the vision clear

- Coordinate activities

- Negotiate with higher authorities, and with the sponsor in particular

- Mediate conflicts

- Identify needed resources

- Set milestones

- Manage the budget

- Ensure that everyone contributes and benefits

- Keep work on track

- Be certain that project goals are delivered on time and on budget

Doesn't this list describe the typical manager's role? With big projects in particular, the two roles are very similar. In these cases, the project manager acts as decision maker, delegator, director, motivator, and scheduler of others' work. He or she is like the traditional boss. On the other hand, the project manager may not have formal authority over some or all of the people who are carrying out the work of the project. For example, suppose you're the project manager of a new HRIS initiative. In this case, the project team members may be drawn from IT, finance, and so forth. You have no direct authority over them; nor do you have access to the traditional forms of leverage, such as pay raises and promotions. You must therefore rely on your leadership qualities to influence team members' behavior and performance.

Project Team Leader

Many large projects are organized to include one or more project team leaders who report directly to the project manager, as shown in figure 3-1. (In small projects, the project manager may serve as both manager and team leader.) In what situations might you serve as a project team leader? Here's one example: your boss is project manager on a large-scale initiative designed to communicate company strategy throughout the firm's business units; you lead the team that's responsible for creating a compelling video in which the CEO explains the firm's new direction to employees around the world. Or maybe your supervisor is managing an effort intended to update the company's recruiting Web site, and you lead the team charged with revising and streamlining all the text on the Web site's pages.

As you might imagine, if you're a team leader, you cannot act like "the boss" and still obtain the benefits normally associated with team-based work. Instead, you must adopt five important roles: initiator, model, negotiator, listener, and coach. You must also be willing and able to pitch in as a working member of the team. Let's take a closer look at each of the five team leader roles.

Leader as Initiator

As team leader, you must initiate action. Though effective leaders don't tell people what to do, they draw attention to the actions essential for meeting the team's goals. Good team leaders are well positioned to initiate action because they usually stand somewhat apart from the day-to-day work of their team—where they can more easily observe the connections between that work and the project's higher-level objectives. While team members are deeply enmeshed in tasks and problem solving, the leader pays continual, close attention to the expectations of the project sponsor, the project manager, and external stakeholders. Using evidence and rational argument, the leader encourages team members to take the steps needed to meet those larger expectations. Not surprisingly, the team leader role is an important function, particularly when the sponsor's and other stakeholders' expectations conflict with individual team members' personal expectations.

Leader as Model

Traditional managers and team leaders can use their own behavior to shape others' behavior and performance. The big difference is that team leaders must rely more heavily on this tactic, since they cannot rely on promotions, compensation, and threats of dismissal to influence team members.

A team leader's behavior is, in fact, a powerful tool. It sets a standard that others feel compelled to meet or even exceed, if only to avoid seeming ineffective or petty. As team leader, you can model team behavior in many different ways. For example, if you believe that your team members should get out of the office and rub shoulders with internal customers, don't just instruct them to do so. Instead, begin a regular practice of traveling to customer locations yourself, creating customer focus groups, and so forth. Your very actions will encourage team members to participate. In a word, you want to model behaviors that exert a direct impact on your team's performance.

Leader as Negotiator

"I'd like Bill to join our performance improvement team," said team leader Sue to Bill's manager. The manager frowned; Bill was one of his best employees. "Being part of the team will involve an estimated four hours of work each week," Sue continued. "And that includes meetings and team assignments."

As you may have realized, most managers don't particularly welcome requests such as Sue's. They understand that a project team has important goals, but so do the managers who are asked to contribute skilled employees and other resources. Complying with a team leader's request can only make their jobs more difficult. Effective team leaders recognize this and use their negotiating savvy to obtain the personnel and other resources they need. The project sponsor can facilitate the process by making it clear that the project's goals are important to the company and that he or she expects managers to cooperate.

The best way to negotiate with resource providers is to frame the situation in a positive way—as mutually beneficial. A mutually beneficial negotiation occurs when both parties recognize opportunities for gain. If you are a project team leader, you will have a better chance of framing your negotiations as good for both parties if you do the following:

- Emphasize the higher-level goals of the organization, and explain how successful team action will contribute to those goals. You'll underscore a point we'll examine in more detail later in this book—that project goals must support organizational goals.

- Emphasize how the other party will benefit by helping the project—for example, by indicating how the project's success will contribute to the other party's success.

To be a successful negotiator, present yourself as trustworthy and reliable, and describe realistic mutual benefits.

Leader as Listener

A good project team leader spends as much time listening as talking. Through listening, you gather signals from the environment—indications of impending trouble, team member discontent, and opportunities for gain. You also look for opportunities to leverage your team members' diverse knowledge, skills, and insights. When team members know you're listening, they'll more willingly share what they know or what they perceive to be happening inside and outside the team. By listening well, you can recommend actions informed by the experience and knowledge of many people.

Leader as Coach

A good project team leader finds ways to help team members excel. In most cases, you can accomplish this through coaching. *Coaching* is a two-way activity in which the parties share knowledge and experience to maximize a team member's potential and help him or her achieve agreed-upon goals. It is a shared effort in which the person being coached participates actively and willingly. Good team leaders find coaching opportunities in the course of everyday business. Their coaching can help members with many routine activities—such as making better presentations, scheduling their work, dealing with conflict within the team, obtaining external resources, setting up a budget, developing skills, or even working effectively in a team environment.

Coaching opportunities are especially prevalent within teams. Why? Many team members must develop particular needed skills as their projects unfold. For example, the scriptwriter you recruited to help your team develop a video that explains the company's new strategy may suddenly find that she must prepare and present a businesslike progress report to senior management. She must develop presentation skills quickly—and coaching from you can help.

Leader as Working Member

A project team leader must also pitch in and do a share of the work, particularly in areas where he or she has special competence. Ideally, that share will include one or two of the unpleasant or unexciting jobs that no one really wants to do. Pitching in solidifies the perception that you're a member of the team, not a traditional boss. The payoff? Greater team cohesion and dedication.

What are the characteristics of a person who can do most, or all, of the things just described? For starters, a project team leader should have the leadership skills we are all acquainted with: the ability to set a direction that others will follow, good communication skills, the ability to give and to accept feedback, integrity, and high standards for performance. Beyond these, he or she should have a positive attitude toward team-based work—and preferably experience with it. If you're a project manager looking for an effective team leader, the last person you'd want to fill the job would be someone who insists on acting like a traditional boss.

The team leader should also enjoy credibility among team members. That means having appropriate skills and experience and a reputation for dealing effectively with others. Lack of credibility can lead to ridicule and a highly dysfunctional situation.

Choosing a Project Team Leader

If you're a project manager, you may designate a team leader if the project is of very short duration, if there is an immediate need for a team (as in a crisis), or if there is an organizational reason for a certain person to be the team leader (such as giving a competent younger employee an opportunity to learn and practice leadership skills). In other situations, the team may select its own leader—or rotate the leadership post and its responsibilities on a regular basis.

One Leader or Several?

For many of us, the notion of team leadership evokes the image of a single leader. To be sure, investing leadership in a single person ensures that authority has an undivided voice. After all, how would a team get things done if it had two bickering leaders? Whose direction would people follow? However, the experience of teams indicates that investing leadership in a single person is not an absolute necessity as long as there is agreement among leaders on means and ends. The only necessity is that leaders are of one mind as to their goal and its importance.

A project that brings together many people representing two or more technical specialties may, in fact, benefit from multiple leadership—particularly if the leaders report to a single project manager. For example, a team whose goal was to establish a new recruiting Web site had a project manager and four area leaders: a technical leader, a user interface leader, a site strategy leader, and a content leader. Each leader reported to the project manager, and each had responsibility for a unique aspect of the project's work. Within these areas of responsibility, team leaders had authority to make decisions and allocate resources. Only when their decisions affected other teams, the project plan, the budget, or the schedule were they required to seek approval from the project manager or other high-level authority. See "Team Leader's To-Do List" for more details about this role.

Project Team Members

The true engine fueling the work of a project is its team membership. Yes, a good sponsor can clear the way and secure resources, and, yes, a good project team leader can motivate performance and keep the work focused. But it's the project team members who do most of

Team Leader's To-Do List

If you're a project team leader, your team is counting on you to:

- Regularly communicate progress and problems with the project manager

- Periodically assess team progress, the outlook of members, and how each member views his or her contribution

- Make sure that everyone contributes and everyone's voice is heard

- Do a share of the work

- Resist the urge to act like a boss

the work. As a consequence, bringing together the right people with the right skills is crucial.

Choosing good team members is probably the trickiest part of team design. A team can acquire its members in one or more of the following ways:

- **Assignment.** The sponsor selects the appropriate people and invites them to participate.

- **Voluntary.** The people most invested or most interested in the work step forward as potential members.

- **Nominated.** People who have an interest in the project nominate individuals who have the right skills and in whom they have confidence.

None of these selection methods is inherently better or worse than others. Each is capable of tapping the right members. But each is equally capable of putting the wrong people on a team, particularly when the organization is highly politicized. Consider these examples:

- The sponsor has selected most of the members of a new Web site design team. Hugh, the sponsor's right-hand man, is one of them. Hugh doesn't know a server from a hyperlink and has nothing in particular to contribute to the team effort. His only purpose will be to report back to the sponsor, who distrusts several team members. For the team, Hugh is excess baggage. Other team members will quickly discover his role as informant and react negatively.

- Ann has volunteered to work on a project that's being organized to reengineer the company's order-fulfillment process. Ann isn't particularly interested in the project's objective, but she sees membership as a way to get face time with Katherine, the project manager and a rising manager in the company. Ann is also concerned that her main rival for a promotion is already on the team. "If he's on that team, I had better be on it too," she reasons. It's clear that Ann's commitment is not to the team's objective but to her own self-interest. As a consequence, her value to the project is questionable.

- Harry has volunteered for the same reengineering project. He has a proprietary interest in the current order-fulfillment process and believes that his organizational standing will suffer if the team adopts a radical makeover of that process. His motivation is self-protection, and his commitment is not to the team's objective but to the status quo.

- Ralph has nominated Muriel, one of his direct reports, to the Web site design team. "This will be a good learning experience for her," he tells himself. Yes, Muriel's participation might be a very good thing for her career development, but will it be a very good thing for the team? Not if she has little or nothing to contribute.

Do you see examples like those in your organization? If you do, watch out. In each example, an individual was put forward as a project team member for a reason that had nothing to do with helping the project achieve its stated goals. Avoid such approaches to member selection while assembling your own project teams.

Skill Assessment

If having the right people on board is so important, what criteria should a team leader look for in selecting members?

Team selection should ideally be determined by the skills needed to accomplish the work. Skill assessment is a two-stage process: the first stage looks objectively at a task and determines exactly what skills are needed to get it done. For example, in examining all the activities that need to be done, you (if you're the team leader) may determine that your team must include members with the following skills: research, instructional design, graphic design, and procurement of consulting services. Together, they represent all the skills and resources needed to achieve the project's goal.

Stage two of skill assessment looks at the people in the organization and determines which of them have the right skills. The right skills may be categorized as technical, problem solving, interpersonal, or organizational.

- **Technical skill.** This category refers to specific expertise—in market research, finance, software programming, and so forth. Technical skill is usually the product of special training.

- **Problem-solving skill.** An individual's ability to analyze difficult situations or impasses and to craft solutions falls under problem-solving skill. Creative people often have habits of mind that help them see resolutions that routinely elude others. Some individuals with specialized training have problem-solving skill appropriate for their field. If you're the team leader, you need problem solvers on your team; otherwise, people will continually look to you for solutions—missing out on the opportunity to leverage the team's diverse knowledge.

- **Interpersonal skill.** This type of skill refers to an ability to work effectively with others—a vital trait for team-based work. In practice, interpersonal skill takes the form of interpersonal chemistry. Let's face it: some people naturally get along well with particular people and not so well with others. For example, a straitlaced person with a formal demeanor and no patience for joking and partying will likely lack the chemistry needed to work well with a group of fun-loving software programmers who come to work on skateboards and end the day with a round of pizza and beer. Businesspeople too often view employees with the same skill sets as interchangeable. Don't make that mistake.

- **Organizational skill.** The final category includes the ability to communicate with people from other units, knowledge of the company's political landscape, and possession of a network. People with these skills help the team get things done and avoid conflict with operating units and their personnel.

When forming project teams, many leaders tend to focus myopically on technical skills. It's so obvious that specific technical capabilities are needed that we focus on them to the exclusion of other skills. As Jeffrey Polzer writes: "This is a sensible starting point because, for example, a software development team cannot work very well without programmers who know the particular coding language to be used in the project; nor can an orchestra succeed without individually talented musicians."[2] Unfortunately, this attention to technical skills often overshadows attention to interpersonal and organizational skills, which, in the long run, may be just as important. For instance, a brilliant programmer may actually retard team progress if she is secretive about her work, is unwilling to collaborate, or generates hostility among other members. In contrast, a person with average technical skills but superb organizational savvy may prove to be the team's most valuable member, thanks to his ability to gather resources, enlist help from the operating units, and so forth.

Polzer cautions that there is still plenty of room on a team for the talented individual contributor who isn't very good at working with others. Such a member's interpersonal weaknesses may be addressed through coaching or other means. Moreover, individuals who are strong on all four skill measures—technical, problem solving, interpersonal, and organizational—are few and far between. Thus, one goal of member selection must be to make the most of the talent available and to take steps to neutralize people's weaknesses.

Most experts on team creation caution that you'll rarely get all the skills you need on the team. Something will always be missing. And in most cases, it is impossible to anticipate every skill needed. As researchers Jon Katzenbach and Douglas Smith note: "No team succeeds without all the skills needed to meet its purpose and performance goals. Yet most teams figure out the skill they will need *after* [our emphasis] they are formed."[3] Thus, the savvy project team leader looks for people with both valued skills and the potential to learn new ones as needed.

Once you've identified a candidate with the right skills for your project team, discuss his or her potential contribution with members you've already chosen and with the project sponsor. Also consult the candidate's supervisor, as team membership absorbs time that the person would otherwise spend on regular assignments. Assuming agreement among all parties, you can then invite the candidate to join.

Adding and Subtracting Members

Be prepared to add new members and possibly bid thanks and goodbye to others over time. New skills and members may be needed as the work changes and the team progresses toward its goal. Consider the example of a team charged with redesigning a company's entire performance management system. This team began as a small core group of five members. Over the six months of its life, it recruited five additional members—each representing specific aspects of the work, such as performance metric design, incentive program development, and so forth. Once this team completed the plan for redesign of the system, it moved to an implementation stage. At that point, still more people were recruited who would play major roles in implementing the new system.

One caution on adding and offloading members: over time, members adjust to the people and the working styles represented on the team. They develop effective patterns for making decisions and communicating—and sometimes do so very gradually. They identify the team with the current lineup of players. This cohesion is undermined when too many people join and exit the team. Newcomers are not fully productive during the time they spend getting oriented. Those who remain must expend valuable time orienting the new members and finding ways to work with them; they must spend still more time filling in for departed team members. The lesson for team leaders? Minimize team membership turnover as much as possible. See "How Many Is Too Many?" for more information on assembling an effectively sized team.

How Many Is Too Many?

The optimal size for a project team depends on the project's goals and tasks. Thus, the best advice about how many people to have on a team is this: have just enough people to do the job and no more. Having too few people will slow you down and possibly mean that you don't have all the requisite skills. Having too many will also slow you down by shifting valuable time and energy into communication and coordination efforts. There is also the problem of commitment. Individual commitment to the team and its goals tends to diminish as more people are added. So recruit as many people as you need to get the job done—but no more.

Authors Jon Katzenbach and Douglas Smith offer these cues to knowing whether your team is small enough:

- Team can convene easily and frequently.

- Members can communicate easily and frequently.

- No additional people are required to get the job done.[a]

a. Jon R. Katzenbach and Douglas K. Smith, *The Wisdom of Teams* (Boston: Harvard Business School Press, 1993), 62.

Note: The appendixes at the end of this book contain worksheets that can help you as you form your team.

Characteristics of Effective Project Teams

Aside from the particular skills that people bring to a project, what else should you look for? The literature on team-based work provides some insights.[4] That literature points to several qualities as ingredients in team or project success. They are:

- Competence

- A clear and common goal

- Commitment to the common goal

- An environment in which everyone contributes and everyone benefits

- A supportive environment

- Alignment of project goals with organizational goals

    Let's look at each of those in detail.

Competence

To succeed, the team should have all the talent, knowledge, organizational clout, experience, and technical know-how needed to get the job done. Any weak or missing competencies jeopardize the team goal. In these cases, teams must strengthen weaknesses or recruit for the missing competencies—something that successful teams learn to do as they move forward.

    As a project manager or team leader, you need individuals who bring critical competencies to the effort. Of course, you may also have to take into account the political realities of your organization. For example, Susan's goodwill could be extremely important if she were in a position to block your team's progress. By making her a team member, you could boost your chances of getting her to buy into team objectives, thus neutralizing her danger to the team.

A Clear, Common Goal

Have you ever been part of a project team that lacked a clear understanding of its purpose? If you have, you probably understand why such groups rarely succeed. It is nearly impossible to succeed when team members cannot articulate a clear and common goal. The situation is even worse when leaders who sponsor and charter teams are unclear or uncertain about what they want done.

One way to test for a clear and common goal is to try the "elevator speech" test. Take each member of the project aside and ask the following question: if you were traveling by elevator between the first and second floors with our CEO and he asked what your team was working on, what would you say? Everyone working on the project should be able to clearly and succinctly explain the goal to the CEO—or to any intelligent stranger. Here are two statements that meet the elevator speech test:

- "We are redesigning our recruiting Web site with three objectives in mind: to make it capable of accommodating each of our different job classifications, to make site updating and expansion faster and less costly, and to enhance the user experience."

- "We are reengineering the entire benefits administration process. If we are successful, 95 percent of incoming employee questions will be handled by a single rep, and 80 percent of all questions will be resolved in three minutes or less."

Can everyone on your team articulate the project's goal with this degree of succinctness and clarity? Would everyone's description of the goal be the same? If you said no to either question, you have a problem. Try to address that problem as a group. As we'll explain later, a project team's goal is generally handed down by higher management, which often sees a problem or opportunity and then wants it addressed. Ideally, management identifies the desired end but leaves the means to people on the team. Still, team members must share an understanding of the goal. Otherwise, they will head in different directions. The consequences? Wasted energy and resources, and ongoing conflict and bickering.

Once they reach a common understanding of the goal, project team members, in concert with the leaders who have defined the desired outcome, should specify the project goal in terms of performance metrics. In the example of benefits administration reengineering, the team specified its goal as follows: "ninety-five percent of incoming employee questions will be handled by a single rep, and 80 percent of all questions will be resolved in three minutes or less." Metrics like these not only define the goal more specifically, but they also provide a way to gauge progress toward the goal. For example, this team could have set up interim milestones such as these:

- Within six months, 50 percent of incoming employee questions will be handled by a single rep.

- Within nine months, 75 percent of incoming employee questions will be handled by a single rep.

- Within twelve months, 95 percent of incoming employee questions will be handled by a single rep.

A team without performance metrics cannot determine whether it has met its goal.

Commitment to the Common Goal

A shared understanding of the project goal is essential, but really effective teams go a step further. Their members are *committed* to the goal. There's a big difference between understanding and commitment. Understanding ensures that people know the direction in which they should work; commitment is a visceral quality that motivates them to do the work—and to keep working even when the going gets tough.

People must see their team's goal as being very important and worthy of their effort. If they lack a compelling purpose, some members will not subordinate their personal goals to the team's goal. They will not identify with the team or its purpose.

Commitment is also a function of goal ownership and mutual accountability. Consider the following example:

> *A number of individuals from different functional areas of a company were brought together to solve a critical problem: their company was losing talented employees to rival firms. The only solution was to find a way to provide high performers with more of what they valued: development opportunities, challenging and varied work, visibility to influential leaders, and so forth.*
>
> *Every member of the project team understood the importance of the goal. They also knew that their economic futures and those of their coworkers and company depended on their success. And because management had not told the team members how they should achieve their goal, they felt a sense of ownership for both the effort and the result— and held each other accountable for that result.*

That's commitment. Don't confuse shared commitment with social compatibility. It's less important that people get along with each other than that they're willing to work together to get things done. A purpose that all team members see as important can overcome any social incompatibilities.

You can recognize shared commitment in the vocabulary used by your team members. When people use *we, us,* and *our* instead of *I, you,* and *they,* team commitment is in the air. Statements like these suggest real teamwork:

- "*We* are making good progress, but each of *us* must pick up the pace."

- "Where do *we* stand with respect to *our* schedule?"

- "*Our* plan is still in the formative stages."

- "Give *us* three months and access to the turnover data, and *we'll* develop a workable plan."

You can more easily achieve team commitment to a common goal if the number of members is small. That seems intuitive. The military, among others, has long recognized the importance of small-group cohesion in generating individual commitment to both the unit and its goals. Soldiers may gripe endlessly about the "damned army" but will often risk life and limb for the well-being of their small unit and its members. For this reason, some experts on teams recommend keeping membership as small as possible, with fewer members being better if all the right competencies are represented.

You can also enhance commitment through rewards. If people understand that recognition, prizes, promotions, bonuses, or pay increases are associated with their success in achieving the team goal, their commitment will increase. By contrast, if they understand that the boss will get the credit and the bulk of the monetary and non-monetary rewards, their commitment will evaporate.

Every Member Contributes—Every Member Benefits

Have you ever been on a rowing team? If you have, you know that every member of the team must pull his or her oar with the same intensity and at the same pace as everyone else. There is no room for slackers or for people who won't keep the right pace. Work teams are very similar. Performance depends on everyone's contribution—pulling for the goal. Individual members who simply show up at meetings to render their opinions but who do no work impair performance and demoralize the active teammates. If team membership has any value, it must be earned through real work. In other words, free riders—members who obtain the benefits of membership without doing their share—cannot be tolerated.

Not every member must put in the same amount of time on team activities or make the same contribution. Variable contributions to projects are a fact of life. A senior manager, for example, may be a regular team member even though he must direct much of his attention to other duties. He may support the project by securing resources or by building support for the team within the organization. While some people might not see this contribution as real work, it is nevertheless important to the team effort.

Also, since members' skill levels are bound to be different, some people will inevitably prove a lot more capable and productive than others. The field of information technology, in particular, includes people with vastly disparate skill levels. So don't become obsessed with free riding.

The project team leader must also do real work. He or she cannot be a team member *and* behave like a traditional boss, delegating all the work to others. Thus, there is a certain element of role ambiguity for the team leader, who must wear a leadership cap some of the time and a team member's cap the rest.

And just as each member must contribute to the team's work, each should receive clear benefits. Benefits can take many forms: the psychological reward of doing interesting and meaningful work, a learning experience that will pay future career dividends, or extra money in a paycheck. In the absence of clear benefits, individuals will not contribute at a high level—at least not for long. The benefits they derive from their regular jobs will absorb their attention and make team duties a secondary priority.

A Supportive Environment

No project team operates in a vacuum. The project is a small organization embedded within a larger environment of operating units and functional departments. It depends on its organizational kin to one degree or another for resources, information, and assistance. The extent to which operating units and departments are supportive, indifferent, or hostile to the project and its goals affects the project team's effectiveness. In particular, the team leader needs to consider these environmental factors:

- **Leadership support.** Support at the top is essential. It ensures a source of resources and helps recruit the right people. Leadership support also provides protection from powerful managers and departments that, for whatever reason, are inclined to torpedo the team effort. One way to secure and keep leadership support is to create what Steven Wheelwright and Kim Clark have eloquently described as "heavyweight teams"—that is, teams headed by people with powerful skills and abundant organizational clout.[5]

- **A nonhierarchical structure.** Team-based work is more likely
  to succeed if the organization does not conform to a rigid
  hierarchical structure. Why? A nonhierarchical structure creates
  habits conducive to team-based work—specifically, a willingness to share information, collaboration across organizational
  boundaries, and employee empowerment. These habits are
  weak or absent in organizations where the bosses do all the
  thinking and directing and everyone else follows orders. Such
  organizations are not team-ready.

- **Appropriate reward systems.** Companies that are new to team-
  based work need to examine their reward systems before launching teams. Often, they must find a different balance in rewards
  for individual and team-based success. Doing so is one of the
  most daunting challenges faced by those who sponsor teams.

- **Experience with team-based work.** Teams benefit when their
  companies and individual members have plenty of experience
  with team-based work. Experience provides insights into what
  works and what does not, how best to organize around a goal,
  how to collaborate, and how to change the team at different
  points in its life cycle. Many companies that rely on team-based
  work provide training on team methods, and with good reason.
  Employees who've worked independently for years must be
  trained in team-based work. Specifically, they need help with
  skills such as listening, communicating with different kinds of
  people, collaborating with people outside their departments,
  and staying focused on the common task.

How supportive of team-based work is your organization? Your
company's team readiness should factor into your decision to attack
a problem or opportunity by assembling a project team.

Alignment

Alignment is the last item on our list of essentials for project team
effectiveness. It refers to the coordination of plans, effort, and rewards
with an organization's highest goals. In an aligned organization,

everyone understands both the goals of the enterprise and the goals of his or her operating unit. In an aligned organization, people pull in the same direction—the one defined by the company's strategic plan. And the reward systems encourage them to do so.

Project teams also need alignment. A team shouldn't even exist unless that team represents the best way to help the organization achieve its goals. So the goals of the project team should align with organizational goals, and the goals of individual team members should align—through the team—with those higher organizational goals. And everyone's efforts should align through the reward systems. This last point is key, and it begins at the top, with the project sponsor. Since the sponsor is accountable for the team's success, some part of his or her compensation should be linked to the team's performance. Moving down the line, the project manager, team leader, and team members should likewise see their compensation affected by team outcomes.

Alignment gets everyone moving in the same direction—the right direction.

To see how one project team demonstrated the many characteristics of a successful team, see "HR in Action: Creating a New Performance Management System."

HR in Action: Creating a New Performance Management System

NetWorks, Inc. is a large international firm that develops communications networking equipment and services for businesses, consumers, and governments. As competition in the industry has stiffened, leaders at NetWorks have decided to launch a major project: an overhaul of the company's existing performance management system. After conducting a workforce survey, the executive team learned that employees' awareness of the company's strategy and their role in carrying it out was alarmingly low. To address these issues, the CEO sponsored a project designed to raise strategic awareness and manage performance in new ways that ensure alignment with the corporate strategy.

Joanne Karohl, director of HR at NetWorks, has agreed to serve as project manager and team leader for the effort. As part of her role, she assembles a cross-functional team comprising the head of NetWorks's strategy management office, the finance director, the IT manager, and the heads of the company's five business units. Each team member has lengthy tenure with the organization and is well familiar with the company's culture, major challenges, and strategic plan for remaining competitive in its industry. Each is also an expert in his or her field. Moreover, most of the members have served on cross-functional teams in the past. Thus, Karohl feels confident that her team collectively possesses the talent and skills needed to pull off this demanding effort. She's especially pleased that the five business unit leaders have agreed to be on the team. Why? She knows she'll need their buy-in if the new system requires them to change the way they evaluate their own and their direct reports' performance.

To ensure that everyone is on the same page regarding the team's goal, Karohl organizes a project launch meeting at which the participants arrive at an agreed-upon statement of their goal: "to develop a performance management system within six months that enables us to easily (1) identify the short-term actions we must take to achieve our long-term strategic goals, (2) monitor strategic performance throughout the organization, and (3) make midcourse corrections to performance as necessary." Arriving at this articulation of the goal takes time and proves frustrating at several points, but Karohl views the effort as well worth it. She does not want her team members to begin the project work until they share a clear understanding of the goal.

Karohl also takes steps to ensure that members each feel personally committed to the goal. She shares articles and case studies showing the link between effective performance management and organizational success. And she uses a blend of

continued

"we" language, sobering facts, and gentle humor to remind the members that achieving the goal will benefit all of them: "We all have a stake in our company's success. And as you well know, the competition in our industry is getting brutal. In my view, the way we handle this project quite literally will have the power to make or break this company. OK—nothing like a little drama to get us started! But we do have a major responsibility to the company, ourselves, our shareholders, and our employees to put NetWorks in the best possible position to stay ahead of our rivals. And this project—if we manage it carefully, and if each of us gives our best—will let us do that."

To further ensure the success of the project, Karohl suggests to the CEO that he use several tactics to demonstrate to everyone in the organization that the project—and the team—has support from the highest echelons in the company. He agrees and commits to delivering a presentation on the new initiative at several upcoming "town hall" meetings that will be Web-cast to all of NetWorks' employees worldwide. He also offers to write several articles praising the project in upcoming issues of the company's internal newsletter.

Finally, Karohl takes several steps to secure alignment within the project team. She decides to offer members the opportunity to earn bonuses as well as several other incentives (such as gift certificates to local restaurants and tickets to cultural events) based on favorable project outcomes. She announces these decisions to the project team. "If we're going to be managing performance differently," she explains to the team, "that's going to require different reward systems for this team than for the other employees. I want to walk our talk by offering you different types of rewards for a job well done on this project."

Karohl's efforts to build a successful project team pay off. Though challenges and difficulties arise as the project unfolds over the next six months, the team ultimately reaches its goal— on time, within budget, and according to the specific quality criteria it had established for itself at the outset of the effort.

Summing Up

In this chapter, you learned the following about the people who participate in a project and their roles:

- A project sponsor authorizes the project, defines the scope of the work, provides resources, and accepts or rejects the final output.

- The project manager receives authority from the sponsor and plays a central role in each phase of the project's life cycle.

- A project team leader reports to the project manager and takes responsibility for one or more aspects of the work.

- Members of the project team do most of the work. They should be selected on the basis of their skills and ability to collaborate effectively with others.

- A team should have just enough people to do the job and no more.

- Successful teams have these characteristics: competence, a clear and compelling goal, commitment to the common goal, an environment within which everyone contributes and everyone benefits, a supportive environment, and alignment of project goals with organizational goals.

Leveraging Chapter Insights: Critical Questions

- Think of a major HR project you participated in recently. Which role did you play? Project sponsor? Manager? Team leader? Team member? How effective were you in that role? When you play that same role on a future project, what (if anything) might you do differently to be more effective?

- Think of a project team you've assembled. Of the defining characteristics of successful teams described in this chapter, which did your team possess? Which were missing? What might you do differently in a subsequent project team to ensure that the team possesses all the characteristics presented in this chapter?

- Think of an HR project your company is launching soon. Whom do you consider the most promising sponsor for the project? The most promising project manager? Do these individuals have the qualities and skills required to excel in these roles? If not, what other individuals might better serve as sponsor and manager?

CHAPTER FOUR

A Written Charter

Your Marching Orders

Key Topics Covered in This Chapter

- *The value of a project charter*
- *Eight things a charter should contain*
- *The problem of ends and means*
- *How to scope a project*

W E'VE ALREADY ESTABLISHED the importance of having a clear objective for your HR project. Having that objective defined, specified, and delivered in written form is very important. But your project team needs more than a clearly stated goal to do its work. It needs an unambiguous sense of the project's scope, the value it should deliver to stakeholders, the time frame within which it must work, and a statement of the resources at its disposal. Together, these constitute the charter that authorizes the project and defines its activities—the subject of this chapter.

A Mandate for Action

Having the right cast of characters on a project team is important. But so is having a *charter* that spells out the nature and scope of the work and management's expectations for results. A charter is a concise written document containing some or all of the following:

- Name of project's sponsor

- Relationship between the project's goals and higher organizational goals

- The benefits of the project to the organization

- The expected time frame of the work

- A concise description of project deliverables (objectives)

- The budget, allocations, and resources available to the project team

- The project manager's authority

- The sponsor's signature

Without a formal charter, the project could head off in a direction that is misaligned with organizational objectives. It could grow in scope without control, a process known as "mission creep." The very act of creating a charter forces senior management to clearly articulate what the project should do—an important duty when senior management is not of one mind, as in this example:

Phil Wilson, the general manager of BestCo's North American division, was the sponsor of the division's effort to reengineer its recruiting operations. As an outspoken critic of the division's current approach to recruiting, he was the right person for the job. He had long been dissatisfied with the time it took to attract and recruit new hires and with the division's frustrating loss of top-notch candidates to competitors. In addition, he thought the costs of the division's recruiting operations were too high. So he put Lila Moss, head of the division's HR group, in charge of a project effort to improve them.

What sorts of cost cutting was Wilson anticipating? What exactly were his complaints about the current recruiting system? What would success look like? Moss attempted to pin him down on those questions, but she wasn't successful. Wilson was too busy to think it all through and too eager to delegate responsibility for the project's outcome. Other division executives were also eager to see improvements, but, like Wilson, they had no clear ideas about the outcomes they wanted. So when Moss quizzed senior managers about the subject, they cited no specific goals. Lacking clear guidance, Moss and the people on her team developed their own goals and criteria for success.

The team pushed forward, and Moss reported progress to Wilson over the course of the ten-month effort. Resources were always a problem, particularly since Moss was never sure how much money she could

*spend and how many people she could incorporate into the team at key
stages. Every request for resources had to be negotiated on a case-by-case
basis with Wilson.*

*The team eventually completed its tasks, meeting all of its self-
declared goals. It had cut time-to-hire by one-third. The percentage of top
candidates accepting a job offer from the division versus going to a com-
petitor rose 20 percent. And the overall cost of recruiting had been cut by
12 percent. The project team celebrated the completion of its duties with a
splendid dinner, after which its members went back to their regular jobs.*

*Senior management, however, was not entirely pleased with the
outcome. "You did a pretty good job," Wilson told Moss. "The improvements you've made are significant, but we were looking for a more
sweeping improvement and larger cost savings." Moss was stunned and
more than slightly angry. "If he wanted these things," she thought,
"why didn't he say so?"*

Situations like Lila Moss's are common but can be avoided
through a charter. Does your project have a written charter? Does it
contain each of the important elements?

Clarifying Objectives

As Moss's case demonstrates, project managers need more than a
broad-brush description of the objectives for which they and their
team, or teams, will be responsible. Ambiguity on the goals can lead
to misunderstandings, disappointment, and expensive rework. Consider this example of a broad-brush objective: "develop a Web site
that's capable of providing fast, accurate, cost-effective product information and fulfillment to our customers." That is how a sponsor
might describe the project's objective in the charter. But what
exactly does it mean? What is "fast"? How should accuracy be
defined? Is one error in a thousand transactions acceptable, or would
one error in ten thousand meet the sponsor's expectations? To what
degree must the site be cost effective? Each of those questions

Tip on Setting Objectives

When defining project objectives, think SMART. In other words, be sure that objectives are *specific, measurable, action oriented, realistic,* and *time limited.*

SOURCE: *Managing Projects Large and Small* (Boston: Harvard Business School Press, 2004).

should be answered in consultation with the sponsor and key stakeholders. (For more on determining objectives for your project, see "Tip on Setting Objectives.")

A thoughtful charter indicates the ends but does not specify the means. The means should be left to the project manager, team leader, and members. Doing otherwise—that is, telling the team what it should do *and* how to do it—would undermine any benefit derived from having recruited a competent team. Richard Hackman makes this point clear in his book *Leading Teams.* "Direction that is unclear or extremely abstract," he writes, "can waste members' time and embroil them in conflicts as they struggle to agree on what they are really supposed to do. Direction that is *too* clear and complete, on the other hand, can lessen members' commitment to the work and sometimes prompts unwanted and even unethical behaviors." According to Hackman, the sponsor must find a balance between giving the team too much and too little specific direction.[1] As he makes clear in figure 4–1, teams do best when the ends are specified and the means are not (upper-right quadrant), when they do goal-oriented work and manage themselves. As he writes: "When ends are specified but means are not, team members are able to—indeed, are implicitly encouraged to—draw on their full complement of knowledge, skill, and experience in devising and executing a way of operating that is well tuned to the team's purpose and circumstances."[2] This is not to say that specifying *both* ends and means (lower-right quadrant) will necessarily lead to failure. That situation more closely describes a traditional, unempowered work group.

FIGURE 4-1

Means and ends

Specify *ends?*

	No	Yes
No	Anarchy	Self-managed, goal-directed work
Yes	Turn-off (worst of all)	Wasted human resources

Specify means? (row label)

Source: J. Richard Hackman, *Leading Teams* (Boston: Harvard Business School Press, 2002), 73. Reproduced with permission.

Making It Time Limited

All objectives should be specific and measurable. If they are not, you'll have no way of knowing whether the project has met its goals. There should also be a time frame within which objectives will be achieved; the project cannot be open-ended. In some cases, the deadline must be firm: a situation with a fixed time and variable scope. For example, in sending a probe to Mars in the summer of 2003, a project team at NASA had a limited window of opportunity. Mars and Earth were in unusually close proximity at that time. By late August, the distances between them would begin to increase rapidly. NASA had to launch its Martian explorer in July or scrub the project. With time as a constraint, the agency had to be flexible about the scope of the space vehicle it was putting together.

Some projects define time as a constant. Consider a software company that decides that it will deliver a new release every three months. Since time is constant, the project team must make adjustments to the scope of its new releases—adding or dropping product features—to ensure that each can be delivered at the end of three months.

The opposite situation is evident in situations with a fixed scope and variable time. As we'll see later in this book, if the scope of the project is set, then a logical deadline can be established only after the project manager and team have had an opportunity to break down each objective into a set of tasks and then estimate the duration of each of those tasks. Nevertheless, the charter should contain a reasonable deadline—one that can be amended as the project team learns more about what it must do.

Getting Specific About Project Scope

Even with a charter in hand, the project manager and key players must spell out the project scope in greater detail. One useful technique for scoping a project is to have key stakeholders and project participants join in a brainstorming exercise that specifically aims to describe what should be within the scope of the project and what should not. Consider this example:

> *Parker & Smith, an office furniture company, had a problem. Its inventory costs were unacceptably high and growing relative to sales. "We now offer twenty different models of filing cabinets," the chief operating officer complained at a meeting with managers from purchasing, product development, manufacturing, and inventory control, "and most of them use unique sets of parts."*
>
> *"That's right," said Ralph Taylor, the inventory manager. "Every time we design a new cabinet, it incorporates fittings and fasteners that aren't common to our other products. As a result, I now have more than three hundred different parts and materials in the stockroom, every one of which I have to track and store. Some of them sit there for years. And that's expensive."*
>
> *The purchasing manager cited another dimension of the problem: "Storage and tracking isn't the only issue. Buying small volumes of many different parts creates paperwork costs for my department and eliminates most of our opportunities for high-volume orders from suppliers—the kinds of orders that produce large discounts."*

Everyone agreed that controlling inventory costs was an important goal for the company, and just about everyone at the meeting had an idea for dealing with it. The question was, How could the group define the scope of the project to rein in costs without agreeing to more objectives than they could reasonably tackle? The COO asked Taylor, the inventory manager, to recruit a project team and find a way.

Within two weeks, Taylor had recruited six key people to the team and convened a three-hour meeting to brainstorm the challenge of high inventory costs. He also invited the COO and a key parts supplier to participate. Each had a different perspective on the problem. Together they tried to determine what should be within the scope of the project and what should not. Table 4-1 contains the output of their discussion.

The example in table 4-1 demonstrates how a team can define the scope of a project and eliminate activities that would dissipate energy and resources. Notice that the team removed two product design proposals from the project's scope even though those ideas had considerable merit. Each would make a worthwhile project in itself, but both were judged to be outside the immediate scope of the current project. This determination demonstrates how project managers, members, and sponsors must make trade-offs among the options they discover. Options are always more numerous than available time and resources.

If the sponsor's expectation specifies the ends to be sought, the project plan specifies the means in actionable terms. The project plan may be the project manager's creation. Ideally, it will represent the best ideas of many, or of all, project team members. With the sponsor's approval, this plan becomes part two of the charter.

A project plan is especially useful for large, complex endeavors because it provides more detail about tasks, milestones, deliverables, risks, and timetables. It serves as a road map, both for the team and other interested parties.

Note: Need a handy tool to help you think through the scope of your project? Appendix A contains a "Defining Your Project" worksheet that will take you through key questions you need to answer.

TABLE 4-1

Parker & Smith defines project scope

GOAL: REDUCE INVENTORY COSTS		
Within the project's scope	***Not* within the project's scope**	**Comments**
Determine the cost savings of reducing the total number of parts by 25%.		"Reducing total number of parts will reduce our storage and tracking costs and reduce complexity. We should know by how much."
	Benchmark current inventory costs against key competitors.	"That would take too much time. Besides, we don't have to know what our competitors are doing in order to achieve significant reductions."
	Develop a plan to design parts complexity out of future products.	"A great idea, but it should be a separate project run by the product development people."
Develop an approved parts list (with opportunities for exceptions when necessary) from which product developers can pick. Estimate the cost savings from such a procedure.		"Most of our fasteners are invisible to customers. There's no reason we cannot design new products from a smaller set of these parts."
	Reengineer our new-product design process.	"A good idea, but it deserves to be a separate project."
Develop a plan for just-in-time parts delivery.		"This will save us on floor space and inventory-carrying costs. We should have done this years ago."

Summing Up

In this chapter, you learned the following:

- A project charter is a mandate for action. It spells out in writing the nature and scope of the work and the sponsor's expectations for results.

- A charter should be unambiguous. Make it specific, measurable, action oriented, realistic, and time limited.

- When you develop a charter, you should spell out the ends, but leave the means to the project team.

- The project manager and key players must specify what is within the scope of the project and what is not.

Leveraging Chapter Insights: Critical Questions

- Think of an HR project you're working on now. Does it have a charter? If so, which of the project charter elements described in this chapter does it contain? Which elements should you add?

- Examine each of the objectives listed in your project charter. Are the objectives "SMART"—specific, measurable, action oriented, realistic, and time limited? If not, what changes might you make in the wording of the objectives so that they meet these SMART criteria?

- Have you clearly defined the scope of your project—what work it will include, and what work it won't include? If not, how might you clarify scope?

- Is time a constraint on your project? Or is it a constant? What does this imply for the flexibility of the project's scope?

CHAPTER FIVE

A Framework for Action

Important First Steps

Key Topics Covered in This Chapter

- *Reaching agreement on how decisions will be made*

- *A method for keeping track of unresolved issues*

- *A procedure for documenting decisions and actions*

- *A plan for communicating*

- *Creating a budget*

L IKE ANY OTHER IMPORTANT venture, your HR project will move along more smoothly if you establish certain procedures and operational mechanisms before the real work begins. For example, how will decisions be made? How will project participants stay in touch and keep up to date? How will unresolved issues be handled? This chapter addresses a number of these organizational issues. Get them in order, and everything else on your project will go more smoothly. And determine the rules at the very beginning. You don't want to find yourself having to make them up as you go along.

Decisions, Decisions

Experienced HR project managers know that decisions constitute a major part of their work. In fact, every project is a set of activities linked together by decisions. Thus, very early in your project planning, you and your team need to agree on (1) how decisions will be made and (2) who will make them. If team members lack consensus, the project will soon get tied up in knots. You—as the project manager or sponsor—may find every little decision parked on your desk. Alternatively, team members will either waste time embroiled in unproductive debate or produce decisions that many of the project's stakeholders won't support. And decisions like these are waiting around every corner:

- Should one minor goal be traded off for another?

- Three new designs for the recruiting Web site are on the table. Which one should the design team select?

- Which consultant should the team hire to help with a specific aspect of the project, and what should be the scope of the consulting engagement?

- The project team is overspending its budget. Which activities should be cut?

- The team is receiving a lot of change requests from other groups in the company, and these requests represent very good ideas. Adopting them will put the team behind schedule and over budget, but taking advantage of these good ideas might be worth the cost. Can the team make this decision, or must it defer to the steering committee?

Within functional business units such as HR, marketing, finance, sales, and so forth, decisions are the domain of the executives and managers who lead those units. These individuals identify the issue for which a decision is needed, seek out and analyze alternatives, and take counsel from appropriate sources. They then make decisions and accept responsibility for the consequences. Decision making within their own scope of responsibility is one of the things that executives are paid to do. Though they may seek consensus and the input of others, they are not bound by others' opinions. By contrast, project teams must approach decisions differently.

Decision-Making Spheres

Project decision making is not as clear cut as decision making within operating units or staff departments. Sponsors and steering committees obviously have decision-making authority over team goals and the level of resources allocated to the team. They also maintain ultimate authority on issues like these:

- Personnel

- Expenditures over a given budget amount

- The use of outside resources

- Changes in organization-wide policy or goals

- Choices affecting customers, such as pricing and specifications

- Changes in the team's deliverables and schedule

But even project sponsors and steering committees must recognize the views of key stakeholders, who may demand a voice in these decisions.

Project managers, on the other hand, should have sole authority over decisions related to project operations and processes as long as they do nothing to:

- Alter the goal or deliverable

- Adversely affect the schedule

- Adversely affect the budget

The same principle about authority applies to team leaders and team members. These participants need the authority to make decisions within their limited spheres *unless* their decisions will have a negative impact on the work of other project teams.

To avoid potential disagreements, be sure that your project team, its sponsor, key stakeholders, and higher management share an understanding of which players and groups associated with the project can make which decisions. (For insight on decision-making protocol, see "Decision Procedures Matter.")

The Who and How of Decisions

If you are a project manager or project team leader, you must help others agree on the who and how of decision making. Who will make what decisions? At the team level, will the team leader or a subset of team members make decisions, or will all members have a

---

Decision Procedures Matter

Research indicates that people care about decision procedures. They want protocol to be fair. And they are much more likely to accept a decision that is unfavorable to them as long as they believe the procedure for making the decision was fair. Trust is a key element in this phenomenon. People must trust those who devise the decision-making procedure. If they see others rigging it and acting out of self-interest, then their willingness to accept decisions—and their commitment to the project—will evaporate.

---

voice? And *how* will decisions be made? Will the majority rule, or must the group reach a full consensus? Will decisions be final? If not, what kind of modification process will the team follow?

Here are some common decision-making approaches:

- **Majority rule.** Participants bring their input to a decision meeting, discuss, and then vote. Decisions that receive more than 50 percent of the votes are adopted.

- **Consensus.** Every member of the team must agree before a decision can be made and adopted. If consensus cannot be reached, new alternatives must be developed and brought back to the group.

- **Small group decides.** A group of individuals with relevant experience and skills is selected to make decisions.

- **Leader decides with input.** The team leader gathers input from team members and then makes the decision.

In selecting a decision-making approach, carefully weigh the trade-offs. The more involved your project team members are in the decision-making process, the more likely they will support the outcome of that process. Thus, project managers and team leaders can use the consensus and majority-rule approaches to build team commitment. But there is a downside: those methods take time. If time is an important issue, consider using different approaches in different situations: perhaps your team could reach an agreement collectively on issues that are most crucial to members but use a more streamlined decision-making approach for other issues.

Whichever approaches you and your team use for decision making, establishing those approaches during the project's start-up stage is vital. Failing to agree on the decision rules will only lead to bickering and dissention. If time and events indicate that those rules are not supporting the project's goals, change them—but in an orderly manner.

Tracking and Disposing of Unresolved Issues

How many meetings have you attended during which important issues were raised but not resolved? Probably plenty. Even when members of a team have agreed that certain issues are important, many such issues are left on the table. Why? Perhaps the team has run out of time. Or maybe participants don't have sufficient information to form an opinion. Or perhaps some individuals need to give the subject more thought. Those are all valid reasons for deferring the resolution of issues. The question is, What happens to issues that you cannot resolve in the course of project work or meetings? Do you just forget about them? Stuff them into a drawer? Send them into orbit? Unresolved issues can clog up the decision pipeline if you don't develop an orderly and systematic way of dealing with them. They can also hold up your project work if a certain task must await a decision before moving forward.

One way to deal with unresolved issues is to enter them into a tracking log. A tracking log has two benefits: (1) it keeps unresolved issues from getting lost, and (2) it provides an assured procedure for their timely resolution. Table 5-1 is just one of many possible versions of tracking logs—this one for a project related to creating an e-learning program at a company.

TABLE 5-1

Tracking log example

Issue	First raised	By (owner)	Comments	Must resolve by
Selection of software supplier	3/05/07	A. Sandoval	Considering three programs	5/21/07
Find new tech team leader	3/09/07	K. McIntyre	Current leader will retire on 5/11/07	ASAP
Whether to attend the June 2007 APRQ conference	3/12/07	J. Johnson	Cost not yet calculated; deadline for application is 4/18/07	4/16/07

But simply creating a tracking log does not eliminate the problem of unresolved issues. Someone simply takes responsibility for them and for bringing them back to the decision forum in a timely way. Both the issue owners and the project manager should share that responsibility of resolving the issues—owners because they are the ones who contend that their issues are important, and the project manager because he or she shapes the decision meeting's agenda.

The important point—and the benefit of using a tracking log—is that the issues that matter won't get lost or forgotten.

Documenting Decisions and Actions

If you participate in several project meetings each day, you probably know how easy it is to lose track of what decisions have been made in those meetings. You might even lose track of who was assigned various postmeeting action steps. Confusion follows:

"I never agreed to that plan. What I did agree to was . . ."

"As we decided several months ago, the HR consultant pool will be limited to the three companies with whom we have been dealing. John, why the puzzled look? Don't you remember that agreement?"

"So we've now shared our plan with each of the affected departments and their personnel. We did meet with each of them, didn't we?"

Do those statements and questions sound familiar? If they do, you need a method for keeping track of the decisions made by your project team. Minutes and progress reports can serve this purpose.

Minutes

When you're managing a sizable project requiring a plethora of meetings and participants, you can easily lose track of what has been done, and what hasn't—who agreed to do what, and who did not. This is why managers of all but the smallest projects should develop a systematic method for keeping track of decisions, assignments, and actions.

Many project teams use meeting minutes—notes recorded by an appointed individual—for this purpose. Project participants review and approve the minutes at their next meeting, making amendments if necessary. Those approved minutes then go into a file, where participants can consult them as needed.

Progress Reports

Minutes are useful and should be taken at every high-level meeting. Simple notes will suffice at lower-level ones. But meetings are not the only forums in which people make decisions and take actions. For every hour that people spend in meetings, many hours of work are being done elsewhere—at least one would hope so! For example, to support a project team that's working on a new product line, people in an R&D lab are busy testing materials and component interfaces. Marketing specialists are surveying potential customers about their needs. Financial analysts are crunching numbers, trying to estimate costs and the value of the new product line to the company. And recruiting specialists from the HR department are gathering information about how many new employees with specific skill sets will be needed to develop and launch the new product line—as well as recommending appropriate recruiting and selection techniques for hiring qualified individuals for these positions. The individuals who are handling each of those activities should report progress and problems to the project manager, who must digest the information and use it to track the progress of the project as a whole.

If you're the project manager, which progress reports do you need? That depends on the situation and the information you require to maintain control and move the effort forward. Like meeting minutes, progress reports should be filed in an orderly way that makes them accessible to whoever needs the information they contain. The specifications of the filing system are less important than the consistency and transparency of the system itself.

Note: In appendix A at the end of this book, you'll find a form you can use or adapt for your project's progress reports.

Creating a Communications Plan

A communications plan is another document you must create at the front end of your project work. The importance of such a plan hinges on how many people, departments, and entities will participate in the project—and how far-flung they are geographically. Small projects that involve a handful of people working in one location may not need a communications plan, except for a regularly scheduled meeting time and place. These people can share information anytime they walk down the hallway or head into the coffee room.

In contrast, consider a large project that brings together dozens of people from many departments, various geographic locations, and different organizations. Getting these widely scattered people to talk with one another and share ideas will prove challenging. If you're leading such a project, you'll need to establish a highly structured and comprehensive communications plan. Without it, project participants won't be able to coordinate their efforts, resolve problems, and hit target delivery dates.

Every project communications plan should include protocols for meetings, e-mail, and reporting. Managers of larger projects should consider creating a project team room and electronic linkages—such as a project Web site, phone conferencing, and videoconferencing—that can help widely dispersed stakeholders and team members stay connected. (For other helpful ideas, see "Tips for Communicating Within Larger Projects.")

Tips for Communicating Within Larger Projects

If you're managing a large HR project, chances are that its working participants will be scattered around the building, if not around the continent or even the world. Some participants may be located at company facilities in other cities or other countries. A few may not even be company employees, but suppliers or employees of a strategic partner. How can you communicate information easily to these people as needed? And how can you help them communicate with each other? Here are a few tips:

- Give a competent person responsibility for creating a project Web site and Web-based newsletter, especially if the time line for the project's completion is long. Use the newsletter to report progress, problems, and upcoming events.

- Use the project Web site to post the charter, assignments, meeting dates, meeting minutes, and other material. People can access that information on a self-serve basis.

- Bundle the e-mail addresses of each work group. Chances are that your e-mail software has a group feature that allows you to send a message to a predetermined set of individuals with a single click. That functionality makes it easy to send information to the people who need it without bothering everyone else with needless e-mail.

Meetings

Projects are punctuated by meetings. Regularly scheduled meetings. On-the-fly meetings. Meetings that deal with emergencies.

Meetings are the *least* favorite activity of busy, action-oriented people. But meetings are also often the best way to communicate information. In addition, meetings provide forums within which project participants can share ideas and make decisions. Indeed, the project's progress generally depends on those decisions. Thus, if your project must have meetings, and plenty of them, it's smart to make the most of them.

At one level, making the most of meetings involves sticking to a regular schedule as much as possible. If people know that project team meetings take place every Monday from 3 to 4 p.m., for example, they can plan their other responsibilities around those days and times. Having a regular schedule also saves meeting organizers the task of finding a time on which many people can agree.

Attendance Policies

You may also want to develop an attendance policy associated with project meetings. Decisions cannot be made when key players are not at the table. Instead, decisions must be deferred to the next scheduled meeting, creating havoc with scheduled work in the process.

The problem of meeting absenteeism is particularly acute when key project participants retain considerable responsibility for their regular jobs. For example, if the company controller is required to spend 85 percent of her time on her regular job, her participation in project meetings will take a backseat to other demands on her time—unless there is a policy about attending. So establish a policy at the outset. If travel is an impediment to meeting attendance, consider using telecommunications technology to link travelers to meetings as they happen. We'll examine this in further detail in just a bit.

Note: Making the most of meetings involves preparing, engaging the right processes during the meeting, and following up on the decisions and agreements made. If you'd like to learn more about these aspects of meetings, see "A Guide to Effective Meetings" in appendix B.

Meeting Technology

There are times when e-mails won't do—when team members simply must get together to talk about their work. In some cases, the ability to communicate verbally is sufficient. In others, people must also be able to see each other or the physical objects that others are working on: a person who has just joined the team, a prototype, or four different color choices for the type in the new company newsletter. Fortunately, we now have plenty of affordable technologies that make each of those different forms of communication possible.

E-MAIL. E-mail is a remarkable communication tool. People can transmit messages almost instantly and at a very low cost from one part of the building to another, or across thousands of miles. They can also attach and transmit word-processing files, photos, scanned documents, and presentation slides at almost the same heart-stopping speed.

Every participant in your project should have an e-mail address and the addresses of all other participants. If you plan to rely heavily on e-mailing attached documents, check for compatibility and compression issues, and establish protocols for use. Be clear about who must be "copied" on what, and don't overdo it. There's probably no need to "cc" every person on the team list with every correspondence you send out; nobody wants to receive massive amounts of irrelevant e-mail. Also make sure that everyone is informed about decisions that affect them and that the people who need to participate in decisions are consulted.

E-mails can help create virtual paper trails and can provide important information down the line if misunderstandings or conflicts arise.

TELEPHONE CONFERENCING. The telephone conference is the quickest and easiest way for a virtual team to communicate verbally. And it has a feature that e-mail lacks: it provides an opportunity for dynamic give-and-take conversations. That advantage makes teleconferencing a better medium when your goal is to discuss, to brainstorm, to resolve problems, or to make decisions.

Many kinds of teleconferencing technologies are now available. Check with your communications service providers about the most current options.

VIDEOCONFERENCING. Videoconferencing is another helpful tool for encouraging connectivity between project participants. It can bring teams together without wasting time or money on meals, travel, and lodging. Project teams located in London, Paris, and Montreal, for example, can see and interact with their colleagues in Rome without leaving their offices. They can view and discuss the same objects and documents in real time. And experts say that videoconferencing produces superior results to phone conferencing (see "Visual Trumps Audio"). Videoconferencing, however, is complicated and requires the help of people with specialized technical skills. For basic video, participants need the appropriate computer, camera, microphone, software, and Internet connection. Unfortunately, systems from

---

Visual Trumps Audio

In their valuable article "Distance Matters," Gary Olson and Judith Olson conclude that attempts to use connective technologies either fail or require major efforts by team members to adjust to using the media technologies. Apart from that blanket conclusion, they note that video connections are far superior to audio alone:

> Our laboratory data show that even for people who know each other and have worked together before, a simple audio connection for conversation and a shared editor for real-time work is insufficient to produce the same quality of work as that done face to face. Those with video connections produced output that was indistinguishable from that produced by people who were face to face. The process of their work changed, however, to require more clarification and more management overhead (discussions about how they will conduct the work, not actually doing the work).

SOURCE: *Managing Projects Large and Small* (Boston: Harvard Business School Press, 2004).

different vendors aren't always compatible with different computers, so if your team opts for video, be sure everyone gets a compatible system.

Bringing People into Contact

Distance matters in team-based work. The greater the physical proximity between project participants, the more likely they are to interact and share ideas on a regular basis. As MIT researcher Tom Allen discovered years ago: "People are more likely to communicate with those who are located nearest to them. Individuals and groups can therefore be positioned in ways that will either promote or inhibit communication."[1] Thus, the physical locations of project team members have a major impact on the depth of communication and knowledge sharing.

Authors Marc Meyer and Al Lehnerd underscore the importance of colocation in their book on team-based product platform development:

> The principles of colocating teams, exposing them to a variety of information, and providing a persistent display of that information, are important . . . Just bringing team members together into one physical place has been shown to improve communication and information sharing. There, small bits of knowledge and information that by themselves mean nothing can be pieced together with other bits to form meaningful insights. Team colocation also fosters bonding between individual members and the commitment needed for focused, fast, high-risk projects.[2]

One effective approach to the colocation issue—even when moving team members' individual work spaces into close proximity is not feasible—is establishment of a project *team room*. A team room is a space dedicated to the work of the team and its members. It functions as a space for meetings, as a place where members can congregate to share ideas, and as a forum where all the physical artifacts and records of the team's work can be displayed or kept. Those artifacts and records may include the following:

- Information on similar projects implemented by HR teams in other companies

- Current versions of the team's project

- Relevant research reports

- A specialized library of books and journals containing information pertinent to the project at hand

The team room may also post these items on the walls:

- A large Gantt chart that plots the project's schedule and milestones from start to finish

- The original copy of the team charter, signed by the executive sponsor

- The team budget, including current variances

This team room should also be equipped with a speakerphone—and perhaps videoconferencing equipment—to accommodate group discussion with off-site members. A whiteboard and paper flip chart should complete the setting. (Other ideas can be found in "Tips for Making the Most of Your Team Room.") Collectively, the team room and its accoutrements facilitate team work and foster team identity.

The team room we've just described may not be feasible if project participants are widely scattered in a large office building or across borders. But you can get some of the same benefits by means of a project Web site. A virtual team room can be set up on the project Web site using four "walls," like those in a real team room:

- **Purpose wall.** This wall includes the team charter, goals, tasks, a list of deliverables, and current results.

- **People wall.** This section identifies the team members and states their roles. Here, users can find out who is involved with different aspects of the project. If possible, attach a photo of each team member and a brief description of his or her particular work and expertise. Putting a face and a bit of history with a name adds an important dimension to virtual team work.

Tips for Making the Most of Your Team Room

A project team room is the natural setting for meetings. But you'll only get the full benefits of the space if people make it a regular gathering place. Here are a few things you can do to draw people to the team room on a regular basis:

- Sponsor periodic brown-bag luncheons in the team room. Use a particular topic, a key internal customer, or a consultant with subject-matter expertise on key aspects of projects like yours as a magnet to bring people together for these informal sessions.

- Create an informal and comfortable space by eliminating traditional meeting room furniture in favor of sofas, coffee tables, and lounge chairs.

- Keep plenty of drawing pads and pens on hand to encourage people to sketch out their ideas.

- Include a small refrigerator stocked with soda, juice, and snacks. Food and refreshments will draw team members into the room, where they will more likely talk with each other.

- **Document wall.** This part of the site contains a schedule of upcoming meetings and their agendas. Minutes of past meetings and any meeting presentations are also stored here. Members can use this wall to post their work for review by colleagues. Those reviews and comments can likewise be posted.

- **Communications wall.** This section contains links and information that connect everyone on the team.

Web sites are great assets, but they require some tending. Someone must monitor and update the site. Depending on the scope of the project, this important job could even be someone's total contribution to the team.

Finding Balance in Process Formalization

Attention to process is important, but don't go overboard. Robert Austin and his coauthors at Harvard Business School advocate a minimalist approach to process formalization. In their view, projects must find a balance between discipline and agility. Formalization of process supports discipline, but it will reduce agility if it adheres excessively to processes. "The companies that have been most successful in balancing discipline and agility," they write, "have neither eschewed process formalization altogether nor let process formalization overwhelm them. Rather, they have developed simple process management tools based on the ideas that the best balance is one that includes the minimum formal specification critical to [process success]."

SOURCE: Lynda M. Applegate, Robert D. Austin, and F. Warren McFarlan, *Corporate Information Strategy and Management,* 6th ed. (Burr Ridge, IL: McGraw-Hill/Irwin, 2002), 278.

Note: Everything we've addressed so far has concerned processes for facilitating project work: how decisions will be made, how communication will be maintained, and so forth. It's possible to create too many, or too rigid, processes. For more guidance on this front, see "Finding Balance in Process Formalization."

Developing the Budget

A *budget* is the translation of plans into measurable expenditures and anticipated returns over a certain period of time. In this sense, the budget serves as the financial blueprint or action plan for the project. For businesses, a good budget can be the difference between success and failure. Why? A good budget—and adherence to it— gives people the resources they need to complete their tasks. Project budgets serve a similar function.

The first question to ask when developing a budget is, What is it going to take—in terms of resources—to successfully complete this project? To determine the project's costs, break it down into the key cost categories you anticipate. Here are the typical categories in which projects generate costs:

- **Personnel.** This is almost always the largest part of a project's budget and includes full-time and temporary workers.

- **Travel.** People may have to shuttle from location to location in the course of their project work. Is everyone on site, or will the team have to be brought together at one locale? Don't forget to budget for meals and lodging.

- **Training.** Will training be required? If the answer is yes, will that training take place on site, or will there be travel expenses involved? If you plan to hire an outside contractor to do the training, the budget must reflect his or her fees and expenses.

- **Supplies.** In addition to the usual—computers, pens, paper, and software—you may need unusual equipment. Try to anticipate what the project will require.

- **Space.** Some people may have to be relocated to rented space. How much room and money will that require?

- **Professional services.** Do you plan to bring in a consultant or seek legal advice? Will you have to buy studies or hire a market research firm? The budget must reflect the cost of each of these.

Since costs are estimated before the work actually begins, completion of the budget gives team members a chance to ask themselves whether they really want to do this project, given the cost. The sponsor, for example, may wish to reconsider the project or reduce its scope once costs are estimated. Likewise, if the sponsor is unwilling to fully fund the budget, the project manager, and anyone else charged with the success or failure of the effort, may wish to withdraw. Projects that are not fully funded are imperiled from the very beginning.

In some cases, the project budget cannot be flexible. A project governed by a contract with a fixed total payment is just one example. Internally operated projects, however, usually have some flexibility, which is often necessary since it is extremely difficult to anticipate every expense. The best projects, after all, are those that alter them-selves as they run into roadblocks and encounter valuable opportu-nities. It is for that reason that many project managers build some wiggle room into their budgets. They ask for 5 percent or so of the estimated budget for that purpose. The extra allowance gives them a limited ability to deal with unanticipated costs without having to beg the sponsor for additional funding.

Once a project has been launched, the project manager can use the budget to monitor progress by comparing the actual results with the budgeted results. This feedback, or monitoring and evaluation of progress, in turn allows the team to take timely corrective action.

Summing Up

In this chapter, you learned the following:

- Your project will link its many activities with decisions—dozens and dozens of them. So before you get under way, determine who will make the decisions and how. Tactics in-clude majority rule, consensus, small-group decisions, and decision by the project manager or team leader.

- During meetings, issues will come up that cannot be resolved then and there. If those issues are important, they must be tracked and brought back to decision makers at an appropriate time. Use a tracking log for this purpose.

- Document decisions as they are made so that people can remember what they've agreed to do.

- Communication is essential in a large, broadly distributed project. Create a workable plan for communicating with proj-ect members. And make it easy for them to communicate with each other.

- Colocate project team members to the extent possible. The closer their physical proximity to each other, the greater the communication between them.

- Telecommunications technologies—including project Web sites, e-mail, phone conferencing, and videoconferencing—can provide communication channels for geographically dispersed project teams.

- Create a project budget. It will help you stay on track.

Leveraging Chapter Insights: Critical Questions

- Think of a project you're about to manage. Given the goals and nature of the project, what might be the best decision-making approach? Why?

- What systems have you put in place to help ensure that project issues don't get forgotten or neglected?

- How will you ensure that all project participants remain informed about what decisions have been made and what actions have been or must be taken?

- Considering the nature of your project, how extensive a communications plan do you need to develop to ensure that participants remain informed and connected?

- What meeting and communications technologies would best enable your project's participants to share ideas, resolve issues, and stay informed of the project's progress?

- Have you developed a budget for your project? If so, how much (if any) wiggle room does the budget contain for addressing unanticipated problems and taking advantage of unexpected opportunities?

CHAPTER SIX

Work Breakdown

From Huge Job to Manageable Tasks

Key Topics Covered in This Chapter

- *Using work breakdown structure to subdivide complex tasks into many smaller tasks*

- *Estimating time and resource requirements for each task*

- *Fitting people to tasks*

ONCE YOU HAVE COMPLETED all the housekeeping processes and set up a budget for your HR project, you are ready to move into the first area of technique: decomposing your large job into a set of manageable tasks.

Many of the objectives addressed through projects are mind boggling in their size and complexity. To those of us who don't work in the construction industry, the job of building an eighty-story office building seems impossibly complicated. How would you create a foundation capable of carrying the weight of a million tons of steel girders and other materials—all of which must arrive on the site at the right time and in the right order? How would you get elevators and running water to the top-most floors? How would you go about organizing, scheduling, and directing a small army of electricians, steelworkers, plumbers, mason, glaziers, and many others?

Seems incomprehensible, doesn't it? Approaching a project this daunting and of this magnitude is reminiscent of the old joke that asks, "How do you eat an elephant?" Though the challenge is intimidating, the answer is simple and commonsensical: cut the elephant into bite-sized pieces. The same approach applies to HR projects large and small—namely, break the objective into a set of manageable tasks. This chapter explains how you can use a technique called *work breakdown structure* (WBS) to do just that. The WBS approach helps you answer these key questions:

- What must we do to achieve our goals?
- How long will it take?
- What will it cost?

Many projects fail because their managers overlooked a significant part of the work or underestimated the time required to complete the work. If you are building and installing a new HRIS, for example, and forget to include the time and cost of training people on it, you won't likely meet all your objectives. But careful scrutiny can save the day. This chapter explains how to break each objective down into its component tasks and make reasonable estimates for the time and resources necessary to accomplish each task.

Work Breakdown Structure

You can use WBS to develop resource and time estimates, assign personnel to your project, track progress, and reveal the scope of project work. You can also use this tool to subdivide complex tasks into many smaller tasks—which in turn can be broken down still further.

To create a WBS, ask this question: what will have to be done for us to accomplish our objective? By asking that same question over and over for each task and subtask, you will eventually reach a point at which tasks cannot be subdivided. Consider this example:

Sharon Carrier has been charged with establishing an HR department in Quinn Associates, a small, growing company. Though Quinn Associates is a small organization, setting up its HR department is a big, big job. At the highest level, Carrier faces these tasks:

- *Evaluating existing personnel files*

- *Creating an employee handbook*

- *Establishing payroll and benefits systems*

- *Setting up recruiting and employee orientation programs*

- *Establishing a corporate communications plan*

- *Staffing the HR department*

Each of those top-level tasks can be broken down into a set of subtasks. And each subtask can be broken down still further. For instance, "Set up retirement plan," a subtask under "Establish payroll/

benefits," can be decomposed into numerous additional subtasks, such as "Request bids from plan administrators," "Review bids," "Contact bid referrals," and "Select administrator."

In our example, Carrier's project team for the new HR department will eventually reach a point at which there is no practical reason to break tasks down further. That point may come when tasks get decomposed into manageable one-week or one-day increments. At that point, work breakdown ends. A WBS typically consists of three to six levels of subdivided activities. The more complex the project, the more levels it will have. As a general rule, stop subdividing tasks when you reach the point at which the work will take an amount of time equal to the smallest time unit you plan to schedule. Thus, if you want to schedule to the nearest day, break down the work to the point at which each task takes a day to perform. (For more on creating a WBS, see "Tips for Doing WBS Right.")

Tips for Doing WBS Right

Many projects run off track because project team members failed to identify all the required tasks and subtasks at the outset. Here are a few tips for getting your WBS right:

- Start with the top-most tasks and work downward.

- Involve the people who will have to do the work. They are in the best position to know what is involved with every task and how those tasks can be decomposed into manageable pieces. The project manager and appropriate team members should analyze every task to determine whether all are necessary and whether some can be redesigned to make them faster and less costly to complete.

- Check your work by looking at all the subtasks and seeing whether they add up to the highest-level tasks. Remember, you don't want to miss anything.

Time and Resource Estimates

Once you're satisfied with the breakdown of tasks for your project, you need to answer a new set of questions:

- How much time will it take to complete each task?

- What will be the likely cost of completing each task?

- What skills will be needed to complete each task well?

About Time

Let's address the time question first. If the task is familiar—that is, it's something that you or other participants in your project have done many times before—estimating completion time is not difficult. Unfamiliar tasks, in contrast, require much more thinking and discussion. Just remember that these time estimates will eventually be rolled up into a schedule for the entire project, so you want to be as realistic as possible. Grossly underestimating the time component will come back to haunt you later. Here are a few tips for making time estimates:

- Base your estimates on experience, using the average expected time to perform a task. The more familiar you or other project participants are with a particular task, the more accurate your estimate will be.

- Always remember that estimates are just that—estimates. They're not guarantees, so don't change them into firm commitments at this phase.

- When presenting estimates to project stakeholders, make sure they're aware of all the assumptions and variables behind those calculations. Consider presenting time factors as ranges instead of fixed estimates. For example, say, "Task A will take eight to twelve hours to complete." Any estimate is bound to be wrong; a range, on the other hand, is more likely to be right because it accounts for natural variations.

- Padding estimates is an acceptable way of reducing the risk of a task (or the entire project) taking longer than the schedule allows. But this practice should be done openly and with full awareness of what you're doing.

About Costs and Skills

Once you've addressed the time issues, revisit each task in your WBS to determine how much each will cost to complete, what resources will be required, and what specific skills will be necessary. The output of this piece of analysis will indicate the level of financial and resource commitments your organization will have to make to successfully implement the project. It will also give you a much better idea of who, based on required skills, will be needed on your project team. If the required skills are not available within the organization, you'll need to fill the gaps by means of training, hiring people with the requisite skills, and/or contracting with independent specialists—all of which you should factor into the project's cost.

Assigning the Work

With your WBS output in hand, you're now in a position to assign the work. Every task should have an identified owner—a person, not a department, who's responsible for the work. And that owner should have enough time in his or her schedule to complete the assignment.

   If you haven't yet assembled your project team, use what you currently know about skill requirements to recruit the right people from inside or outside your company. If someone has already assembled the team, or if outside recruiting is not allowed, you'll have to do the best you can with the available talent. That means assessing people's skills and matching them as carefully as you can to the task list, using training to fill in skill gaps. If you have worked with the team members before and know their individual strengths well enough, make the assignments yourself.

If the project sponsor or someone else has assigned the team and you are unfamiliar with members' individual capabilities, create two lists: one with the names of all the people assigned to the project team, and another with all the skills required to successfully complete the work. At your next project team meeting, go through these lists. Encourage people to talk about their own skills, and give the group responsibility for initially assigning people to the listed tasks. Determining assignments in a group setting enables team members to gain familiarity with one another's skills. It also ensures that the right person gets assigned to each task and that the team members become aware of the finite resources they have available.

If team members cannot think of anyone qualified to handle certain tasks, you'll have to think about training or recruiting. If members assign an individual to a great number of tasks, be certain that this person has the time to do all of that work. Overloading a team member is analogous to creating a plan that relies on a particular machine to operate thirty hours per day! It simply won't work. But it happens. All too many companies discover that their projects require one or more people to work virtually around the clock. Some ill-thought-out project plans have actually required a person to be working in two different geographic locations at the same time!

Also check to see whether any team members are not being asked to do enough. Everyone needs to contribute.

An Extended Example

Now that you've reviewed the basic concepts for the work breakdown structure, let's see how one company put it to use to launch an HRIS project. This case illustrates one approach to specifying tasks and related subtasks and the assignment of time estimates to each. For the sake of simplicity, cost and skills requirements have not been included.

Table 6-1 shows examples of the major tasks of the project and how they might be broken down into level 1 and level 2 subtasks.

TABLE 6-1

HRIS work breakdown structure

Major task	Level 1 subtask	Level 2 subtasks	Level 2 subtask duration (days)
Conduct needs assessment	Assess proposed system's interface with current systems	• Survey other HR departments for their best practices • Interview HR staffers to define process flows and functionality	2 2
Create system specifications	Specify database functionality	• Write separate specs for each module (benefits, recruitment, etc.) • Specify data-entry and retrieval processes	4 3
Design system	Design report formats	• Design ad hoc report formats • Design standard report formats	3 2
Develop system	Ensure system's security	• Engage technical security specialist • Create security plan	5 4
Install system	Develop user training program	• Develop online tutorial • Create hands-on training	10 5
Evaluate system	Assess effectiveness of modules	• Assess recruiting module • Assess applicant tracking module	3 3
Total duration (days)			46

Source: Adapted from Steven J. Gara, "How an HRIS Can Impact HR: A Complete Paradigm Shift for the 21st Century," SHRM White Paper, November 2001.

For simplicity's sake, we've shown just one level 1 and two level 2 subtasks for each major task. In addition, each subtask is assigned an estimated time duration, the total of which is forty-six days. This does not mean that the total time needed to complete the project is forty-six days, since some tasks can be completed in parallel.

Note: Appendix A at the end of this book contains a work breakdown structure worksheet like the one shown in table 6-1. You can use it to specify the many tasks in *your* HR project.

Shall We Proceed?

Completion of the work breakdown structure is an important milestone in the project-planning process. The outcome of WBS is a rough estimate of how much time will be required to complete the project. You can also use your WBS to estimate the cost and skills that are necessary for completion. Taken together, these calculations represent important information that the project's decision makers and key stakeholders did not have when they first commissioned the project. Thus, they should consider whether they really want to proceed, asking themselves these questions:

- Can we afford the project?

- If the project succeeds, will it be worth the cost?

- Do we have the skills needed to succeed?

- Will the project finish in time to make a difference for our business?

Since the organization's investment in the project will be relatively small at this point, those questions are very appropriate. Moreover, abandoning the project because of a "no" response to any of the above questions would not be terribly painful.

Abandonment, of course, is not the only option if time, money, and skills are insufficient. The other option is to alter the scope of the project itself. If there is insufficient time to hit an important target date, such as the first day of your company's annual benefits open-enrollment period, or if the project is too costly, you should think about reducing the project's objectives. For instance, perhaps your company doesn't need the full suite of HRIS modules available, and you could reduce the project scope by whittling down the number of modules to only those that are essential. Producing part of the project may be better than producing nothing at all. If the requisite skills are not available, think about delaying the project launch until a time when training or recruiting can provide the skills.

Does your company take a second look at its project plans at this point? It should. Are company executives flexible with respect to project objectives when sufficient time or other resources are lacking? They should be.

Summing Up

This chapter presented the following points:

- Work breakdown structure is a technique used to decompose high-level project goals into the many tasks required to achieve them.

- Once WBS is complete, project managers can estimate the time and cost required to complete each task. They can also assign people to the tasks they've identified.

- You can stop breaking down tasks into subtasks when you reach the point at which the work will take an amount of time equal to the smallest time unit you want to schedule. That might be one day or one week.

- Your WBS exercise may reveal some challenging conclusions: the project will cost more than it's worth, the organization lacks the skills needed to do the job, or the project will take too long to complete. These revelations should make management think twice about proceeding.

Leveraging Chapter Insights: Critical Questions

- Consider a major HR project you'll be leading. If you haven't already done so, list all the major tasks that need to be completed in order for the project to succeed.

- Break each major task into level 1 and level 2 subtasks, and estimate the number of days each subtask will require.

- Look again at all the tasks you've listed. What skills will be required to carry out the tasks? Does your organization currently have people who possess the needed skills? If not, what steps might you take to obtain the skills?

- Given your WBS, what resources will be required for the project to succeed? Does your company have the requisite resources?

- Considering skills, resources, and timing, does it make sense for your company to proceed with the project as laid out in the WBS? If so, why? If not, why not?

CHAPTER SEVEN

Scheduling the Work

Putting the Horse Before the Cart

Key Topics Covered in This Chapter

- *The steps of the scheduling process*
- *Checking for bottlenecks*
- *Using Gantt and PERT charts*
- *The critical path*

S CHEDULES MATTER. You can use them to sequence and control the activities required to carry out your HR project. You can also use them as measures against which to appraise your team members' performance as they carry out their work. Without a schedule, your project might linger for month after month, consuming resources and missing opportunities.

This chapter introduces a practical process you can follow to create a workable and realistic schedule for your HR project. That process has four steps:

1. Identifying and defining tasks and subtasks through the work breakdown structure method

2. Examining the relationships between tasks

3. Creating a draft schedule

4. Optimizing the schedule

Since we've already covered the first step in chapter 6, let's examine each of the others in this chapter.

Examining the Relationships Between Tasks

Many tasks are related in some way and, as a result, must be performed in a particular sequence. Consider how you normally go about enjoying a cold bottle of beer on a hot summer day. Three tasks are usually involved: (1) opening the bottle, (2) pouring the beer from the bottle into a glass, and (3) consuming the brew. Ahh! There is a dependent relationship between these three activities. Obviously we cannot do step 2 before we've completed step 1, and we cannot perform step 3 until 1 and 2 have been completed. If time is an issue, we could eliminate step 2 altogether, drinking directly from the bottle. But step 1 would continue to be an antecedent to step 3.

Many workplace activities are similarly dependent on other activities. Remember the project we introduced in chapter 6—in which Sharon Carrier is planning to create an HR department for her small company, Quinn Associates? The members of Carrier's project team must carry out certain activities in a specific sequence. For example, to create the employee handbook, they must obtain samples of other companies' handbooks before they can write a draft and then have the draft reviewed by the executive team and legal experts. And to establish payroll and benefits systems, they need to review providers' services before they can select providers and then set up the systems. Because of dependencies, these tasks must be scheduled in a linear manner. But note that certain tasks—such as developing the employee handbook and setting up payroll and benefits systems—can follow parallel tracks simultaneously because these activities are not dependent on each other. Recognizing opportunities to work different activities in parallel, as in this example, is one way you can reduce the overall time required to carry out your project.

Once your project team has evaluated the relationships between tasks, you can diagram them on a whiteboard or, better still, label Post-it notes with the names of discrete tasks and arrange them in the correct order on a large wall. The Post-it note approach is the better choice because it enables you to make changes easily. After some brainstorming and moving of notes from here to there, you and your team will eventually arrive at a satisfying arrangement of dependencies.

Different Dependencies

In some cases, tasks logically have a linear, *finish-to-start* relationship. One task must be finished before another can start, as illustrated below.

| Design component |—| Build component |—| Test component |

Other tasks have a *lagging* relationship. Here, one task must await the start and partial completion of another, as shown below. For an example of a lagging relationship between tasks, consider the development of a new computer system. The software developers must wait until some, but not all, of the hardware development is done. After that point, much of their work can be done in parallel.

| Hardware development |

| Software development |

To learn more about determining tasks' dependencies, see the accompanying box entitled "Different Dependencies."

Creating a Draft Schedule

Now you and your project team have all the information you need to create a draft schedule: a list of tasks, an estimate of the duration of each task, and knowledge of task relationships. We use the term *draft* here because you'll likely need to fine-tune the schedule once everyone has had a chance to review it. The schedule itself should:

- Indicate start and completion dates for all activities

- Recognize all task duration estimates

- Recognize task relationships

Gantt Charts

Many project managers use a *Gantt chart* for scheduling work. A Gantt chart is essentially a bar chart with the tasks listed in the left-hand column and fitted into appropriate time blocks. These blocks indicate when tasks should begin, based on task relationships, and when they should end. You can create a Gantt chart using an electronic spreadsheet or a project management software program, such as Microsoft Project. You can also use different colors to indicate which team members are responsible for each block.

Gantt charts show the following:

- Project status (by shading out tasks already completed)

- Estimated project duration

- Estimated task duration

- Task sequences

The popularity of the Gantt chart stems from its simplicity and from its ability to show people the big picture at a glance. What the Gantt chart does not indicate are the relationships between various tasks. So schedulers must take extra care to reflect those relationships in the time blocks as they enter the items.

The Critical Path

Another important piece of information not shown in the Gantt chart is the *critical path*. The critical path is the set of tasks that determines total project duration. It is the longest path through the project, and any delays along it will delay the completion of the entire project. In this sense, there is zero slack time within the critical path. While some tasks can be sequenced with much flexibility, critical-path tasks are locked in by task relationships.

To identify the critical path, let's revisit Sharon Carrier's project for setting up an HR department. As described in figure 7-1, her project team broke major tasks into subtasks and determined which sequences of tasks could be performed in parallel. Take another look

FIGURE 7-1

HRIS project PERT chart

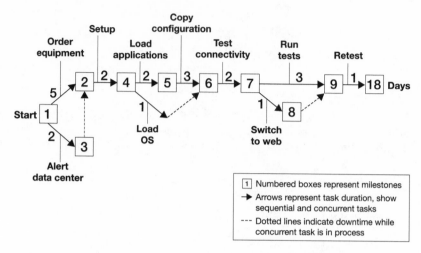

Source: *Harvard ManageMentor on Project Management* (Boston: Harvard Business School Publishing, 2002), 25. Used with permission.

at figure 7-1. This graphic makes up part of what's called a *network diagram*. Unlike a Gantt chart, a network diagram reveals all the dependent relationships between tasks. It also reveals the critical path. Note in figure 7-1 that developing the employee handbook ends on 5/30, while setting up payroll and benefits systems ends on 5/20. Team members working on the payroll and benefits systems could spend ten days beyond the number of days budgeted for them and still not affect the scheduled completion of the project. Nor would the total project schedule be shortened if members completed their work on non–critical-path activities ahead of time. The reason? Tasks on the critical path determine total project duration.

PERT Charts

Some project managers use PERT as an alternative to the Gantt method for scheduling. PERT stands for *Performance Evaluation and Review Technique*. Figure 7-1 shows an example of a PERT chart for part of an HRIS project. Each task in a PERT chart is represented by a node that connects with other nodes, or tasks, required to complete the project. A PERT chart may show many parallel or interconnecting networks of tasks, indicating the need for periodic reviews of the project's progress. Unlike the Gantt chart, it indicates all the important task relationships and project milestones. (Note: The terms *PERT chart* and *network diagram* are practically synonymous.)

Which scheduling tool is best for your purpose? The best method is the one that you are comfortable with and that does the job. Don't be lured into using something just because everyone else does or because it's the latest thing. Take a hard look at how you like to work, and use the scheduling method that best fits your habits.

To assess which method might suit you best, look at the system you use for tracking and scheduling your own work. Are you satisfied with it? If you are, this system may be the way to go for tracking and scheduling your HR project. But remember that a system's usefulness also comes from its ability to inform all the members of your project team of what is going on and to keep them aware that they are part of a larger effort.

For other ideas on scheduling your project, see "Tips for Creating a Draft Project Schedule."

Tips for Creating a Draft Project Schedule

Want more guidance on fine-tuning your project schedule? Follow these guidelines:

- Develop a list of specific tasks.

- Assign a deliverable to each activity—for instance, "test version of HRIS recruiting module."

- Use deliverables as a basis for creating a project schedule with realistic milestones and due dates.

- Identify bottlenecks that add time to the schedule.

continued

- Determine ways to eliminate bottlenecks, or find ways to work around them.

- Establish a protocol for updating and revising the schedule.

- Keep all stakeholders involved in and informed of the project's progress and all schedule modifications.

Optimizing the Schedule

The final step of the scheduling process is optimization. Here, the project manager and team take a very critical look at the draft schedule and seek ways to improve it—that is, to make it more accurate, realistic, effective, and efficient. Like a writer looking for ways to eliminate unnecessary words from his sentences and to add necessary transitions, the project manager should look for the following:

- **Errors.** Are all time estimates realistic? Pay particular attention to time estimates for tasks on the critical path. If any of these tasks cannot be completed on time, the entire schedule will be off. Also, review the relationships between tasks. Does your schedule reflect the fact that some tasks may have to start simultaneously and that others cannot start until some other task is completed or partially completed?

- **Oversights.** Have any tasks or subtasks been left out of the work breakdown structure? Has time for training and maintenance been overlooked in the schedule?

- **Overcommitments.** A review may find that some employees would have to work ten to twelve hours per day for months on end to complete the tasks assigned to them in the schedule. Likewise, a piece of equipment may be booked in the schedule for output in excess of its known capacity. If you find these overcommitments, redistribute parts of the load.

- **Bottlenecks.** A *bottleneck* is any task that causes the work feed-ing it to pile up. Think of an auto assembly line that has to stop periodically because the people who install the seats cannot keep up with the pace of the line. The usual way to handle this is (a) to improve the work process used in that task (i.e., to speed it up) or (b) to shift resources into that task—for example, by adding more people or better machinery.

- **Imbalances in the workload.** A schedule review may indicate that some team members are being asked to carry more than their share of the load while others are being asked to do very little. Balancing the load could reduce the overall schedule.

- **Opportunities to reduce the schedule.** Because tasks on the critical path define the duration of the entire project, look very carefully at them. You may be able to shorten them by shifting more of your resources to them, as in the bottleneck problem. It may be possible to take these resources from non-critical-path tasks. For example, if you have four people working on a task that has four to five days of slack time, shift some or all of those people onto a critical-path task for several days.

Using Scheduling Software

A number of software packages are available to help you develop and manage your schedule. To figure out which software is best for you, get recommendations from users. Then check their work habits against your own to see whether the software is a good fit. Unless you are already familiar with the software, build time into your per-sonal schedule to learn it. Mastery may require that you can get reli-able training and technical support for the program.

Software is a wonderful tool when you know how to make the most of it. It can keep track of times and tasks; produce clear, eye-catching schedule charts; and so forth. It is helpful but not infallible. It won't check for faulty time estimates or dependencies you may have overlooked in putting together the schedule. So review every task in the schedule carefully with another team member or stakeholder before entering it into the software.

Any project-planning software you intend to use should do the following:

- Handle development of and changes to Gantt charts and network diagrams, including PERT charts and calculations of critical paths

- Provide on-screen previews of information before printing

- Produce schedules and budgets

- Integrate project schedules with a calendar allowing for weekends and holidays

- Create different scenarios for contingency planning and updating

- Check for overscheduling of individuals and groups

Summing Up

In this chapter, you learned the following:

- Once you've identified all your project's tasks and subtasks, it's important to examine the relationships between tasks to see which must follow a particular sequence and which can be worked in parallel.

- A draft schedule includes the start and completion dates of all activities, recognizes task durations, and illustrates the dependencies between tasks.

- Gantt charts provide a useful visualization of project status, estimated project and task duration, and task sequences. However, they do not reflect underlying task dependencies or the critical path.

- The critical path is the longest path through a project. It represents the total project duration.

- Any delay along the critical path will derail the entire project.

- PERT charts and network diagrams serve the same purposes as Gantt charts but also indicate the critical path and all important task dependencies.

Leveraging Chapter Insights: Critical Questions

- Select an HR project you've begun managing. Which sequences of activities must be performed in a specific order? Which sequences can be carried out in parallel? Which series of activities represents your project's critical path?

- Which scheduling method do you find most useful for depicting the tasks and time frames required by your project? Gantt charts? PERT charts? Other methods? Why? Would shifting to a different method from the one you're using offer important advantages? If so, what would those advantages be?

- If you've drafted a schedule for your project, examine it for typical problem areas. Do you see the potential for bottlenecks? Overcommitments? Unfair distribution of work? Other problems? What changes might you make to your draft schedule to fine-tune it?

- Are you considering using scheduling software to plan this and other HR projects? If so, how might you ensure that you get the most from the software? Should you arrange for training? Talk with other users to make sure a particular application would be the most appropriate for you?

CHAPTER EIGHT

Adjustments and Trade-Offs

More Fine Tuning

Key Topics Covered in This Chapter

- *What to do when a project cannot meet all the expectations of the sponsor and other stakeholders*

- *Challenging assumptions, deadlines, resource allocations, and stated deliverables*

- *Reevaluating the schedule, its underlying tasks, and task assignments*

W E'VE ALREADY EXPLORED how to break down a complex HR project into a manageable set of component tasks and how to schedule those tasks. When you carry out these two key project activities, you'll likely uncover discrepancies between the objectives stated in the project charter and the outcomes that the project team can deliver. The work breakdown structure exercise, for example, may reveal that company personnel are incapable of completing certain tasks. Likewise, scheduling may indicate that the project cannot be finished within the time frame that key stakeholders anticipated. Faced with these discrepancies, you and your team must make adjustments and trade-offs. This chapter discusses a number of options for fitting an HR project into constraints such as time and skills.

When Your Project Won't Fit

Some projects cannot be realistically completed within the time frame or budget initially conceived by sponsors and key stakeholders. Work breakdown structure and scheduling bring these problems to the surface. You need to confront such problems head-on by bringing them to the attention of the sponsor and other key stakeholders. Consider this example:

Antonia Pena, the vice president of HR at Pittsburgh-based EvanCo, Inc., has received a directive from her executive team to identify fifty

employees who would be willing to permanently relocate to the com-
pany's new facility in Minneapolis. The ultimate objective of the project
is to relocate these individuals in time for the facility's grand opening—
just six months away. Pena and her project team have just completed
the final, optimizing step of the scheduling process. They reviewed their
work breakdown structure, adding several subtasks that someone had
overlooked in the draft schedule. They reassessed the time anticipated for
each task, with particular attention to those on the critical path. And
they did whatever they could to redeploy resources to make the schedule
as short and as realistic as possible. But they couldn't get the schedule
to conform to the steering committee's expected completion date.

"We have a big problem," Pena told her team. "To keep our
relocating employees motivated and positive about the move, we want to
provide them with flexibility. That means letting them sell their homes
here and buy new ones in Minneapolis before relocating—so they don't
have to move twice. But the real estate market here has just turned
sluggish. Homes are staying on the market for many more months than
they did in previous years. That's likely going to put us behind schedule
by at least a month. Carla will go ballistic."

Carla Henderson was the CEO. Pena recalled her last meeting
with Henderson. "This is a hugely important project for us," Hender-
son had told her. "We need to have the new facility fully staffed up
six months from now with fifty of our best performers ready to hit the
ground running. Otherwise, our business can't continue operating
smoothly."

Pena would have to tell Henderson that the project team would
not be able to get all fifty relocated employees in place by the time the
new facility was ready to open its doors for business. What else could
Pena do?

Pena's situation is not uncommon. Project ideas emerge from
many sources: brainstorming sessions by senior managers, serendipi-
tous discoveries in the laboratory, the emergence of a market threat,
and so forth. Each of these sources produces a request for action. The
executives who sponsor projects are, if nothing else, action oriented
by experience. They give orders and expect their subordinates to

follow through. However, the careful planning that follows (work breakdown structure and scheduling) is bound to uncover contradictions that action-oriented executives may have overlooked. What sponsors and other key stakeholders expect cannot always be achieved under their initial terms—despite project team members' efforts to make it happen.

What can be done under these circumstances? In the example just described, what should Pena say to Henderson?

Challenging Assumptions

Most projects are formed on a foundation of assumptions. For example, "There is $1 million available to complete the project—and no more." "We have to limit the number of people on the project to twenty-five." "The project must be completed by March 30 of next year." "The new product must be no larger than six inches by ten inches by four inches."

Where do these figures and specifications come from? Some may come off the top of someone's head without a great deal of thought—not the product of careful reflection, measurement, or calculation. Almost certainly, neither the sponsor nor any of the key shareholders produced these figures through the careful work breakdown structure and scheduling exercises demonstrated earlier. Let's reflect on some of these key assumptions.

The Deadline

Consider Henderson's drop-dead date for relocating the fifty employees to the new facility. According to Henderson, all fifty individuals *had* to be relocated in time for the facility's opening. But if that didn't happen, would the company's operations suffer as badly as Henderson believes? And if so, would there be some other way to fully staff the new facility in six months, even if some relocating employees hadn't yet arrived at the new office? Those questions must be answered. There is a possibility that Henderson's assumptions aren't completely accurate.

Available Resources

A project's charter should state the resources available for the work. But faced with a problem like Pena's and the importance of the outcome, the project manager, sponsor, and stakeholders should discuss the possibility of supplementing the originally allotted personnel, funding, and so forth. Giving the project more resources might bring the schedule in line with stakeholder requirements. For example, perhaps Henderson would approve bonuses paid to relocating employees who are having trouble selling their homes, to motivate them to move more quickly than they planned.

Project managers have several options for freeing up more resources for use on their initiatives:

- Expand the project budget

- Assign more employees to the project, particularly to tasks on the critical path

- Outsource one or more tasks to qualified vendors or suppliers

- Buy, instead of build, components whose development will add time to the schedule

But in selecting from these options, decision makers face a trade-off: when you shift resources from one organizational activity to another, you must determine whether exchanging one value for another will produce a better overall outcome.

Facing up to trade-offs is one of the most common and important challenges of project management—one that many managers fail to master. Too often, project sponsors such as Henderson at EvanCo demand that the project manager meet their impossible requirements and then express disappointment when the manager fails to deliver. When the project manager tells them, "Given the available time and resources, I can do X or Y. Which do you want?"

the stakeholder replies, "Both." When the project manager cannot provide both, he or she takes the blame.

The best antidote to this problem? Make necessary trade-offs visible, and involve your project's stakeholders in the resolution. Indeed, stakeholders *must* take responsibility for these trade-offs.

Project Deliverables

The third area in which a project manager might seek a scheduling solution involves the deliverables stated in the project charter. Those deliverables might be a finished product (e.g., a bridge ready to receive vehicle traffic), a plan ready for implementation (e.g., a complete marketing plan for the coming calendar year), a working prototype, or (as in Pena's case) a new facility fully staffed with existing employees. Whatever the deliverable happens to be, its specifications may be negotiable to some degree, especially if the sponsor and key stakeholders cannot or will not relax the deadline or contribute more resources to the cause.

Of course, whether and how specifications can be altered depends entirely on the situation. In the group-move case, Pena spoke with Henderson about the requirement that the new facility be fully staffed on opening day:

> "My team has revisited the schedule," said Pena, "and we believe that we can have the new facility fully staffed in time for the grand opening. However, to do that, we will have to relax one of the specifications given to us in the charter."
>
> "Which one is that?" Henderson asked.
>
> "The part about staffing only with existing employees," Pena replied. "If we force all fifty people to move before they've sold their houses here and bought new ones in Minneapolis, we will probably lose some of our best performers. After all, the job market's brisk in this area, and they've got other options. I propose using contingent staffers to fill any positions at the new facility that remain open owing to our people's trouble selling their homes."

"Well, it's not an ideal solution," Henderson replied. "It may increase our costs, and I'm concerned that the contingent staffers won't be able to hit the ground running."

"That's understandable," Pena said, "but even if all fifty of our people made the move on time, they, too, won't be fully up to speed on opening day. Remember: they're moving to a whole new area, so for many of them, it's going to feel as if they're working for a totally different company. They'll all need a while to settle in and won't operate at peak capacity anyway. I don't think that putting a few contingent people in place is going to drastically affect our operational efficiency."

"You're probably right," Henderson conceded. "In the end, we do want to keep all fifty of our people positive about the move."

"Good," said Pena. "If you can live with this as a deliverable, we can meet your schedule."

The discussions that project managers, key stakeholders, and sponsors have around the issues just described require that people are willing and able to set priorities. Is the delivery date the highest priority? Is it secondary to the original set of deliverables? If more resources are needed to make the project work, from which other activities should they be taken? Those are questions with which decision makers must grapple.

Revisiting Tasks and Times

There is a good chance that challenging assumptions about your project's deadline, available resources, and deliverables will uncover opportunities to adapt the project to the schedule. In some cases, you may need to relax more than one of those constraints to obtain the right fit. But there is also a chance that none of those solutions will help—in which case you and your project team must revisit your earlier work. Consider these tactics:

- **Reevaluate your work breakdown structure.** Is every one of the tasks and subtasks listed in the WBS necessary? Get rid of any that are not, as long as their deletion will not imperil the project. Are the estimated times needed to complete these tasks realistic, or have some been padded? If any are overstated, make them more realistic.

- **Reevaluate your initial assignment of tasks.** Are the current owners of each task the best possible choices? If not, try to recruit individuals who can do these jobs faster and better. You may ruffle some feathers, but that's life if you want to get your project finished on schedule. The project sponsor's organizational clout might be useful in obtaining the services of these high-performing individuals. Sponsor intervention becomes particularly important when managers resist any attempt by a project manager to move their best employees away from their regular departmental duties.

- **Redirect resources to get the highest possible performance.** Are any of your best people or other resources tied up in activities that aren't on the critical path? If they are, do some thoughtful shuffling. Then reestimate the time needed to complete the affected tasks. You may find that this reshuffling has improved your schedule.

- **Streamline key tasks.** Business's experience with process reengineering during the 1990s demonstrated something of profound importance: many tasks could be made faster and better through redesign. Bank loan applications that once took ten days were completed in a few hours without any decrease in quality. Customer orders that once took several days to process and pack were shipped the same day. There may be opportunities to do the same with tasks on your project's critical path. Have you examined those tasks from a redesign perspective?

Theoretically, those practices should go into the final, optimizing step of the project scheduling process. But if that step fails to align the schedule with the charter's requirements and if the sponsor will not allow any adjustments, you'll have to approach the job with greater determination.

Summing Up

In this chapter, you discovered the following:

- If it's clear that a project cannot produce the deliverables or meet the deadline specified by the sponsor, attack the problem head-on through discussion with him or her. Don't ignore the problem.

- Revisit key assumptions about deliverables, deadline requirements, and project resources. It may be possible to satisfy the sponsor and stakeholders by making adjustments to those elements.

- Revisit the work breakdown structure and your initial assignment of tasks to identify unnecessary steps and opportunities to get jobs done faster and better.

Leveraging Chapter Insights: Critical Questions

- Select an HR project you're currently managing that has encountered problems meeting all of the sponsor's and other stakeholders' expectations. What is the nature of the problem? For example, do you anticipate having trouble meeting deadlines? Staying within budget? Not coming through on a deliverable?

- Which assumptions—on the part of the project sponsor and key stakeholders—might merit reconsideration so as to redefine the constraints of the project?

- If stakeholders aren't willing to redefine deadlines, to allocate more resources to the project, or to reconsider deliverables, how might you identify additional strategies for fitting the project to the stakeholders' expectations? For example, can you reassign certain tasks to different people in order to get those tasks done faster and therefore meet the original project deadline? What other solutions might you identify?

CHAPTER NINE

Managing Risk

Scanning the Hazy Horizon

Key Topics Covered in This Chapter

- *Identifying and prioritizing risks
  to the project plan*

- *Avoiding and minimizing risks*

- *Developing contingency plans*

E VERY HR PROJECT PLAN includes assumptions—about task performance by project team members, the time required to complete key tasks, the future availability of resources, the collaboration of allies, and so forth. Risks lurk in each of these assumptions. What if the techies in the IT group cannot produce a workable Web site for your HRIS project? What if a key member of the project team is hospitalized for a month—or leaves the company? How would the project be affected if an HR consulting firm you've hired to handle part of your project falls a month behind schedule? Managers of all sorts who are handling complex projects grapple with risks like these every day:

- **Financial resource risk.** A financial manager, foreseeing a possible cash flow shortage, reduces the risk by collecting receivables ahead of schedule, putting a hold on all discretionary spending, and making sure that a bank credit line is available.

- **Human resource risk.** Informed that a key employee, Jack, has been interviewing with other companies, Mary, his boss, takes some initial steps toward finding a replacement. "Who could fill Jack's shoes tomorrow if need be?" Mary asks herself. "If no one is quite ready, what training or experience would our best internal candidates for the job need to become ready? What might we do to persuade Jack to stay with our company?"

- **Supply risk.** A purchasing manager for an original equipment manufacturer, fearful that the supply of a key component may be extremely tight six months in the future, reduces the risk by building a buffer stock.

- **Quality risk.** A real estate developer awards contracts to different building contractors. Knowing from past experience that many low-cost bidders will cut corners to finish within budget, the developer builds quality specifications into every contract and monitors compliance on a regular basis.

Each of those managers recognized the risks to their operations and took steps to mitigate those risks. Doing so is part of their jobs. As an HR project manager or participant, you must do the same.

What Is Risk Management?

Risk management is the part of project planning through which you identify key risks and develop plans to prevent them and/or mitigate their adverse effects. In reality, there are two types of risk management. People who use risk management type 1 assume a certain amount of clairvoyance—they expect that it is possible to anticipate developments that could compromise the project plan or schedule. Managers who use risk management type 2 recognize that some adverse developments cannot be anticipated. There can be no contingency planning around all forms of risk. The only remedy is to build a robust management framework that's capable of dealing with the unexpected—whatever it might be. This chapter focuses on the first form of risk management; type 2 risk will be developed more fully later.

Risk management in the traditional, type 1 sense has three essential aims:

1. To identify and prioritize risks to the project

2. To take actions to avoid or minimize key risks

3. To develop contingency plans to handle potential setbacks

   Let's consider each of those activities.

Identifying and Prioritizing Project Risks

The most obvious way to deal with risk is to conduct a systematic audit of all the things that could go wrong with your project. A risk audit involves the following three steps:

1. **Collecting ideas widely.** People's perspectives about risk differ greatly. Some foresee perils that others miss entirely. By talking with many people—project team members, people in the operating units or on the corporate staff, customers, and suppliers—you may harvest some surprising information. For example, by talking with the IT manager who's handling the technical functionality of the new e-learning program you're managing, you may learn that she's been having difficulty getting bids in from the software consultants she's considering using to help her with the project. This development suggests a possible risk to the overall project schedule.

2. **Identifying internal risks.** Internal risks can take many forms. For example, consider understaffing. One key resignation in your project team could cause the initiative to collapse. Poorly trained or unorganized personnel represent another source of internal risk. For instance, suppose you're counting on managers in key positions to serve as mentors to new hires in a new employee mentoring program you're developing. If some of those managers turn out to be busier than expected during the time they're scheduled to serve as mentors, they may make only a halfhearted attempt to fulfill their mentoring duties. And your program may fall flat.

3. **Identifying external risks.** An external risk may take the form of an emerging new technology that will render your new recruiting Web site, for example, outdated. An impending regulatory change may pose another risk. Also consider economic changes—such as a downturn in the real estate market that makes employees unwilling to relocate to a new company facility because they'll have difficulty selling their homes. External risks are many and often hidden. Some large technology companies maintain small "business intelligence" units to identify these threats.

As you conduct your risk audit, pay particular attention to areas with the greatest potential to harm your project. Depending on the project, these areas might include new legal compliance obligations, technical breakdowns, labor market volatility, or conflicts in relationships with customers, suppliers, and unions. Ask yourself where your project is most vulnerable. Then consider these questions: What are the worst things that could go wrong in these areas? Which risks are the most likely to surface? For more help on examining potential risks, see "A Method for Quantifying Risk."

A Method for Quantifying Risk

Your risk audit will likely identify dozens of risks to your project. Naturally, some will be more dangerous than others—that is, their potential for damage will be greater. At the same time, some risks are more likely to occur than others. Thus, risk has two factors you must consider: potential negative impact and probability of occurrence. You can use them to prioritize your audit list. Here are four steps for auditing risk:

1. Estimate the negative impact of each risk. Express it in monetary form. For example, "The cost of a one-month delay would be $25,000."

2. Assign a probability to the risk (0 percent to 100 percent). For example, "The risk of a one-month delay is 40 percent."

3. Multiply the monetary impact by the probability. Example: $25,000 × 0.40 = $10,000. Statisticians call this resulting number the "expected value." In effect, it is the dollar impact weighted by the probability of its occurrence.

4. Rank-order your audit list by expected value.

A rank-order list will give you greater insights into the risks you face.

Taking Actions to Avoid or Minimize Risks

Once you have audited your situation and identified the key risks, you will be better positioned to do something about them. In the most drastic cases, a project manager may alter the project's scope to avoid risks that his or her organization is not prepared to confront. For example, a sausage maker, fearful of bacterial contamination somewhere in the production or distribution channel, may decide to produce only precooked and aseptically packaged meats. In another case, the project manager may take positive steps to prevent risks from emerging as full-blown crises. For instance, if you are concerned that a key project member, Brenda, may leave the company, you might use the following tactics to eliminate the risk or minimize its consequences:

- Make sure that Brenda has a visible and attractive career course ahead of her within the company.

- Prepare other employees to fill Brenda's shoes in the event that she leaves.

- Don't give Brenda responsibility for too many important tasks; instead, distribute important tasks among several reliable project team members. Doing so will diversify your risk.

Still other risks identified in your audit can be minimized through thoughtful planning. For example, consider this scenario:

You and your project team are managing the creation of an HRIS for your company. At the start of the project, you're considering which modules to include in the system—career development, benefits, job evaluation, equal employment opportunity, safety / Occupational Safety and Health Administration, recruitment, payroll, employee self-service, training, labor relations, and so forth.

You know that the members of the project's steering committee often change their minds on desired outcomes as projects they're sponsoring begin to unfold. Right now, they're advocating adopting the full suite of possible modules for the HRIS. But you know that if you take this approach and then the steering committee members decide that some of the modules aren't needed after all, you'll have expended huge sums of money, and plenty of time, researching and creating specs for a fully integrated system. The risk of wastage is too great.

To mitigate the risk, you do a little additional research into how other companies have handled this part of the HRIS decision process. You discover that many organizations have adopted a smaller package of standard modules featuring only the payroll, benefits, employee self-service, and recruitment modules. These companies claim that starting with the smaller package has enabled them to more easily address technical problems while setting up the system, to gain familiarity with using the HRIS, and to add more specialized modules later as needed.

You build a compelling business case for taking this more cautious approach, and then you present your case to the steering committee. You share the convincing anecdotal accounts you've assembled and the sobering statistics you've gathered about the high costs of adopting the full suite of modules at the outset of an HRIS project. Thanks to your careful preparation, the steering committee agrees to start off with the smaller package.

Note: For more tips on performing a risk audit, see "Brainstorm the Possibilities."

Brainstorm the Possibilities

Brainstorming sessions that include many people with different functions and different perspectives is usually the most productive approach to identifying risks and finding ways to minimize their impact. There is real power in numbers, since no single person can foresee the dozens of things that could go wrong in a project, especially a large one. As you brainstorm, develop a list of serious risks, and then unify similar risks into manageable groups. Try to identify the underlying basis for those risks. For instance, the basis of risk for the HRIS project is the steering committee members' propensity to change their minds after a project has begun. Once you understand the sources of risk, you'll be in a better position to avoid them.

Developing Contingency Plans to Handle Potential Setbacks

Some risks cannot be avoided. Others can be reduced, but only in part. You need to develop contingency plans for these unavoidable and uncontrollable risks. A *contingency plan* is a course of action prepared in advance to deal with a potential problem; it answers this question: "if _____ happens, how could we respond in a way that would neutralize or minimize the damage?" Here are two examples of project contingency plans:

- The Acme Company set up a two-year project to modernize its manufacturing facilities. Senior management regarded the two-year deadline as extremely important. Recognizing the real risk that the deadline might not be met, the sponsor agreed to set up a reserve fund that could be used to hire outside help if the project fell behind schedule. This contingency plan included a monthly progress review and a provision that falling three or more weeks behind schedule would trigger the release of the reserve funds. In addition, two managers were charged with the job of identifying no fewer than three vendors who had the capacity to help out with the project.

- TechnoWhiz, Inc. was banking on its software project team to develop a new version of its integrated business application suite, one that would include all the bells and whistles, as well as seamless linkages to the Internet. Not wanting to miss the announced release date and expensive marketing rollout, the team developed a contingency plan for dealing with any unfinished elements of the program—and the probability of having some was high. That contingency plan was straightforward: any feature not ready at the time of the official release would be offered at a future date to all registered users of the new version as a downloadable add-on. Staffing for development of add-on elements was planned in advance, with budgeting contingent on the amount of needed work.

The real benefit of a contingency plan is that it prepares your project and company to deal quickly and effectively with adverse situations. When disaster strikes, managers and project members with such a plan can act immediately; they don't have to spend weeks trying to figure out what they should do or how they will find the funds to deal with their new situation. The what and how of their response will be contained in the plan.

Has your project identified its risks? Does it know which have the greatest expected value? Has it developed contingency plans for dealing with them? See "HR in Action: Planning for the Worst at Elliot Printing" for an example of HR-related contingency planning. And then read "Make Someone Responsible for Each Serious Risk and Its Management" for more helpful advice on preparing for potential risks.

HR in Action: Planning for the Worst at Elliot Printing

Nina Glass, HR director for Elliot Printing, knew that competition in the industry was reaching brutal levels. She also knew that the company's union contract would be coming up for review in six months. Because workers had been grumbling about pay rates, she was worried that union leaders would present stiff demands for higher pay rates—rates that the company couldn't afford. Mulling over worst-case scenarios, she envisioned Elliot Printing being put in a position where it would either meet the union's expensive demands or face a crippling strike. She proposed a project to the rest of the executive team: work out a contingency plan for running the company without its union people.

The executive team agreed that such a plan would be valuable. Glass received approval to assemble a team to develop the plan. To select members, she first identified nonunion supervisors working in the most potentially affected areas of the company: the

continued

press room, trimming and packing line, and shipping room. She also invited the sales manager to join, since customers might be concerned about the company's ability to deliver orders during a strike. The CFO constituted another valuable team member because she could handle the financial aspects of a possible strike. Finally, the head of Elliot Printing's public relations department joined the team. He had deep connections with the local media and could act as public spokesperson for the company if needed.

During the team's first meeting, members identified fronts on which a strike would produce problems—such as production deadlines, customer relations, community relations, stress on nonstriking employees, physical security, and so forth. Each team member agreed to meet with the nonunion people in their respective units and to gather their ideas for combating these problems.

Next the team prioritized the list of problems, selecting stalled production lines as the greatest challenge. However, according to the production supervisor, the company's printing presses—though immense—were relatively easy to operate. "A few weeks of hands-on training and supervision would enable other employees to operate the machines," he said. Several nonunion employees proved willing to learn, so Glass contacted the equipment manufacturer to arrange for training services.

As these and other components of the contingency plan took shape, the project team ran the ideas by the company's attorney for comments and suggestions. Since the details seemed sound, the team decided to test the plan under simulated conditions, practicing each component as if a strike had indeed occurred. For example, the PR director delivered a speech to the project team and a small number of other employees announcing the "strike," explaining its causes, and laying out the company's plans for resolving the impasse and ensuring that all company operations would proceed smoothly. Listeners offered suggestions for improving the speech for public consumption. And employees who had been attending evening training sessions on the printing equipment applied their learning to a simulated print job on a Saturday morning.

Six months passed. Knowing that they had a sound contingency plan in place, company executives went into the union contract review negotiations with confidence. Ultimately, they and the union leadership worked out a three-year deal—and there was no strike. Though Elliot Printing didn't have to roll its contingency plan into action—at least this time—Glass and the rest of her project team knew that the mere existence of the plan put the company in a strong position to deal with its worst nightmare—should it ever become reality.

SOURCE: Adapted from *Crisis Management: Master the Skills to Prevent Disasters,* Harvard Business Essentials (Boston: Harvard Business School Press, 2004), chap. 3.

Make Someone Responsible for Each Serious Risk and Its Management

Just as every task on your project's schedule should have an owner, every key risk should be someone's responsibility. That person should monitor the assigned risk, sound the alarm if it appears to be moving from being a potential problem to a real problem, and take charge of the consequences.

For example, suppose you're developing an employee handbook, and you've identified the following risks: (1) one or more of the managers who have agreed to review the draft of the handbook might deliver their comments late, putting the project behind schedule, and (2) the freelance writer you've hired to draft and revise the handbook may produce less-than-high-quality work, threatening the accuracy and readability of the handbook's contents.

You assign a project team member to own each of these risks. One person agrees to check with reviewing managers frequently

continued

during the review process to ensure that they meet their deadlines for submitting comments. And another person commits to evaluating the earliest versions of the writer's work to catch and address any quality problems immediately. Thanks to these assignments, you and your team stand a better chance of dealing promptly with problems should they arise.

Summing Up

In this chapter, you discovered that:

- Risk management identifies key risks and develops plans to prevent them and/or mitigate their adverse effects.

- A risk audit identifies things that could go wrong.

- Brainstorming sessions that involve many people with different functions and perspectives are usually the best way to conduct a risk audit.

- You need to develop contingency plans for important risks that cannot be avoided or greatly reduced.

Leveraging Chapter Insights: Critical Questions

- Consider an HR project you're about to launch. What are the internal and external risks inherent in the project? And whom might you contact to brainstorm ideas for possible risks?

- When you rank-order the risks you've identified, which are the top three most-pressing risks?

- What steps might you take to avoid or minimize the risks you've identified? Are there changes you could make to the project plan to mitigate those risks? If so, what are they?

- For risks that can't be avoided or significantly mitigated, what contingency plan might you put in place? Whom would you invite to help you develop the contingency plan? And how might you test the plan to ensure that, if the worst does happen, the plan will work as intended?

CHAPTER TEN

Project Adaptation

Dealing with What You Cannot Anticipate

Key Topics Covered in This Chapter

- *Three sources of unanticipated project risk*

- *How management inflexibility on budgets and deadlines has led to disastrous surprises*

- *A model for adaptive project management— and when to apply it*

I N WARFARE, initial battle plans begin falling apart with the first skirmishes. Combatants are forced to respond to moves that were not—or could not—have been anticipated. Challenges and opportunities reveal themselves as events play out. Big, complex HR projects—even those that are well planned—experience something very similar. Internal customers' requirements change even as the project team is working to satisfy them; the team discovers that it is aiming at a moving target. Participants encounter unforeseen opportunities to do something of greater value for customers in the course of executing the existing project plan. Project prototypes lead to dead ends or reveal the need for more development. A key consultant working with the team is pulled away for a month to serve another client. Project participants are learning about a new technology and its capabilities even as they attempt to install it.

Each of those examples is a development that you and your project team may not have anticipated, no matter how smart or prepared you were in the beginning. In chapter 9, we explained a traditional form of risk management that emphasizes risks that can be anticipated and addressed through avoidance and contingency plans. In this chapter, we turn to risks that are less likely to be anticipated. Consider a project involving the development of a new e-learning program for your company's workforce. You may end up dealing with new and unfamiliar technology that you haven't yet mastered. And because the technology is new, your internal customers may not be able to articulate the deliverables they expect from the initiative. The project's unfolding is punctuated by dead ends and disappointments—as well as valuable discoveries.

The traditional framework of project management has not been particularly useful for dealing with hard-to-anticipate risks. The tools offered in earlier chapters—work breakdown structure, time estimates, and scheduling methods—definitely help, especially when project personnel are familiar with the tasks and technologies with which they must engage, and when outcomes are highly measurable. As author and Harvard Business School professor Robert Austin has stated: "Conventional project management methodologies work best when the chances are really good that the project will unfold as anticipated during its planning stages, when there is little that can happen during the project that planners can't see coming, when you can formulate responses to contingencies in advance. In other words: when there is not much genuine discovery going on."[1] Austin points to building construction as an example, where the range of potential problems often can be anticipated and solutions planned in advance. The traditional tools of project management, however, are less useful when uncertainty is high. Something more is required: adaptability.

This chapter provides practical advice for dealing with hard-to-anticipate risk—that is, it explains how you can (and should) be prepared to adapt and learn as a project unfolds and as participants make discoveries and encounter unanticipated problems and opportunities.

Sources of Unanticipated Risk— and Their Consequences

The risks that project managers cannot anticipate generally come from three sources:

1. New and unfamiliar technology (e.g., development and installation of totally new enterprise software)

2. Work that lies outside the experience of the project planner and project team (e.g., a team of HR professionals who have

never experienced a merger or acquisition before must decide
how to blend two previously separate HR departments)

3. Project magnitude (e.g., transforming a struggling company's
   entire organizational culture so as to enable it to survive
   changes in the business landscape)

The consequences of the risks inherent in those three sources
largely make themselves felt during the implementation phase of projects. Those consequences can be huge in terms of project cost, schedule slippage, and disappointing results. Managers of Boston's infamous
Big Dig highway project, for example, were forced to reveal in 2001
that the venture was several *billion* dollars over budget and a year or
more behind schedule. In another example, a major financial services
company reported receiving no benefit from hundreds of millions of
dollars invested in a new IT system; the project was a total loss.

Another consequence of applying the traditional project management discipline to situations with high uncertainty—where
things are likely to go wrong—is a tendency for participants to remain silent about problems. Being on time and on schedule are so
important that some people are afraid to come forward with the
truth about inevitable problems with budgets, schedules, and technical roadblocks. Admitting to a problem is the equivalent to admitting
to a personal failure. You can almost hear the project sponsor saying,
"You agreed at the very beginning that you could get the job done
in six months if you had a $300,000 budget and a team of five peo-
ple. So why isn't the job finished?"

Not surprisingly, many people simply ignore their project's problems, hoping that a breakthrough or stroke of good luck will make
things right in the end—which almost never happens. Others hope
that problems and their consequences will not come to light until
much later—or that their personal connection with those problems
will remain invisible. For example, software developers may be tempted
to take shortcuts because most nonspecialist managers don't know how
to trace complex systems problems to their sources.[2]

In a case that involved one of the Big Three U.S. automakers, a
new, three-year, multi-billion-dollar vehicle platform project was

under tremendous pressure from higher management to be completed on time. The company's engineers and designers were attempting something they had never done: introducing a compact car that could go head-to-head with those built by Japanese rivals. As the project entered its final months, it was clear to people in the trenches that the new vehicle had major problems, yet no one wanted to acknowledge them. Senior management wouldn't tolerate any bad news. So the new vehicle was pushed on from one development stage to another with all of its defects. For example, when it failed its low temperature start-up test, someone fudged the numbers, giving it a passing grade. When a preproduction model arrived at the company's outdoor track for road testing, engineers altered its carburetor and filled the tank with a special fuel; the car could not make it around the track without that assistance. Management was clueless about the vehicle's problems—which became devastatingly clear once it entered the market.

In a comparable case, this one involving a major U.S. manufacturer, managers for a multi-million-dollar IT implementation project deliberately silenced systems analysts who had discovered substantial technical problems. The systems analysts were saying, "This won't work. The plan must change." These were words the project managers didn't want anyone to hear. After all, they had a plan, and the plan had to be implemented. In the end, their failure to heed the analysts' warnings—and to adapt the plan to a new reality—cost the company millions.

The disasters experienced by these companies might have been avoided or mitigated if people had not been so locked into their plans. What happens when projects at *your* organization encounter serious and unanticipated problems?

The Adaptive Management Approach

Is the object of your project or its implementation shrouded in uncertainty? Is it based on a new technology or material with which your team is unfamiliar? Are the tasks involved different from anything your team has dealt with in the past? Is the project substantially larger than any others in your experience?

If you answered yes to one or more of those questions, the traditional management tools—work breakdown structure, time estimates, and scheduling methods—might not be optimal. You may have to consider a more adaptive approach.

As we've seen, the traditional model for project management is a linear progression of activities: define and organize, plan and schedule the work, manage execution, and close down. Feedback loops provide opportunities for learning to flow back into different components of the model. But, really, this model is linear: it assumes that project planners have identified the tasks that must be done, the associated costs, and the required time. The traditional model is workable for many, if not most, projects, but it's less helpful for those with high levels of uncertainty. But what might you use in those exceptional cases?

In their research of large IT implementation projects, Lynda Applegate, Robert Austin, and Warren McFarlan found that some companies—notably Cisco Systems and Tektronix—have enjoyed success with adaptive project management models that do the following:

1. **Approach tasks iteratively.** Members engage in small incremental tasks. They evaluate the outcomes of those tasks and make adjustments moving forward.

2. **Have fast cycles.** Long lead times interfere with the iterative approach.

3. **Emphasize early value delivery.** Instead of delivering value at the project's end, deliverables come earlier and in smaller pieces. This encourages feedback and the incorporation of learning into subsequent activities.

4. **Staff the project with people who are capable of learning and adapting.** Some people are faster learners than others and are more amenable to change.

5. **Put less reliance on decision-making tools that assume predictability.** Return on investment, net present value, and

internal rate of return are useful decision tools, but only when future cash flows are reasonably predictable—which is not the case in projects with high uncertainty.[3]

Cisco refers to its project approach as "rapid iterative prototyping." Here, many tasks are viewed as probes—learning experiences for subsequent steps. This tactic is analogous to the notion of the "cheap kills" that research and development personnel use to sort through many possibilities quickly and at low cost. When the right solution is not apparent, they try a number of simple experiments to separate promising and unpromising options. Even failed experiments provide insights into what will work. This experimental, adaptive approach to project management requires project leaders and team members who are curious, open to learning, and eager to cycle their learning into each new step as the project unfolds. (Cisco may have coined the term *rapid iterative prototyping,* but the concept is as old as the lightbulb. To learn more, see "Rapid Iterative Prototyping— Nineteenth-Century Style.")

The adaptive approach points to a new role for project sponsors. In the traditional model, the sponsor says, "Here's what I want. To get it, I will provide your project with a budget of $2 million and eighteen people." Writing for *Science*'s Next Wave, Robert Austin suggests a different approach, one that conforms more closely to the approach used by venture capitalists (VCs). Venture capitalists, Austin notes, seldom give entrepreneurs a big pile of cash at the beginning of their work. Instead, VCs stage their commitment as their entrepreneurial partners produce results.[4] For example, if the entrepreneur has a start-up software company with a plan to develop a breakthrough application, the VC will provide only enough cash for the project to move forward to the next level. If the entrepreneur succeeds in reaching that level, the VC will review progress and develop expectations for the next step. Here, the results of the just-completed step provide new information for the VC, who will finance the following step if the prospects look favorable.

The venture capitalist advances cash to probe and seek feedback— that is, to purchase information, learn, and reduce uncertainty. Each

Rapid Iterative Prototyping—Nineteenth-Century Style

Thomas A. Edison, America's innovation icon, never used the expression *cheap kills* as far as we know. And he certainly never heard the term *rapid iterative prototyping*. He did, however, practice both.

In 1878, Edison jumped into the race to develop the first practical incandescent lamp. Many others were already in the field, but he reasoned that he stood a chance to win.

Edison knew—as did his competitors—that passing an electrical current through a wire or other conductive filament would make it glow brightly. He also knew that higher voltage would make the filament glow more brightly, but that it would also cause the filament to burn up more quickly. A key challenge, then, was to find a filament material that would glow brightly without quickly burning up.

What material should he try? No amount of advanced planning could have answered that essential question. So Edison and his Insomnia Brigade of assistants (so called because of their boss's demanding work hours) set out on a course of cheap kills. They tested thousands of filaments in a vacuum—filaments made from chromium, aluminum, papers coiled in various ways, and other materials. They eventually found a material that worked well—a piece of carbonized cotton thread.

Edison beat his many competitors to the patent office, and his practice of making cheap kills, or rapid iterative prototyping if you will, made his success possible.

SOURCE: Adapted with permission from James M. Utterback, *Mastering the Dynamics of Innovation* (Boston: Harvard Business School Press, 1994), 58–62.

investment gives him or her an option to remain in the game—if there is a game! In effect, the financier pays to preserve the option to do more.

In this adaptive model, key project activities move forward through a series of learning experiences as represented graphically in figure 10-1.

FIGURE 10-1

The adaptive model of project management

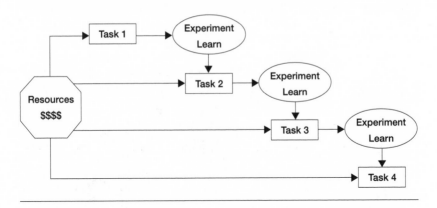

The adaptive model does not apply to every project, but it's recommended when the level of planning or execution uncertainty is high—that is, when the project faces risks that may not be anticipated, or when the range of potential outcomes is very wide. How uncertain is your current HR project? Is your company ready for this adaptive approach? Are you? See "HR in Action: Processing a Turnaround" for an example of how one HR leader used the adaptive approach.

HR in Action: Processing a Turnaround

Of all the sources of unanticipated risk, project magnitude arguably proved the biggest for the HR team at Xerox Corp. With the company facing a steep financial slide in 2000 (marked by ballooning debt, a plummeting stock price, and dwindling cash), Xerox's HR had to simultaneously pull numerous levers in order to turn the struggling organization around. These levers included massive layoffs and complex buyout packages, combined with major divestitures and focused retention strategies— all applied to a vast international organization. It was about as hefty a turnaround project as one can imagine. But by managing the project through the adaptive approach, the HR group helped

continued

put Xerox back on solid footing. Indeed, by the end of 2003, net income had jumped to $222 million (from just $19 million the previous year), and share price had soared to between $14 and $15 (from a mere $4 earlier in the year).

How did Xerox HR apply the adaptive approach? For one thing, the team looked for opportunities to make experimental changes that delivered results quickly. For example, it consolidated and expanded the HR service center. Whereas the center used to handle only transactional work, it also began providing research and analysis to HR operations throughout the company and handling employee relations issues for most U.S. employees. At the same time, the company added Web-based processes to handle routine work. The payoff? HR could reduce headcount while still delivering valuable service to managers and employees. This experiment turned out to generate the biggest savings of all for Xerox.

As another example of the value of rapid experimentation, the HR group swiftly enacted a series of retention strategies to keep the company's best performers loyal during this time of profound change. One strategy had Xerox's charismatic new CEO traveling around the world three times in just two months to let high performers know that "we can't survive without you." Another strategy called for a cash "stay" bonus. Still another entailed giving the most valued employees the job assignments and learning opportunities (an international stint, profit-and-loss responsibility, a general management position) they needed to eventually take on executive leadership positions. These rapid tactics paid big dividends: 97 percent retention of high performers in the first twelve months.

The HR team also leveraged participants' ability to adapt and learn. For instance, it assigned some compensation experts to the new shared service structure at corporate HR, kept others in HR operations within the business units, and redeployed still others to different functions altogether. These individuals' willingness to go where they were needed and to broaden their expertise proved essential to the turnaround. As another example of leveraging the power of learning, HR formed strategy alignment workshops at which five hundred employees worldwide discussed potential obstacles to the company's success and ideas for removing roadblocks. Attended by the CEO, the workshops enabled Xerox to harvest the creative thinking of a wide range of employees.

Though many components of Xerox's turnaround effort were painful, the HR team's use of the adaptive approach enabled it to begin generating results quickly, learn from mistakes, and ultimately guide the company away from disaster and toward an impressive recovery.

SOURCE: Tom Starner, "Processing a Turnaround," *Human Resource Executive,* May 16, 2004.

Summing Up

In this chapter, you learned the following:

- The traditional project model is not particularly adaptive when the level of unanticipated risk is high.

- Unanticipated risks have three general sources: new and unfamiliar technology, a new kind of work, and a project magnitude that is substantially larger than those with which the team has experience.

- Insistence on strict adherence to budgets and deadlines can be dangerous when uncertainty is high; it can make people ignore or conceal problems, as well as miss valuable opportunities.

- The adaptive project management model encourages people to do the following: engage in small incremental tasks, evaluate their outcomes and make adjustments, avoid long lead times, emphasize early value delivery, staff projects with skilled people who are capable of learning and adapting, and put less reliance on decision-making tools that assume predictability.

Leveraging Chapter Insights: Critical Questions

- Review the projects you're currently managing or participating in—as well as projects that may be coming your way in the near future. From these many projects, which one has the most potential for unanticipated risks? Why?

- What are the sources of unanticipated risk in the project you identified above? Consider unfamiliar technology, new skills, and project magnitude.

- In your view, does the project you've identified merit use of the adaptive management approach? Why or why not?

- If you were to use the adaptive management approach for your project, how might you design small experiments from which to draw lessons? In what ways could you deliver value early as the project unfolds? How might you assemble a project team of individuals who have a large capacity to learn and adapt? Who comes to mind as you consider candidates for team membership?

CHAPTER ELEVEN

Getting Off on the Right Foot

Project Needs to Keep in Mind

Key Topics Covered in This Chapter

- *The importance of the project launch meeting, and topics to address*

- *Integrative mechanisms that encourage collaboration and trust between project team members*

- *Norms of team behavior*

W HEN YOUR HR PROJECTS get off on the right foot, they have a greater likelihood of success. Project planning, a formal charter, work structure breakdown, careful scheduling, and risk management are all part of ensuring an effective start to your initiative. But there's more, and it's covered here.

Once you've formed your project team, created the charter, and scheduled the work, you need to do several additional important things before work commences. First, the project needs a launch—a special event that marks the official beginning of the work. Second, you must attend to a number of important issues associated with team-based work. (At the end of the day, project management is very much about leading teams. Indeed, team-based work lies at the heart of every project.) Finally, you'll need to establish the norms of behavior that make collaborative, team-based work possible and communicate those norms to all participants in the project.

Why Launch Meetings Matter

An official project launch represents the first project milestone, telling everyone, "We begin this journey together, and we begin now." If conducted properly, the launch has substantial symbolic value.

The best way to launch a project effort is through an all-team meeting, one with appropriate levels of gravity and fanfare. Clearly, before the launch meeting, you and other stakeholders in the project will have already engaged in extensive discussion and planning. But those informal get-togethers are no substitute for a face-to-face meeting attended by all the project team members, the sponsor, key stakeholders, and, if appropriate, the highest-ranking official of your organization.

Physical presence at this meeting has great psychological importance, particularly for geographically dispersed teams. Members of such teams may have few future opportunities to convene as a group. Being together at the very beginning of the long journey and getting to know each other at a personal level will foster commitment and bolster participants' sense that this team and project are important. It's difficult to imagine anyone feeling part of a group with common goals if he or she is not in the physical presence of teammates at some point. If certain people cannot attend the launch meeting because of their geographic location, every effort should be made to give them a virtual presence through videoconferencing or, at the very least, speakerphone.

The sponsor's attendance at the launch meeting is imperative. His or her presence and demeanor speak volumes about the importance— or unimportance—ascribed to the project's mission. As experts Jon Katzenbach and Douglas Smith write:

> When potential teams first gather, everyone monitors the signals given by others to confirm, suspend, or dispel assumptions and concerns. They pay particular attention to those in authority: the team leader and any executives who set up, oversee, or otherwise influence the team. And, as always, what such leaders do is more important than what they say. If a senior executive leaves the team kickoff to take a phone call ten minutes after the session has begun and he never returns, people get the message.[1]

At your project's official launch meeting, strive to accomplish the following tasks:

- **Be very clear about who belongs to the project team.** Acknowledge each member by name if the group is not too large. There may be core members, and there may be peripheral members who participate for a limited time or in a limited way. But all are members. Do not tolerate any ambiguity on this point. Welcome to the launch meeting all those who will contribute to the project.

- **Explain the project charter and its contents.** The sponsor or project manager should explain the goal, deliverables, and timetables as documented in the charter.

- **Seek unanimous understanding of the charter.** Just because the leadership explains the goal, deliverables, and so forth, there's no assurance that every team member will interpret them in the same way. Engage people in discussion about the charter with the goal of getting agreement and consensus.

- **Have the sponsor explain *why* the project's work is important and *how* its goals are aligned with larger organizational objectives.** People need to know that they are part of something with important consequences for themselves and the organization; otherwise, they won't make their best effort. This discussion should aim to satisfy that need.

- **Describe the resources available to the team and the non-team personnel with whom members are likely to interact.** That group may include other company employees, employees of alliance partners, suppliers, or customers.

- **Describe team incentives.** In addition to their normal compensation, what will members receive if team goals are met or exceeded?

- **Make introductions.** Unless people are already acquainted with each other and familiar with others' special skills, use the launch meeting as an opportunity for personal introductions. If the group is of a reasonable size, ask participants to introduce themselves, to say something about their background and expertise, and to explain what they hope to contribute to the effort.

By the end of the launch meeting, people should have a clear sense of direction, the importance of the team's goal to the organization, the ways in which success will be measured, and the rewards they'll earn for their efforts. They should know who is on the team and what each is capable of contributing. And they should begin to think of themselves as members of a real team. A sense of belonging and of contributing to a common goal can develop only with time and through shared experiences. Nevertheless, you can plant the seeds at the launch meeting.

Creating Integrative Mechanisms

Simply throwing people into a launch meeting, giving them collective goals, and handing out free T-shirts with a team name and logo creates a team in name only. Effective project teams are created through collaborative activities: joint work, idea sharing, the give-and-take that typically surrounds important decisions, and the exchange of information. You can facilitate these team-building activities through integrative mechanisms.

Integrative mechanisms include regularly scheduled meetings, communication links such as newsletters, project Web sites, and the physical colocation of team members. Off-site social events can also help build team identification and group cohesion. Each of these mechanisms, in effect, encourages people to talk with one another, understand each other at a personal level, share ideas, analyze and critique alternative strategies, and build the bonds of trust and friendship that make team-based work stimulating and productive.

What integrative mechanisms is *your* HR project using?

Establishing Norms of Behavior

Turning an assemblage of individuals into an effective project team cannot be done overnight. Individuals come to the effort with personal agendas. Many view their new teammates as competitors for promotions, recognition, and rewards. Still others may harbor personal grudges against one or more of the people with whom they have been thrown together. And there is always an individual or two who lacks the social skills required for group work.

Personal agendas, internal competitions, grudges, and poor social skills are present to some degree on every team, and they can undermine project effectiveness if they're not contained or neutralized. The diversity of specialties and work styles that you've probably brought to the team through great effort may also make collaboration more difficult. Technical specialists, for example, may speak an unfamiliar jargon. That behavior may set them apart from their teammates, because many people don't trust what they find unfamiliar.

One of the best ways to manage these problems is to set down clear norms of behavior that apply equally to all. As described by Jon Katzenbach and Douglas Smith, authors of *The Wisdom of Teams*, a popular book on team-based work, the most critical rules pertain to:

- **Attendance.** Members and leaders must understand that the team cannot make decisions and accomplish its work if individual members fail to show up for meetings or joint work sessions. If you are the project manager or leader, people will follow your example. Thus, if you're chronically late or absent, they will mimic your behavior.

- **Interruptions.** Decide to turn cell phones off during meetings and work sessions. Taking a call during a team session indicates that the call is more important than what the team is doing. Also make it clear that people are not to interrupt others during meetings. Everyone has a right to speak.

- **No sacred cows.** Agree that no issues will be off limits. For example, if a process-reengineering team knows that a change will upset a particular executive, its members should not be afraid or reluctant to discuss the issue. Avoiding the issue because of the executive's possible objections will signal that the team and its efforts are pointless.

- **Constructive criticism.** Problem solving is bound to produce competing solutions. The champions of these solutions must understand that they are empowered to represent their views but are forbidden to undermine those of others through deception or the withholding of relevant data. Team players must also learn how to vent disagreement in constructive ways.

- **Confidentiality.** Some team issues are bound to be sensitive. Team members will not discuss those issues freely unless they are confident that what is said within the team stays within the team.

- **Action orientation.** Teams are not formed to meet and discuss; those that do are simply gab sessions that accomplish nothing. Their real purpose is to act and produce results. Make that clear from the very beginning. In the words of Katzenbach and Smith, an action-oriented team means that "everyone does real work" and "everyone gets assignments and does them."[2]

How should you define your group's norms of behavior? That depends on the group's purpose and its members' personalities. But certainly any effective set of norms should be clear and concise. It should also include the basics: respect for all members of the group, a commitment to active listening, and an understanding about how to voice concerns and handle conflict.

To guarantee the free flow of ideas, some groups may want to go further—for example, making it explicit that anyone is entitled to disagree with anyone else. They may also want to adopt specific guidelines that:

- Support calculated risk taking

- Establish procedures about acknowledging and handling failure

- Foster individual expression

- Encourage a playful attitude

Whatever norms your group adopts, make sure that all its members have a hand in establishing them—and that everyone agrees to abide by them. Members' participation and acceptance will head off many future problems. Also, be aware that norms sometimes emerge in unanticipated ways, even if guidelines are explicitly discussed at the beginning of the team project. For example, if some egos are bruised during the team's initial meetings, you may observe subtle hostility between the affected individuals in subsequent interactions. That hostility will probably manifest itself through second-guessing, criticism, sarcasm, and other counterproductive behaviors. As a leader or team member, you should discourage such actions and remind everyone that mutual respect, open discussion, and collaborative behavior are the expected norms.

Careful attention to designing a project launch meeting, creating integrative mechanisms, and establishing agreed-upon norms of behavior can strongly determine the success of your project. See "HR in Action: Launching a Leadership Development Project" for an illustration of how one organization took specific steps to ensure a positive outcome for a major HR initiative.

HR in Action: Launching a Leadership Development Project

Lotte Soretto, HR director at consumer-goods conglomerate Berman-Tighe, knew that her company's leadership development efforts needed overhauling. In particular, the professional development and educational opportunities the firm offered to managers and executives had been too ad hoc in the past: people signed on for courses and degree programs without discussing whether these learning opportunities related to the skills and capabilities the company needed at different levels in its leadership hierarchy. Soretto received approval from Tom Gormley, her CEO, to manage a new initiative that had a bold objective: articulate the requirements of each level of leadership in the company, and redesign learning opportunities to ensure that those requirements were met. Gormley agreed to serve as the project sponsor.

At the project launch meeting, Soretto introduced each member of the project team, along with Gormley and several other members of the executive team. She invited each participant to describe his or her background and expertise and to explain what each hoped to contribute to the project. Gormley then stood up and delivered a rousing speech about how the new initiative would benefit the company. "All of you here today," he said, "are playing a crucial role in helping us put the right people in the right places to push Berman-Tighe to new heights." After Gormley spoke, Soretto went over the project charter, confirming the goal of the initiative, the intended deliverables, and the schedule for completion. Several participants asked questions, such as "How flexible are the two midrange deadlines?" and the group members clarified their understanding of the charter through the resulting conversation.

Soretto wrapped up the launch meeting by detailing the resources the team could draw on as they moved the project forward, including the project budget, personnel that would be available to the team to provide assistance, and office space that the team could use freely. She also reminded team members of the "pot of gold" waiting for them if their efforts came in on time and within budget and generated results in the form of positive responses to newly trained leaders' 360-degree feedback surveys. In addition to their usual salary, team members would receive cash bonuses and an all-expenses-paid trip to the tropics if they met or exceeded their goals.

To further ensure a successful start to the project, Soretto asked the company's IT manager to create a project Web site. About half of the project team members worked in far-flung parts of the company, and the site enabled them to stay in touch with one another as the project unfolded. The site contained a team roster listing every member's role and contact information, links to documents such as the charter and meeting minutes, and a chat room where members could discuss issues and

continued

arrive at decisions. Soretto also got team members to agree to meet weekly—using videoconferencing technology for off-site members—to go over the project's status.

Finally, during the first few weekly team meetings, Soretto initiated discussion of the behavior norms for the team. Members agreed to arrive at meetings on time and to attend consistently, as well as to avoid interruptions and distractions during team meetings. They also defined guidelines for resolving conflicts within the team. These guidelines included bringing complaints directly to the individuals involved, rather than engaging in gossip or backstabbing; using "I language" (such as "I can't do my part of the project when you submit paperwork late" versus "You're doing sloppy work"); and blending advocacy with inquiry ("I think this solution is ideal; does anyone see it differently?").

Thanks to Soretto's efforts to give her project a positive start, the leadership development effort ultimately generated valuable benefits for Berman-Tighe. The project team operated smoothly, and when members came into conflict over an idea or some other aspect of the work, they proved able to resolve it amicably and productively. Moreover, a year after the project was completed, the company had a much clearer description of the skills needed in each leadership position, as well as the development opportunities available for each leadership level. And managers, executives, and individual contributors who were being groomed for leadership positions were signing on for educational programs specifically keyed to the skills they needed to develop. A year later, when participants in the new development programs conducted 360-degree feedback surveys of their leadership abilities, the results indicated significant progress on criteria such as "ability to communicate company strategy," "genuine interest in direct reports' professional development," and "capacity to set direction and delegate." The positive launch that Soretto engineered had translated directly into measurable business results.

Summing Up

This chapter offered the following guidelines:

- Launch your project with an all-team meeting. Everyone should be there, including the sponsor. During that meeting, explain the charter. Stress the importance of the team's goals and the ways in which they fit with larger organizational goals.

- Use integrative mechanisms to transform a group of disparate individuals into a cohesive team. Regularly scheduled meetings, communication links, physical colocation, and social events can help you build team identification, group cohesion, and collaboration.

- Smooth over incompatibilities and make the most of personal differences by creating norms of behavior and getting others to accept them. Showing up at meetings on time, completing assignments on schedule, helping teammates when needed, providing constructive criticism, and demonstrating respect for different viewpoints are examples of positive norms of behavior.

Leveraging Chapter Insights: Critical Questions

- Think of an HR project you're about to lead. In what ways might you organize an effective launch meeting for the project? What might the project sponsor say and do at the launch meeting to get things off on the right foot? How might you set a positive, inspiring tone during the meeting?

- Which integrative mechanisms might you use to create cohesion and collaboration in your project team? Consider regularly scheduled meetings, communication links such as newsletters and project Web sites, the physical colocation of team members, and off-site social events.

- What norms of behavior will be important to establish for your project team? What process will you use to define those norms and gain everyone's commitment to upholding them?

CHAPTER TWELVE

Keeping on Track

Maintaining Control

Key Topics Covered in This Chapter

- *Using budgets, quality checks, and milestones to monitor and control work*

- *Making the most of conflict*

- *Getting people to collaborate*

- *Communicating progress and possibilities*

- *Handling problems*

MANY OF THE CONCERNS of HR project managers and project team leaders are the same concerns faced by all managers: getting results through people and other resources. To accomplish their aims, managers in every functional area must keep people motivated and focused on goals, mediate between the people above and the people below, and make decisions. They must also monitor and control adherence to schedule, budget, and quality standards; deal with people problems; and relentlessly facilitate communication.

This sounds like a big job—and it is! Moreover, it describes what HR project managers must do during the third phase of the project life cycle: managing execution. This chapter focuses on the key responsibilities you'll need to embrace during this phase.

Monitoring and Controlling the Project

In some respects, the manager of a project is analogous to the thermostat that monitors and controls the temperature in your house. Think for just a moment about how that thermostat functions. It is constantly sensing the temperature inside the building. If it senses that the air temperature is within a preset range, say 69 to 71 degrees Fahrenheit, it thinks that all is well and does nothing. It takes action only if it senses a temperature outside of the desired range. If the temperature is too high, the thermostat signals the air-conditioning system to start working. If the temperature is too low, it signals the heating system to switch on. The thermostat continues monitoring the temperature, and once the building's temperature is back within the desired range, it sends another signal, telling the air conditioner or furnace to stop.

Management has analogous sensors and uses them to monitor activities under its control. It uses budgets to gauge the pace of spending relative to set targets, it checks the quality of output to sense whether work processes are functioning correctly, and it uses periodic milestones to assure itself that the work is on schedule. Let's examine each of these monitoring and control mechanisms.

The Budget

The basics of setting up a budget were presented earlier. Here we'll explain how you can use the budget to monitor your project activities. You monitor by comparing the actual results for a given time period with your project's budget. If evaluation reveals that the project's spending is right on target, with actual results matching the budget's expected results, then no adjustment is required. However, if actual results differ from the expected results, then, simply put, you—the project manager—must take corrective action. For example, if your team had expected to pay outside HR consultants $24,000 in July but you find that actual payments totaled $30,000, you need to investigate the reason for this discrepancy and possibly correct the situation.

The difference between actual results and the results expected by the budget is called a *variance*. A variance can be favorable, when the actual results are better than expected—or unfavorable, when the actual results are worse than expected. We see both favorable and unfavorable variances in table 12-1.

What should you do if monitoring detects unfavorable budget variances? One approach is a strategy of hope—that is, hope that the variance is simply a random deviation that will not repeat itself in the future. No smart manager will rely on that strategy. Overspending in one budget period, even to a moderate degree, may be a symptom of an underlying problem—one that will grow larger if

TABLE 12-1

Monthly project budget report: July

Project spending categories	Actual results	Budgeted amounts	Variance
Supplies	$2,000	$2,500	+500; favorable
Outside consultants	$30,000	$24,000	−6,000; unfavorable
Travel	$7,700	$9,000	+1,300; favorable

left unattended. So when you see a significant budget variance, investigate. Why did it occur? Is it likely to repeat itself? What corrective measures are called for? If you're under budget in several categories, does the total of those favorable variances cover a larger unfavorable variance in another category? If so, perhaps you can live with the situation. As you address problem variances, don't attempt to do it yourself; instead, enlist the people closest to the problem.

Is your current HR project close to going over budget? Learn about the common pitfalls of budgets—and their remedies—in "Tips for Monitoring Budgets."

Tips for Monitoring Budgets

When monitoring actual costs against your budget, watch out for these common factors; they can send your project over budget:

- Inflation during long-term projects

- Unfavorable changes in currency exchange rates

- Failing to get firm prices from suppliers and contractors

- Unplanned personnel costs, including overtime, incurred in keeping the project on schedule

- Unanticipated training costs and consulting fees

SOURCE: *Managing Projects Large and Small* (Boston: Harvard Business School Press, 2004).

Quality Checks

Quality checks are another approach to keeping any HR project on track. To make a quality check, you examine some unit of work at an appropriate point to ensure that it meets specifications. For example, if the project is building a new recruiting Web site, you may want to have components of the software system tested as they are developed to be certain that they function according to plan. You should not wait until the very end of the project to do this testing. By that time, any substandard work would cost enormous amounts of time and money to fix.

Periodic quality checks, like the building thermometer, indicate conditions that are out of specification. Once these problems are identified, the project team can find the causes and fix the processes that created the problems in the first place. That sort of monitoring and corrective action ensures that subsequent task output will meet quality standards, keeping your project on track.

Milestones

Travelers in an earlier era used engraved stones placed along the road to assess their progress. "Cambridge: 17 Miles," one might read. The English-speaking world refers to these as "milestones." We use figurative milestones to mark passages in our life: graduation from high school or college, marriage, the founding of a new business, the "big 4-0" birthday, and so forth. Projects use significant events as milestones to remind people of how far they have come and how much further they must go. These significant events may be the completion of key tasks on the critical path. Here are a few examples:

- The sponsor's acceptance of a complete set of employees' requirements for a new benefits self-service system

- The automation of payroll processes in a newly created HR department

- The successful testing of a prototype HRIS

- The incorporation of final revisions into a new employee handbook

- The identification of all individuals who will be affected by a planned reduction in force

- Completion of a plan for merging two HR departments after an acquisition

- The first successful practice run of a new disaster recovery plan

- And the ultimate milestone: completion of the project

Make sure to highlight milestones in your project schedule and use them to monitor progress. Also use them as occasions for celebrating progress when celebration is called for. Some project teams recognize milestones with a group luncheon, a trip to a sporting event, or some other enjoyable event.

Strictly speaking, every task on your project schedule represents a milestone, but some are more significant than others. The more significant markers have greater psychological appeal for team members. Use them to rally participants, and share words of encouragement like "We are now very close to completing the Web site's specifications. Let's keep up the pace and get it done on time."

Building a Suitable Monitoring and Control System

Budgets, quality checks, and milestones are basic monitoring and control devices that apply generally to projects. But there may be others that apply very specifically to your situation. Do you know what they are? If you don't, here is some advice for selecting and implementing them:

- **Focus on what is important.** You will need to continually ask questions like these: What is important to the organization? What are we attempting to do? Which parts of the project are the most important to track and control? What are the essential points at which we need to establish controls?

- **Build corrective action into the system.** Your control system, like the thermostat in our initial example, should emphasize response. If control data doesn't trigger a response, then your system is useless. Your system must use information to initiate corrective action; otherwise, all you are doing is monitoring and not exercising control. If quality is below standard, set up an ad hoc group to determine the cause, and fix the problem. Do the same if any of the project's teams have fallen behind schedule. Be very careful, however, that control doesn't lapse into micromanagement. Encourage the people closest to the problem to make the correction.

- **Emphasize timely responses.** You need to receive information quickly in order to devise effective responses. Ideally, you'll want real-time information. In most cases, though, weekly updates suffice.

No single control system is right for all projects. A system that's right for a large project will swamp a small one with paperwork, while a system that works for small projects won't have enough muscle for a big one. So find the one that's right for your project. Also watch for an all-too-common problem that can crop up in any project: mission creep, or the tendency for project goals to change and expand. "Beware of Mission Creep" offers tips for handling this situation.

Beware of Mission Creep

Throughout the project, be on guard against mission creep—unwittingly giving in to pressure to do more than has originally been planned for. As you find out each stakeholder's definition of success, you may feel pressure to accomplish too much. Don't get caught up in trying to solve problems that lie beyond the scope of your project—even legitimate or urgent problems that your company needs to address. For example, a project organized specifically

continued

to overhaul a company's performance management approach should not get sidetracked into trying to develop better ways of formulating strategy. That's a different job requiring a very different set of skills. Remember: it's all right to change the project's objectives midstream, but do so with your eyes open, not unconsciously—and only after making sure all your stakeholders are willing to go along with the new objectives.

Dealing with People Issues

A quick scan of the most popular books on project management would give you the impression that the subject is mostly about task analysis, measuring techniques, scheduling methods, and the use of software to plot and maintain a course. But that impression would be wrong. Yes, the techniques offered in this and other books are very useful. But *people*—particularly those working in teams—are at the heart of project work. Men and women who labor and solve problems together, who share information, and who accept mutual responsibility for success or failure play a much more vital role in a project's success than mechanical techniques do.

The people issues that matter for project work are extensive and are best addressed through books and training programs devoted to team management. (The accompanying sidebar, "Tips for Making the Most of People," is a good overview to start with.) Nevertheless, we address two key people issues here: conflict and collaboration. Managing both of these effectively is essential for keeping your HR project on track.

Mastering Conflict

One of the thorniest people issues faced by project managers is conflict between team members. Individuals brought together from different parts of an organization to complete a mission always present opportunities for conflict. Ironically, one of the important character-

Tips for Making the Most of People

If you are a project manager or team leader, you will be more successful in reaching your milestones if you adopt this advice about dealing with people:

- Be very selective in recruiting. Bring in people who view the project's goals as important. These people will be more predisposed to concentrating on achieving goals than to thinking about the differences they have with other team members.

- Engage members in activities they find interesting and valuable. This too will keep them focused on results.

- Publicly recognize the contributions of individual members. Doing so will make them feel appreciated, valued, and part of the group.

- Recognize the value of differences and how they serve the common goal. Unique skills and singular insights contribute to success.

- Create opportunities for members to know each other. Whether it's through off-site recreation, lunches in the team room, or something else, give people opportunities to get to know each other at a personal level. Doing so will help them cut through stereotypes (like, "those finance people are hard to work with") and find bases for collaboration.

- Get people working together! Working together side by side can build team spirit.

istics of a well-structured team—diversity of thinking, backgrounds, and skills—is itself a potential source of conflict. For example, the IT members of a team working on a project designed to create a recruiting Web site may believe that having lots of interesting and cutting-edge features is essential to the success of the project. They may feel impatient with the HR director's concern that users of the site might be overwhelmed by the large number of different features. "We should take advantage of the technology's power and build in the most sophisticated features we can," the IT folks say. "Not so," says the HR director. "Ease of use is our primary concern." And so the conflict begins.

To turn conflict from a negative to a positive force, you must encourage members to listen to each other, to open themselves up to different viewpoints, and to objectively question each other's assumptions. At the same time, you need to prevent conflict from becoming personal or from going underground, where resentment simmers. Here are three steps for making the most of conflict:

1. **Create a climate that encourages people to discuss difficult issues.** Disagreement builds and produces no positive results when people fail to deal with the conflict's source. Some people call this matter "the moose on the table." It's there, but nobody wants to acknowledge it or to talk about it. Make it clear that you *want* the tough issues aired, and that *anyone* can point out a moose.

2. **Facilitate the discussion.** How do you deal with a moose once it has been identified? Use the following guidelines:

   • First, acknowledge the issue, even if only one person sees it.
   • Refer back to group norms on how people have agreed to treat each other.
   • Encourage the person who identified the moose to be specific: "What, exactly, do you see as the problem here? How is that problem affecting our work as a team?"
   • Keep the discussion impersonal. Do not assign blame. Instead, discuss *what* is impeding progress, not *who*.
   • If the issue involves someone's behavior, encourage the person who identified the problem to explain how that behavior affects him or her, rather than to make assumptions about the motivation behind the behavior. For example, if someone is not completing work on time, you might say, "When your

work is delivered late, the rest of us are unable to meet our deadlines," not "I know you're not really excited about this product, but that shouldn't be an excuse for wrecking our schedule." Likewise, if someone is chronically late for scheduled meetings, don't say, "What makes you think you're so important that you can show up late for meetings?" Instead, try something like this: "Your lateness means we can't start on schedule. That wastes the time of five or six other people and prevents us from completing our meeting agendas."

- Team members should also know how to give feedback to you. If they sense a lack of leadership, they might say, "When you don't provide us with direction, we have to guess what you want. If we guess wrong, we waste lots of time," not "You don't seem to have any idea what we should be doing on this project." A good project manager or team leader knows how to receive feedback, even when it's negative.

3. **Move toward closure on conflict by discussing what can be done.**

  - Leave meetings with concrete suggestions for improvement, if not a solution to the problem.
  - If the subject is too sensitive and discussions are going nowhere, adjourn your meeting until a specified date so people can cool down. Or, bring in a facilitator. A good facilitator can help warring parties settle their differences in a positive way.

Generating Collaborative Behavior

Collaboration is the bedrock of a project team's effectiveness. It makes a team greater than the sum of its parts. But collaboration doesn't always occur naturally.

Have you ever watched a basketball game in which one player took a shot just about every time he got his hands on the ball? His teammates passed the ball whenever they were badly positioned or closely guarded by opposing players. But the "ball hog" never passed, even when a teammate was within easy striking distance of the basket. This is one type of noncollaborative behavior you have to watch for on your project team. Why? Because noncollaborative behavior will slow down your project.

Specifically, check to see whether team members are sharing the work or whether one person is trying to do it all. Even if this prima donna is a high performer, his or her behavior will discourage participation by others and slow overall progress. Also, watch for anyone, including a team leader, who:

- Appears to be taking undue credit for the team's accomplishment

- Is always pressing to get a larger share of team resources

- Is secretive or unwilling to share information

- Turns disagreements over goals or methods into interpersonal conflicts

That last point deserves special attention, because interpersonal animosity will throw your project off track. According to team expert Jeffrey Polzer, relationship conflict distracts people from their work and erodes their commitment to the team and its goals. "Some teams can't get through a meeting without an angry outburst, overt criticism, and hard feelings," he writes. When this happens, team members may respond by withdrawing from debates, attempting instead to preserve their relationships by avoiding confrontation.[1]

If you observe this kind of relationship conflict, take action to stop it. Do whatever is necessary to bring the feuding parties together, to examine the conflict in an objective manner, and to seek a resolution. If either or both parties are too stubborn or too singleminded to work things out, think about getting those individuals off the project.

Note: Conflict and collaboration are not the only people problems that you must address in keeping your HR projects on track. You may also encounter problems associated with the team structure, individual team members, and the quality of work. For solutions to those problems, check table 12-2, on pages 184–185.

Maintaining Communication

We've already explored the importance of creating a communications plan as part of the larger project management process. Meetings, newsletters, reports, and one-on-one encounters are powerful mechanisms for disseminating information, sharing ideas, and encouraging productive dialogue. They also help your HR projects stay on track.

To understand how to use communications to keep a project on track, think about the information that different project participants need to accomplish their missions:

- **The sponsor.** The sponsor needs periodic status, or progress, reports from the project manager. These should indicate where the project and its various initiatives stand relative to the schedule, the budget, and quality measures. A written report is the usual medium of communicating this information. (Note: Appendix A at the back of this book contains a sample project progress report.) The sponsor will also want to know about current and anticipated problems, change requests, and new opportunities discovered in the course of project work. Regular meetings are the best way to report these issues. The sponsor can use the meetings to guide the project manager and authorize certain activities.

- **The project manager.** In a sizable HR project, the manager must delegate substantial responsibility to one or more team leaders. There may be, for instance, a team leader in charge of technical activities, another for information-gathering initiatives, yet another for tracking legal concerns, and so forth. The project manager will look to these leaders for the same type of reporting that he or she provides to the sponsor. Once again, regular progress reports and meetings are used to share information, authorize action, make decisions, and keep the project on track.

- **Project team members.** Project managers and team leaders use communications to direct and control activities with team

TABLE 12-2

Troubleshooting guide

Problem	Possible causes	Potential impact	Recommended action
Team structure problems			
Team member leaves	• Didn't get along with teammates	• Impact may be slight if a new person with the same skills can be recruited • Could create a crisis if you cannot find a person with the same skills	• Cross-train team members • Use the opportunity to bring in a person with even more know-how • Avoid the problem by having backups for key positions
Lack of skills/ missing skills	• Certain skills overlooked during planning • Need for new skills discovered in the middle of the project • Organization was not prepared to take on the project	• The project will not move forward as fast as it should or it might stall	• Have team member trained in the needed skills • Hire outside consultants or contractors who have the skills
Interpersonal problems			
Inflexible team members	• People think that their way is the only way to operate • Anxiety over trying new approaches	• Progress slowed or blocked	• Indicate your expectation of flexibility at the very beginning • Work one-on-one to reduce anxiety over using new approaches • Look for flexibility when recruiting members
Conflict within the team	• Different working styles and areas of expertise • People are not prepared by training or experience for team-based work	• Progress, commitment to goals, and team cohesiveness will suffer	• Get people to focus on project goals and solutions • Build commitment to goals • Break up cliques • Counsel or remove agitators from the project

Problem	Possible causes	Potential impact	Recommended action
Productivity problems			
Time wasted on wrong tasks	• Poor time management • People are not prioritizing tasks • Weak management	• Tasks on the critical path will suffer	• Manager should make priorities clear
Poor quality work	• Quality standards not understood • Inadequate skills	• Project will fail to meet expectations of stakeholders • Costly and time-consuming rework will delay the project	• Recruit people who have the skills required to produce the requisite quality • Apply skill training where needed • Managers should communicate quality expectations from the very beginning
Team member burnout	• Schedulers have overcommitted members • Failure to create jobs with sufficient variety • Failure to communicate the importance of tasks	• Schedule delays • Poor quality work • Poor morale	• Avoid overscheduling individuals • Communicate the importance of key tasks • Build variety and learning into job assignments
Schedule problems			
Tasks are falling behind schedule	• Miscalculated task durations in the planning stage • Reason for schedule problem unknown	• Will continue to get worse, putting the project further and further behind schedule	• Face up to the planning miscalculation, and readjust the schedule if possible • Create and implement a solution to the problem, and then monitor progress very closely • Working with people closest to the problem, seek the cause

Source: Harvard ManageMentor on Project Management (Boston: Harvard Business School Publishing, 2002), 42–44. Adapted with permission.

members. Individual members can inform management about barriers to progress, newly discovered opportunities, and where best to direct resources. But communication must be a two-way street. Team members need to know what the general status of the project is, which decisions have been made that affect their work, and how they should proceed in ambiguous situations. Meetings are generally the best forums for these information exchanges.

- **Stakeholders.** A sound stakeholder communications system is also important. These people will want continuous updates on project status and progress.

Handling Problems

A big part of keeping a project on track is handling the myriad problems that inevitably surface. A marketing or other functional manager agitates for expansion of your project's mission. Several tasks take longer to complete than expected. Two team leaders fight over resources, splitting team members into hostile camps. Like pestering mosquitoes, problems like those can eat up your time and attention. It's impossible to provide advice about each of these problems in a book of this size, so, once again, see the brief ideas listed in table 12-2.

Projects generally experience four classes of conflicts: team structure problems, interpersonal problems, productivity problems, and schedule problems. The troubleshooting guide in table 12-2 identifies some fairly typical issues, their possible causes, their potential impact, and recommended action. Though it is by no means complete, you may find it useful.

Summing Up

In this chapter, you learned the following:

- Budgets are useful tools in controlling and tracking project performance. Variances point to areas where you should intervene or investigate.

- Conduct periodic quality checks to identify problems; then identify and deal with the causes.

- Use completed milestones as opportunities to celebrate project progress.

- Watch out for diversity; it is a source of both strength and potential conflict.

- Discourage conflict and noncollaborative behavior.

- Use your communications system to sense problems and signal responses.

Leveraging Chapter Insights: Critical Questions

- Think of an HR project you're leading. How do the costs of the project compare to what you've budgeted? Where do you see variances? How might you investigate to find the source of any unfavorable variances?

- What quality checks are you using to periodically assess the project's progress? What types of quality problems have you encountered? How might you best address these problems?

- What are your project's most important milestones? Have you and your team celebrated achievement of these milestones? If not, you may be having trouble maintaining energy and morale among your team members. To address this, what steps might you take to ensure that milestones are celebrated?

- How would you describe the conflicts experienced between members of your project team? Would you say that these conflicts are productive or destructive? If destructive, what techniques might you use to transform them into more productive exchanges?

- Have you spotted any troubling noncollaborative behavior among members of your team? If so, how might you foster more collaborative behavior?

- What communication mechanisms have you put in place to ensure that every project participant receives the type of information he or she needs? How might you improve those mechanisms?

- What types of problems have you encountered most while leading this project? Team structure problems? Interpersonal problems? Productivity or scheduling problems? What might be causing the trouble? How is each of these problems affecting your team? And what actions might you take to address the issues?

CHAPTER THIRTEEN

The Closedown Phase

Wrapping It Up

Key Topics Covered in This Chapter

- *The value of the project closedown phase*

- *How to evaluate a finished project*

- *Documenting project work for future learning*

- *Using a special session to capture and pass along lessons learned*

- *Capping the project with a celebration*

CLOSEDOWN SHOULD BE the final phase of every HR project. At this point, your team delivers, or reports, its results to the project sponsor and stakeholders and then examines its own performance. Many managers are inclined to gloss over this phase because they are unaccustomed to closedown activities. After all, their regular jobs are ongoing. And being action-oriented people, they're eager to move on without looking back once a job is finished. (In other cases it's hard to determine when a project has been completed and it's time for closedown. For more on this dilemma, see "Not All Projects Have a Clear Ending.")

Not All Projects Have a Clear Ending

We generally think of projects as having a clear beginning, a period of work, and a clear closedown. But not every project fits that tidy mold. Some simply move from one phase to another. A new employee handbook, for example, may shift immediately to planning and work on the revised version to reflect expected changes. The same project many assign some of its people to the development of soon-to-be-created sections that will ultimately be added to the handbook in a later edition. Even in such instances, however, closing the books on the initial project should coincide with the closedown activities explained in this chapter.

Closedown is worth doing despite managers' busy schedules. It helps you and your team get through the psychological issues that go hand-in-hand with important work-life transitions, and it is particularly important when team members have devoted themselves to a project for long periods of time. Closedown provides an opportunity to thank people who have contributed—both team members and the many other individuals who supplied advice and resources at some point in your project's life.

More important, the closedown phase gives everyone a chance to reflect on what has been accomplished, what went right, what went wrong, and how the outcome might have been improved. Such reflections are at the core of organizational learning—which can and should be shared with other projects sponsored in your organization.

The closedown activities examined here are performance evaluations, documentation, lessons learned, and celebration.

Performance Evaluation

Through performance evaluation, you assess how well the project performed relative to the three key factors included in its charter and any subsequent amendments:

- **Objectives or deliverables.** Have all objectives been met? Have project deliverables met the mandated specifications? For example, if the charter required the delivery of a complete recruiting plan for attracting more minority applicants— including data on the size of the potential minority applicant pool, a listing of sources and methods for targeting minority applicants, and so forth—the plan submitted by the project team should be evaluated against each of those details.

- **Schedule.** Did the project complete its work on time? If it did not, the project team should do two things: (1) estimate the cost of its tardiness to the company and (2) determine the cause of the schedule delay and how it could have been prevented.

- **Cost.** What did it cost to complete the project? Was that cost within budget constraints? If the project ran over budget, determine what caused the overspending and how that variance might have been avoided.

Ideally, an independent party that's capable of making an objective assessment should participate in postproject evaluation.

Documentation

Every large project produces reams of documents, such as meeting minutes, budget data, the closedown performance evaluation, and so on. These documents are part of the historical record; collect and store them so you can draw on them later.

Why bother with documentation? It's a source of learning. Consider this example:

The minority recruiting strategy project finished its work two years ago and did a praiseworthy job. Its deliverable—a complete recruiting plan for attracting more minority applicants—was credited with the 15 percent increase in the number of minority candidates expressing interest in job openings at the company.

Now Helen Young, an HR manager at the same company, has been given the job of organizing and leading an analogous project, this one aimed at improving recruiting of older workers. Not wanting to reinvent the wheel, Young and core members of her project hope to learn from the earlier project experience. "Let's see how that team organized and scheduled work and how it tracked progress," she suggests.

And so Young and her team spend several days poring through the stored documents of that earlier project. They pick out useful reporting templates, research reports, and Gantt charts. They also interview the former project manager and several key participants. "This information will make our planning phase much easier," Young notes.

Then one of Young's coworkers, Stephen Corliss, makes an important discovery. "A report I found in the file cites a meeting between our people and Steiger Associates, a major HR consultancy," Corliss says.

"According to this report, Steiger's proposal looked promising, but our people went with Hire Power, another consultancy, instead."

"And we all know what a poor job Hire Power did on the research part of the minority recruiting project,"Young chimes in. "Make a copy of that report, Stephen. We'll want to have Steiger Associates on our list of possible consultancies for this project."

In this case, Young's team found several useful pieces of information in the previous project's documentation: a proven approach to organizing work, reporting forms, and a potential new provider of consulting services. Your project may likewise be a gold mine of useful information for subsequent project teams—but only if you gather all important documents and store them in accessible formats.

Lessons Learned

Writing in the *Harvard Business Review*, Frank Gulliver identified learning as one of the important values of project work—a value overlooked by many. "If your company is like most," he writes, "you spend thousands of hours planning an investment, millions of dollars implementing it—and nothing evaluating and learning from it." [1] Not every organization is that shortsighted. The U.S. Army has maintained its Center for Army Lessons Learned for decades. The center's mission is to learn whatever it can from every type of combat operation and turn that learning into practical advice that it then disseminates to soldiers in the field. It actively solicits input from battle-tested soldiers on everything from urban warfare maneuvers, to the appropriate uses of body armor, to the effectiveness of high-tech systems under adverse field conditions, as experienced in mountainous Afghanistan.

The center also looks outside the army's own experience for important lessons. For example, it documents tactics used by combatants in other parts of the world and evaluates these tactics' usefulness for U.S. military leaders and soldiers.

Most businesspeople believe that they are light-years ahead of the military in matters of management. But lessons learned is one area in which private industry can learn a lesson of its own. And plenty of those lessons can be found in project team operations and their supporting reports. (Gulliver himself learned lessons through a project with BP. For details on his findings, see "Four Lessons Learned at BP." Other helpful advice can be found in "Putting Learning to Work.")

Lessons learned should be part of every closedown operation. Project participants should convene to identify what went right and

Four Lessons Learned at BP

In an article in *Harvard Business Review*, Frank Gulliver points to four main lessons that he and British Petroleum, now known as BP, learned through systematic postproject appraisals (PPAs). These are:

1. **Determine cost more accurately.** Prior to implementing PPAs, BP planners inaccurately predicted the scope of their project. In most cases, this led to unrealistically low project budgets.

2. **Anticipate and minimize risk.** The company learned from its experience with acquisitions and plant expansions that project planners should take the extra time needed to study market issues.

3. **Evaluate contractors.** PPAs led to the establishment of a contractor evaluation unit dedicated to judging contractor qualifications and monitoring their performance.

4. **Improve project management.** At the recommendation of PPAs, the company set up a projects department to help its engineers develop the know-how to become skilled project managers.

SOURCE: Frank R. Gulliver, "Post-Project Appraisals Pays," *Harvard Business Review,* March–April 1987, 128–130.

what went wrong. They should make a list of their successes, their mistakes, their unjustified assumptions, and things that could have been done better. That list should become part of the documented record.

Here is a partial list of questions you and your project team should address at a lessons learned session:

- In retrospect, how sound were our assumptions?

- Did we bother to test key assumptions?

- How well did we seek out alternatives?

- What about our time estimates—did we under- or overestimate task duration?

- Were our meetings productive or time wasters?

- And the ultimate question: if we could start over again tomorrow, which things would we change?

Make a systematic list of these lessons, grouped by topic (e.g., planning, budgeting, execution, etc.) and organized in a form similar to table 13-1. Make that document available to all subsequent project teams. Next to the deliverables, these lessons may be the most valuable output of your project experience.

Putting Learning to Work

One way that you can put learned lessons to work is to establish staffing continuity between the projects your company launches. For example, if your HR department has just completed an implementation of one HR software installation project, make sure that, skill requirements permitting, several veterans of that project are assigned to the next one. These veterans will bring lessons from the first project with them and will be sources of experience and know-how for first-time project members.

TABLE 13-1

Project lessons learned

Project phase/task	What worked	What didn't work	Ways to improve
Planning/time estimates		Consistently under-estimated time to complete tasks. Wrecked our schedule.	Must be more systematic in making estimates. No more top-of-the-head guesses. Get expert advice.
Execution/budget control	Biweekly budget reporting identified variances before they could get out of hand.		Underestimated the budget for out-sourced software development. Next time include one of our internal IT people on the team.

Source: Harvard ManageMentor on Project Management (Boston: Harvard Business School Publishing, 2002), 54. Used with permission.

Celebration

If you followed the advice given earlier, you formally began your project with a launch meeting and perhaps some attendant festivities. The sponsor attended that event and drew a mental picture of the journey you and your team were about to begin and a review of what the project aimed to accomplish. Perhaps the CEO was present to explain the importance of the project to the company and to all of its employees.

In closing down the project, do something very similar, with the same selection of individuals reflecting on what your team has done and on the project's impact on the company. If the project was a success, be sure to invite whichever customers, suppliers, and nonproject employees helped during the journey. If the project failed to deliver on its entire list of objectives, highlight the effort that people made and the goals they did achieve.

Use the occasion to thank all who helped and participated. Then pop the corks and celebrate the end of your project.

See "HR in Action: Closing Down an Employee Mentoring Project" for an example of how one HR professional ensured effective completion of her project.

HR in Action: Closing Down an Employee Mentoring Project

Sheryl Grenier, an HR manager at Marston Enterprises, sat back in her chair and breathed a huge sigh of relief. The employee mentoring project she had been leading for the past four months was finally completed. She and her team had poured enormous amounts of energy and time into the effort, and numerous other projects and tasks had stacked up in the meantime for each of them. Grenier eyed the towering pile of folders on her desk and the appointments and deadlines penciled in her planner. She wanted nothing more than to clear her head and then grapple with the next big initiative on her plate: a legal compliance audit that she had promised to complete by the end of the quarter.

But Grenier understood the importance of taking time to conduct a proper closedown of the mentoring project. To get the ball rolling, she e-mailed all the members of her team to arrange a performance evaluation. At the meeting, the group tallied up how they did with respect to the project's objectives, the schedule, and the budget. "Well," noted Simon Hodges, the IT manager responsible for creating online chat rooms for mentor-protégé pairs operating in different company locations, "we seem to have hit all the important goals of the effort. The chat rooms are up and running, and people are actually using them." Cody Lee, a line manager who had agreed to participate in the program pilot, added her impressions: "We've certainly delivered on our objective of ramping up new hires more quickly. The new protégés we've been following have all generated measurable business results faster than the previous round of hires."

"This is all good news," agreed Grenier, "though of course we were late in completing the analysis of the criteria for matching mentors to protégés." Recalling that part of the project, the team members determined that the delay stemmed from the unexpected absence of a key participant. "Next time, we'll put a backup in place so that we don't lose ground," Lee suggested. "On

continued

the other hand, we came in slightly under budget—so that's something to be proud of!"

Grenier then asked each team member to compile all forms of documentation that the team had created during the course of the project and to submit them to her within one week. "We had some excellent help from our consultant, and we did a good job of tracing the critical path of the project," she explained. "I wouldn't be surprised if the HR folks in our German division decided to set up a similar program. If they had access to our files, they could avoid reinventing the wheel."

"Even more reason to document our lessons learned and add that to the historical record," Hodges added. The team members began brainstorming what did—and didn't—work well during each phase of the project and exploring strategies for handling things better on the next effort. "One thing we could have done better was to manage mission creep more proactively," said one participant. "We caved in to several line managers' requests that mentors also provide training to some new hires, and that meant a lot of us had to work overtime to make it happen. Next time, we'll have to draw the line more firmly around the project's boundaries." The group discussed additional ideas for improving inefficiencies and listed all the solutions offered.

As the team wrapped up the evaluation meeting, Grenier asked members to get their calendars out once again. "Let's pick a date to have a celebratory lunch," she said. "We've accomplished a lot, and I'm looking forward to enjoying some relaxed time with you all."

Back in her office, Grenier phoned Harold Becker, the chief HR executive and sponsor of the project, and invited him to attend the lunch. "This crew did a great job," she told him. "I'm hoping you'll be able to say a few words about the results the project has generated for the company. The team will appreciate knowing that you recognize the value of their contribution."

"Will do," agreed Becker. "I'd be happy to attend."

Summing Up

In this chapter, you learned the following:

- Evaluate project performance on the basis of chartered objectives or deliverables and adherence to schedule and cost.

- Collect and store project documentation to create a record for future learning.

- At the end of the project, use an informal meeting to brainstorm the many things that led to success and failure. Make a systematic list of those items and make it available to future project personnel.

- Use a closedown meeting to mark the formal end of the project, to celebrate successes, to recount lessons, and to thank all participants.

Leveraging Chapter Insights: Critical Questions

- Think of an HR project you and your team have just completed. How would you evaluate the project's performance? Consider its objectives or deliverables, the project schedule, and the actual spending versus budgeted spending. How did your project stack up to expectations?

- What documents did you and your team generate while moving the project forward? Which do you think might be most useful to another project team grappling with an analogous project in the future? Why? Would some documents be helpful for any project team? If so, which ones?

- What lessons did you and your team learn while working on the project? What might you do differently on future projects to leverage lessons learned and generate a better outcome next time around?

- How will you design an effective celebration to mark the formal completion of the project? Whom will you invite to speak at the event? What will you counsel them to say? What might you do to help project participants feel appreciated and valued and able to move on to future efforts?

CHAPTER FOURTEEN

Managing Varied HR Projects

Achieving Your Desired Results

Key Topics Covered in This Chapter

- *Starting an HR department*

- *Conducting a legal compliance audit*

- *Developing an employee handbook*

- *Designing an employee orientation or mentoring program*

- *Implementing an HRIS*

- *Creating an employee expatriation program*

- *Outsourcing HR activities*

- *Winning executive support for your HR project*

Y OU'VE SEEN the big picture of the project management process—everything from defining and organizing the project to planning the work, managing project execution, and closing down the effort. You're ready to take a closer look at the unique considerations and challenges associated with specific types of HR projects. In this chapter, we present a range of HR-related projects that you may find yourself leading during your career. For each project type, we provide practical strategies, guidance, and tips for surmounting the special management challenges associated with that project. We also offer case studies showing how other HR practitioners have handled such projects—and the steps they took to ensure the initiatives' success. And finally, we provide suggestions for how to win executive approval and support for HR projects and expenditures.

The following chapter, chapter 15, will turn to projects in which you're likely to play a strong supporting role—such as assisting with HR-related issues during a merger or acquisition and developing a disaster recovery plan. Like chapter 14, chapter 15 will also provide guidance, tips, and case studies.

With all of this in mind, let's turn now to HR projects you may lead.

Starting an HR Department

Many small companies and start-ups operate without a formal HR department: perhaps the founders hire outside experts to oversee payroll processing and tax returns, and individual managers handle recruitment, selection, and compensation negotiations. The CEO's secretary may compile and maintain employee records and job descriptions. An attorney may come in periodically to review company operations, ensure legal compliance, and handle any legal matters that need attention. But some companies, even while they're relatively small, decide to establish an HR department to achieve efficiencies and lay a foundation for future growth. A formal, well-run HR department can help ensure that the right human resource policies and strategies are in place to support the company's goals and accommodate an expanding workforce.

If you're charged with setting up a new HR department in your organization, you can expect to experience both stimulation and challenge while leading this project. You may feel overwhelmed by the huge number of decisions that must be made—such as the following:

- What will the department's mission within the organization be?

- How will we measure its value?

- What services will it provide to the rest of the company?

- Which processes will it handle itself and which will be handled by outside experts?

- How will personnel records be maintained?

- What role will the department play in high-level matters such as strategy formulation, compensation and benefits programs, retention efforts, training, and succession planning?.[1]

To manage this complexity, some experts recommend using the following seven-step process:

1. **Define your HR department's purpose.** Through informal interviews with key staff members and management, as well as your own observations of how different HR activities currently are handled in your organization, define the purpose of the soon-to-be-created HR department.[2] The department's purpose should directly support the organization's high-level

goals—whether those goals involve improving efficiencies, cutting costs, enhancing the level of workforce talent, or some other objective. The purpose should also specify how the department's effectiveness will be measured (e.g., by changes in turnover rates and other HR-related metrics) and to whom it will report.[3] In addition, the purpose must specify the focus of the department: Will it serve in an administrative capacity? Provide statistics and reports? Ensure general compliance with employment laws? Constitute a strategic component of the business and have status equal to that of the finance, sales, manufacturing, and other major departments?[4]

2. **Present your project plan to the rest of the management team.** Share your ideas for the HR department's purpose with other company leaders. Explain how long you expect it to take to establish the new department, what the project will cost, and what the payoff will be—in terms such as increased employee satisfaction and performance, lower costs, greater profits, enhanced ability to attract talent, and so forth. Specify the key goals that you plan to accomplish within the first six or twelve months, as well as the qualifications needed for the individual heading the new department and any additional staff members serving in the department.[5]

3. **Review existing personnel files.** Determine whether all the necessary documents are in place and whether a lack of documents or a series of errors in existing reports poses any legal liability for your company. An employment attorney or reference guide can help you make these determinations as well as centralize files and safeguard their confidentiality.

4. **Consider an employee handbook.** If your company has already cobbled together an employee handbook, review it to decide whether it needs updating or replacing. Obtain samples from other similar companies to use as benchmarks for yours. Have an attorney review the final draft of the handbook. Then give all employees a copy, have them sign a document acknowl-

edging that they've received it, and retain the document in their personnel file.

5. **Improve payroll and benefits processing.** Research payroll- and benefits-processing companies that can handle these HR activities skillfully and affordably. Consider purchasing HRIS software that can help free up your and other HR staff members' time for more important matters.

6. **Develop HR policies that make a difference.** Decide what kinds of benefits offerings, compensation strategies, recruiting and retention approaches, and new-employee orientation programs can best help your company achieve its goals. For example, would an employee wellness program enable your organization to attract more of the types of job applicants it needs to compete with rival companies? How might you use orientation programs to get new hires up to speed more quickly? What training and professional development opportunities could improve retention of valued employees? How do your company's compensation packages compare with standards in your industry or geographic area? What rewards and recognition programs might help your company improve workforce performance?

7. **Create communication channels.** Launch an employee newsletter through which your department can keep the company's workforce informed about company strategy, top performers, the thinking behind new change initiatives, and other important matters. Also decide how you'll communicate vital business information—such as turnover and retention rates, training programs' costs and results, and employee absenteeism— to management. In these communications, be sure to explain how performance on such metrics is affecting your company's bottom line.

Clearly, all of these steps require extensive time, effort, and thought. Don't hesitate to ask HR colleagues in other organizations for their assistance and advice, as well as to hire outside experts if resources allow. In addition, be sure to involve line and operational managers in establishing HR policies, procedures, and processes that will affect the functioning of their departments. You'll stand a much better chance of gaining their trust, cooperation, and confidence in your abilities and counsel by including them in these key decisions.[6]

Each HR professional who sets up a new human resource department faces unique project management challenges. See "HR in Action: Starting an HR Department at Missouri Consolidated Health Care Plan" to find out how one HR manager handled the task.

HR in Action: Starting an HR Department at Missouri Consolidated Health Care Plan

When Lorraine Mixon-Paige, HR manager at Missouri Consolidated Health Care Plan (MCHCP), set up an HR department for her organization, she deftly addressed a series of unique challenges. In August 1993, MCHCP branched off from Missouri's public retirement system in accordance with a state bill passed earlier that year. The new company's mission was to focus solely on health care. "We had 50 employees who branched off from the larger system," Mixon-Paige explains. "These included managers, claims processors, call center representatives, and administrative people. We needed an HR department to both manage the existing employees and help us recruit to reach our goal of about 130 employees. We also had to ensure that our employees had the skills needed to communicate our new focus to customers—to ensure that they understood that we were no longer their retirement system but instead were providing health-care plans. It was a process of creating a new brand."

To establish MCHCP's human resource department, Mixon-Paige drew from her previous employers' policy manuals and developed policies related to standard HR matters such as antidiscrimination. She also added new policy areas specific to the medical insurance industry, such as confidentiality of patient information. In addition, she designed recruitment strategies for attracting employees who fit MCHCP's culture, in which people felt a strong sense of ownership for their jobs. And finally, she extracted information from the previous organization's personnel files to create complete files for employees of the new organization.

One particularly thorny challenge came in the form of morale problems among some of the original fifty employees. "Some of them had trouble adjusting to new ways of doing things," Mixon-Paige acknowledges. "They'd say things like, 'We used to do it this way at the old business.'" By setting up frequent, regular meetings with managers and monthly all-staff meetings featuring question-and-answer periods, Mixon-Paige sent the message that the new organization needed to chart its own path and establish its own identity. She and one other HR staff member also established, and now handle, new-hire orientation, compensation programs, job classification, recruitment, and all other HR services.

When asked what advice she might offer fellow HR practitioners who are establishing new HR departments, Mixon-Paige counsels against "writing yourself into a corner by creating overly specific personnel policies. Employees take these as gospel, and if the business changes, they may find it difficult to adapt to revised policies." She cites promotion and pay-raise policies as examples where generality should trump specificity. By keeping promotion and wage-increase criteria more general, she says, companies can revise policies to reflect shifting business realities. But with HR policies with legal ramifications—such as antidiscrimination policies—"that's the time to be very specific."

SOURCE: Lorraine Mixon-Paige, telephone interview by Lauren Keller Johnson, July 19, 2005.

Conducting a Legal Compliance Audit

We're living in an age of ever more complex employment laws and regulations. Simultaneously, certain HR-related activities such as termination practices and performance evaluation methods have become hot buttons in many organizations. Companies today put themselves at major financial risk if they ignore any noncompliance problems related to these laws and employment issues. To minimize these risks, many organizations purchase employment practices liability insurance. Many also conduct voluntary HR compliance audits—either on an annual basis as an internal checkup or in response to significant changes in the organization's processes or in federal or state laws.[7]

An HR audit is an objective assessment of a company's HR policies and practices for the purpose of evaluating whether specific practice areas are in compliance with legal requirements and/or whether they're generating the strategic results (such as reduction in employee turnover or workforce diversity) the company wants. An audit can help a company avoid legal liability and identify areas of concern that need immediate attention before an employee files a lawsuit or governmental regulators come knocking. It can also enable an organization to sharpen its competitive edge by improving key HR practice areas such as recruitment and retention of valued talent.

An effective audit comprises two parts: (1) evaluation of the company's strategic and operational HR policies, practices, and processes and (2) an assessment of HR outcomes, such as number of unfilled positions, turnover, employee satisfaction, diversity, and so forth. Both parts of the audit are conducted through questionnaires, a review of documents, and interviews with specific managers and employees to assess the current practice of HR policies.

An HR professional or other individual (such as the company's CEO, CFO, or risk manager) may sponsor the audit project, while in-house HR professionals or an outside attorney or HR consultant can conduct the audit. And according to Ronald Adler, president and CEO of Laurdan Associates, Inc., an HR consultancy based in Potomac, Maryland, the audit team may comprise members of the

HR department, the company's general counsel and CFO, unit managers, the organization's risk manager, and possibly an HR consultant.[8]

If you're leading an HR compliance audit team, you and your team will likely take the following seven steps to plan and execute the project:

1. **Determine the scope of the audit.** Will you conduct a comprehensive review of all HR practice areas or focus on one or two that you believe need attention?

2. **Develop the audit questionnaire.** Identify key areas served by your HR department, and list all the questions needed to ensure a comprehensive review of those areas. Some companies that have asked a law firm to conduct the audit use the attorney's checklist as their questionnaire. Other organizations develop their own questionnaire or use HR audit tools developed by HR consultancies.

3. **Collect the data.** Use the questionnaire as your road map to review the areas identified as within the scope of the audit.

4. **Benchmark your findings.** Compare your findings with HR benchmark standards, such as internal company data, national standards, or practices at other similarly sized firms. Metrics that often get benchmarked include absenteeism rates, number of days to fill a position, cost per new employee hired, turnover, and so forth.

5. **Provide feedback about the results.** Summarize your findings and recommendations for your senior management team, rating each compliance problem area as high, medium, or low risk.

6. **Create action plans.** Develop plans to implement the changes suggested by the audit findings.

7. **Foster a climate of continuous improvement.** Use constant observation and continuous improvement of your company's HR policies, procedures, and practices to ensure that it achieves and maintains its competitive advantage.

As you might imagine, leading an HR audit project can be time consuming and expensive, depending on the scope of the effort. (Note, though, that some insurers provide an audit as a free service to their client companies.) Moreover, this type of project presents its own unique management challenges. Adler cites the following as particularly important considerations to keep in mind while leading an audit project:

- **Buy-in from top management.** If you're the project sponsor, it's vital that you win support for the audit from other members of the executive team. Why? If they're not on board with the effort, you'll have difficulty getting the resources needed to implement any corrective actions suggested by the audit findings. To gain top management's buy-in, explain the potential costs of ignoring compliance problems. Also point out the audit's ability to help your company improve its HR strategies—and thus hone its competitive edge.

- **Discoverable information.** If your audit is conducted with internal resources or an outside consultant who is not a lawyer, everything connected with the audit is subject to discovery in any litigation relating to employment practices. For this reason, many companies decide to retain a lawyer to conduct the audit—even though neither the audit nor the attorney is a requirement. By using a lawyer, you may be able to safeguard your audit's results against disclosure through attorney-client privilege.

- **Project governance.** While planning the project, you'll need to work out a series of governance issues—such as how often your team will meet, whether you'll produce interim reports (and if so, what their content will be), who will collect and store the information gained through the audit, who will see the findings, and who will implement any required corrective measures.

- **Expectations management.** Many audits create expectations among employees that the company will act on the information gained—especially if that information is acquired through employee surveys and interviews. However, you may decide that action isn't necessary on every opinion or fact you gather. To manage employees' expectations, show that you're not just stashing the audit report in a drawer after the project is complete. Instead, share some of your findings with employees, through a general meeting or a written communication. Ask your CEO to share his or her thoughts about the audit results with the workforce.

- **Attention to outcomes.** Though it's vital to examine HR policies and procedures during an audit, it's even more important to examine the outcomes of those policies and procedures. For example, use the audit process to determine the actual number of women and minorities in your workforce—to see whether your equal employment opportunity policy is generating the desired results. Policies in themselves are useless unless they lead to the outcomes your company needs to execute its strategy and improve its competitive position.

- **Corrective actions.** Some of your audit findings will suggest the need for required corrective actions—that is, steps your company must take to comply with a particular law. Other findings may point out important misalignments between your company's current policies and recent changes in its strategic direction. With still other findings, the decision whether to make a policy change is completely subjective. For example, perhaps you're not legally required to improve your turnover rate—but doing so would yield some benefit for your company. Separating your findings into these categories can help you prioritize the actions you'll take to address any problem areas.

Developing an Employee Handbook

Most companies have some form of employee handbook or personnel policies manual. Such a document offers numerous advantages. For example, the handbook enables your company to:

- Educate employees about company products, customers, commitment to the community, competitors, and other topics relevant to employees' work

- Establish a positive image as an employer, responsible citizen, provider of valuable goods and services, and generator of economic value for society

- Ensure consistency in the administering of policies and procedures

- Describe the work environment in which employees will carry out their responsibilities

- Provide a quick, easy reference source for employees' questions about the company

- Communicate respect and caring for employees, balanced with firmness regarding company policies and values[9]

In addition to these benefits, a well-written employee handbook can help supervisors maintain consistency in their management of direct reports. By clearly communicating expectations and the employer-employee relationship, the handbook can also help reduce the need for employees to seek out union representation. And clear rules about how work should be conducted in your organization can support disciplinary action and help your company avoid charges of unlawful discrimination.[10]

But preparing (or revising) an employee handbook can also present you, the project leader, with unique challenges. For example, you need to decide what content to include and when it's time to revise an existing handbook. You also must find ways to make the handbook as readable, clear, and engaging as possible. And you have to strike a delicate balance between crafting a warm, caring tone and avoiding promises your company can't keep (such as guaranteed employment). In addition, you'll need to assemble a project team comprising the right individuals—and often call on your persuasion skills to obtain their time and expertise. None of this is easy. But by giving your handbook project the time and careful thought it deserves, you'll create a document that can provide important advantages for your company.

Let's take a closer look at the special challenges of preparing an employee handbook and consider strategies for addressing these challenges:

- **Project team.** According to Michael Lotito, a partner at law firm Jackson Lewis, you'll need specific individuals to serve on your handbook project team. "Typically you'll have several people from HR," Lotito explains, "but you should also have someone from the benefits department, from public relations or communications, from legal, and from employee orientation. High-level operations executives, such as the COO, should be involved, as well as someone from your company's complaint resolution group." Not everyone needs to be involved with every phase of the handbook's development, Lotito notes. But you should draw on the entire team's expertise to ensure that you're covering all the appropriate topics in the document.[11]

- **Content.** The best employee handbooks state their organization's philosophy, strategic plan, beliefs, key human resource policies (such as support of a smoke-free environment and equal opportunity employment), orientation information for new hires, and legal obligations of the company and its workers and their mutual responsibilities. Many handbooks also contain a welcome letter from the CEO or other high-level officer. Sections may address topics ranging from legal issues (e.g., an employment-at-will statement and equal employment opportunity policy) and brief descriptions of employee benefits, to grievance procedures, career development opportunities offered by the company, and guidelines regarding solicitation in the office.[12]

- **Process.** Prepare a preliminary copy of your handbook, using a template and filling it out by gathering the required information and drafting the different sections using a consistent writing style. (Lotito notes that many law firms and some state chambers of commerce provide suites of labor employment law products and services, such as handbook templates, that you can build on and translate into your own style.) Have the draft reviewed by all levels of management, and consider submitting it to employees for their comments. Top management will make the final decision about what's included. Have an employment attorney inspect the draft to ensure that it doesn't establish unintended contractual obligations to employees.[13] According to Lotito, the project time line can vary: "At the average company that has fewer than a hundred employees, the process might take about three months. If you're updating an already fairly comprehensive handbook, you may need less time." If people express reluctance to contribute to the project because of time constraints or a lack of appreciation for the handbook's value, Lotito explains, call on your power of persuasion and influence. Reiterate the importance of the document and your appreciation and need for their expertise. Include money in the project budget for a celebration of the handbook's completion—where you acknowledge contributors' efforts and express your gratitude for their help and participation.

- **Delivery.** The final handbook will be printed in a format in which pages can be revised as policies, procedures, and laws change, and one copy will be presented to each employee. Require employees to sign a statement saying that they have read and understand the material in the handbook.[14]

- **Writing style.** Aim for a clear, welcoming, and accessible tone, using language pitched at the eighth-grade level. Ensure that the phrasing you use reinforces your company's values. For example, if your organization is committed to teamwork, make statements emphasizing employee cooperation and mutual support. If a core value is informality, present a less formal dress code and avoid emphasizing formal hierarchy and titles.[15] Though a positive and friendly tone is important, don't water down or hide disclaimers and reservations of management's rights. Examples of important disclaimers include "This handbook does not create, express, or imply an employment contract," "This employer reserves the right to make changes to the policies, procedures, and other statements made in this handbook," and "The handbook supersedes any previous handbook or unwritten policies." When it comes to balancing warm communication and litigation avoidance, always make sure your company's legal needs are protected first.[16]

- **Revision cycle.** Three developments should serve as a trigger for revising your handbook: changes in federal and state law, new technologies (which have required companies to describe policies regarding use of e-mail and monitoring of computers in the workplace), and shifting social practices (which can mean adding policies regarding personal appearance, smoking, or employee dating). Constantly review such developments to ensure that your handbook remains up to date.[17]

- **Versions.** As Lotito explains, if your company operates in multiple states or countries, you'll need to make some crucial decisions. Specifically, will you create one version of your handbook that covers the full range of policies and legal requirements in every location? Or will you develop a core version of the handbook and augment it with a special supplement for each location? Which approach would best reflect your company's values? "In the U.S., some states have more protected categories of employees than others," Lotito notes. "For example, California law includes sexual orientation as a protected category. Even if sexual orientation is not a protected category in another state where your company operates, you may decide to define it as such because doing so reflects the company's values."

Another example cited by Lotito involves family and medical leave. The Family and Medical Leave Act (FMLA), as you know, applies to companies that have fifty or more employees within a seventy-five-mile radius. If one of the sites where your company operates has fewer than fifty employees, will you still offer family and medical leave according to the FMLA?

Companies that have offices around the world face even more complex decisions. For instance, "France and Germany have extensive union penetration," says Lotito. "You may not have the legal right to create a handbook without consulting union leadership. And sexual harassment laws differ across countries. But if your core values or code of conduct stipulates avoidance of sexual harassment, you may want to include a clause to that effect in your handbook—even if you aren't required to do so by local laws."

Managing development of an employee handbook doesn't end with the physical printing and distribution of the document, maintains Lotito. He also advises using the handbook to "make your company's vision, mission, and values come alive" and encouraging widespread use of the document. For example, "mention the handbook to managers and employees at every opportunity. Encourage managers to bring out the document during monthly staff meetings and discuss a 'policy of the month' with their employees." The goal? To help managers and employees throughout your organization gain extensive familiarity with the document.

Designing an Employee Orientation and Mentoring Program

Well-designed employee orientation and mentoring programs can generate enormous value for your organization. Through employee orientation, you acclimate new hires and indoctrinate them into your company's culture. Using mentoring programs, you create ongoing development opportunities for employees as they master their jobs and gain more experience at your company. The payoff? Newcomers become productive quickly, form positive social relationships, and feel connected to the company—all of which helps improve retention. They also gain familiarity with company policies and procedures, strengthen their skills, and communicate more with managers.

But to capture such value from your orientation and mentoring programs, you need to apply your project management savvy. Let's consider the unique challenges of managing development of an effective orientation program first. We'll then take a closer look at the challenges of designing a mentoring program.

Managing Development of an Orientation Program

Whether your company already has an orientation program in place or not, new hires are getting oriented—finding out how things work in the company, what the culture is like, and what the explicit and tacit rules and norms are. To ensure that newcomers acquire the right knowledge, your orientation project should comprise the following eight steps:

1. **Evaluate current orientation processes or programs.** Closely examine the current processes or programs through which the company orients new hires.[18] By interviewing recent hires and managers, as well as getting their input through anonymous surveys and focus groups, find out what's working well and what isn't. How knowledgeable are employees about the company's policies and procedures; mission, values, and strategy; culture; and their role in helping the company succeed? To what extent have they formed valuable connections with their bosses and colleagues? To what extent do they feel welcomed and valued by the organization?

2. **Develop success measures.** Determine how you'll measure the impact of changes to your current orientation efforts or implementation of a new orientation program. For example, will you examine changes in turnover rates among employees who have been with the company for up to two years? Evaluate employee morale and job satisfaction? Assess employees' understanding of company policies? Such measures can help you gauge the effectiveness of your orientation project after it's completed and has been implemented for some time.

3. **Consider program design.** Decide how you'll design your orientation program. The most effective programs contain visual components (e.g., overhead slides showing the organizational chart), auditory elements (e.g., spoken presentations by session facilitators), and opportunities to practice and reinforce new knowledge in fun, interactive ways (such as quizzes and contests to test new hires' familiarity with company policies). The best programs also repeat key information numerous times, over several sessions rather than an intensive, one-hour meeting. In designing your program, also consider asking both recent and more seasoned employees from different parts of the company to share their experiences with joining the firm. This is an excellent opportunity to present additional "commercials" for your firm. Finally, consider offering light refreshments during orientation sessions. Food can lend any meeting a less formal air and can help participants form social bonds more easily.

4. **Determine program topics.** An effective orientation program covers the following topics: your company's history, products and services, and sales; key customers and competitors; mission, strategy, and values; policies and procedures; organizational culture and structure (how the enterprise's different units work together to carry out its work); key officers and unit heads; performance evaluation system; professional development opportunities; and layout of the office or facility.[19]

5. **Design a start-date kit.** Prepare a kit containing information new hires will need on their first day on the job. The kit should include company literature, an organizational chart, a map of the building, a list of local resources (such as banks, restaurants, and day-care facilities), a glossary of company-related acronyms and terms, lists of internal resources or individuals (to whom new hires can go with questions related to benefits, payroll, and so forth), instructions for using e-mail and the telephone sys-

tem, and current training offerings. Equally important, the kit should include your employee handbook.[20]

6. **Enlist managers.** Managers throughout your organization can—and should—play a key role in your orientation project before their new hires have even arrived. As part of your project, remind hiring managers to contact a new hire soon after he or she has accepted an offer of employment to communicate their pleasure, welcome the newcomer, and confirm the start date and other practical information (such as where to park and whom to contact upon arriving at the office).[21] Hiring managers should also prepare each newcomer's work space ahead of time and assign him or her a "buddy." Buddies are fellow employees who can further help a new hire get acclimated by taking him or her to lunch on the first several days, explaining where to get office supplies, introducing the person around, and offering encouragement.[22]

7. **Design follow-up actions.** Plan to check on new hires' progress during the first weeks and months following orientation. For example, ensure that supervisors have reserved space in their calendars to answer new hires' questions as the employees ease into their new job responsibilities. And check that managers are encouraging new employees to share any issues, frustrations, or concerns.[23]

8. **Constantly improve your program.** Using the metrics you've selected early in your orientation project, continually measure the results your program is generating. If you're not getting the intended results, find out why—then engineer changes in your orientation efforts to address any gaps.

To learn how HR professionals at one company have successfully managed an employee orientation project, see "HR in Action: Acclimating New Hires at The Container Store."

HR in Action: Acclimating New Hires at The Container Store

At Dallas-based storage and organizational products maker The Container Store, the HR staff uses project management skills to design and implement innovative employee orientation strategies. For one thing, they view orientation as a process that begins long before a new hire's first day on the job—indeed, it begins during job interviewing. "Full-time employees have a minimum of three interviews with three different people," says Barbara Anderson, director of community services and staff development. "We have a quirky culture, and spend a lot of time talking about how and why we do business the way we do."

The company also emphasizes repetition in its orientation efforts. Consider its multiple-session Foundation Week orientation program, in place since 1996. Each session reinforces what new hires learned in the previous session. "By the end of the week," Anderson says, "the new employee has heard the most important things five different times from five different people." The sessions cover topics such as company philosophy, selling techniques, and customer service—which employees learn through discussions with their managers and through observing how product gets into the stores and onto the shelves and how salespeople greet customers.

The Container Store also helps new hires feel a sense of achievement and rite-of-passage experience when Foundation Week is completed. "We have a ceremony that cheers on the new employees," explains Anderson. "And that is when they get their apron. The psychological effect of having to wait for that apron is incredible."

The company's careful and creative approach to new-hire orientation has paid big dividends. For two consecutive years, the organization occupied the top spot on *Fortune* magazine's list of the 100 best companies to work for in the United States. And whereas industry turnover rates range from 33.6 percent to as high as 124.3 percent, The Container Store boasts a rate of just 25 to 30 percent—even among part-time and seasonal employees.

SOURCE: Adapted from Carla Joinson, "Hit the Floor Running, Start the Cart . . . and Other Neat Ways to Train New Employees," SHRM Employment Management Association Forum, Winter 2001.

Managing Development of a Mentoring Program

Like a well-designed orientation program, a thoughtfully developed mentoring program can help your company improve retention, job satisfaction, productivity, and morale. Through such a program, mentors help protégés acquire often intangible skills that are essential to their professional development—such as decision making, time management, or assertiveness—but that are not listed in their formal job descriptions.[24]

According to Donna L. Horkey, PHR, of HR consultancy Missing Link Consultants, Inc., the biggest challenge in managing development of a mentoring program lies in finding mentors. For example, a manager who you think would make an excellent mentor for an employee may claim that he or she is too busy to commit to a mentoring relationship. Another manager may be reluctant to let a talented employee take on a long-term assignment in another department for fear of losing him or her.

Horkey, also the author of *Mentoring: The Missing Link to Supercharge Your People*, offers guidelines for addressing these challenges:

- **Help potential mentors expand their scope of concern.**
  Remind them that part of their responsibility is to do what's best for the company—not just for their own department. "Tell them that if your organization doesn't groom its employees for greater challenges and give them opportunities to develop, another company will," advises Horkey.

- **Appeal to managers' egos.** Many people may respond positively to your request that they serve as a mentor if you appeal to their ego. Explain to a potential mentor that a particular employee needs to learn more about time management, for instance, and say, "You have real skill in this area—you're the best in your unit. I know that this person can learn a lot from you."

- **Clarify the parameters of the mentoring relationship.** To ease concerns about time, reassure potential mentors that their protégé won't be their "child" forever. The average mentoring relationship proceeds for about six months and requires no more than a few hours every few weeks, says Horkey. Also show a willingness to arrange mentoring relationships to accommodate busy managers' concerns. For instance, perhaps a breakfast meeting every other week between mentor and protégé will be sufficient. And make it as easy as possible for mentors to participate—for example, by providing them with forms they can fill out to document their protégé's progress. You'll find it far easier to get the information you need to evaluate the effectiveness of your mentoring program.

- **Control the mentor-protégé matching process.** Match mentors and protégés according to the skills protégés need to learn and the individuals who can best help them develop those skills. Also, a person's boss should not be his or her mentor. "Matching mentors and protégés from different parts of your organization can create good cross-pollination and cross-functional awareness," says Horkey. In addition, avoid allowing managers to volunteer for mentoring or to pick their protégés. If left to their own devices, a manager might select a protégé just because he or she likes the person—not because the manager can offer the skills assistance or knowledge the employee most needs.

Implementing a Human Resource Information System

An HRIS enables a company to keep an accurate, complete, and up-to-date database that it can use to generate reports, maintain records, and automate routines and tasks, such as job application tracking.[25] Companies can select any number of modules for their HRIS—such as benefits, career development, job evaluation, equal employment opportunity, safety/Occupational Safety and Health Administration, recruitment, payroll, employee self-service, training, and labor relations. System software can be purchased off the shelf or customized to a company's existing IT platform.

When managed and implemented effectively, an HRIS can help a company track and analyze important information—such as costs per hire, costs of termination, and time and attendance—to identify productivity and profitability problems. Additional benefits include saving time through automating processes, such as benefits administration, and reducing costs by streamlining processes, such as report generation and compensation management.[26]

But as you might imagine, managing development and implementation of an HRIS is an enormous, expensive undertaking. Fail to anticipate and address the unique project management challenges posed by an HRIS, and you risk seeing your effort miss deadlines, go over budget, and disappoint the internal customers who will use the system.

Experts offer numerous suggestions for managing your HRIS implementation project skillfully. Here are some particularly helpful guidelines:

- **Secure an executive sponsor.** Your executive sponsor—whether a single individual or steering committee—supports you throughout your management of the project, not just in getting funding. The sponsor also helps remove obstacles and explains and defends your project team's efforts when needed.

- **Avoid project mission creep.** Be clear about why the HRIS is being implemented and what you want the system to do for your company. Keep these goals in mind as you select software vendors and system modules, decide whether to customize any software, and evaluate system designs and functionality options. If a manager asks you to expand the scope you've defined, your ability to deliver on time and within budget may be at risk. Let your executive sponsor make the decision.

- **Leverage your existing systems.** Build on your current software and processes where possible. You'll save money and time and avoid compatibility problems later.

- **Don't forget training.** Early on, develop a plan for training end users to begin using the new system once it's implemented. Often, HRIS vendors train the project team, but your company will likely be responsible for training end users.

- **Involve users.** Engage end users in testing early versions of the system and providing their feedback on how the system is working. They will ultimately have to live with the system that's implemented, so involving them early in development can help stave off frustration in the future.

- **Manage change.** When a company implements an HRIS, people throughout the organization may have to make changes in how they do their work. As part of managing your HRIS project, determine how you will manage those changes and gain people's buy-in for the new processes. One helpful strategy is to put the most resistant individuals on your project implementation team—so they know their input is valued and can more easily embrace the idea of change. Ask your executive sponsor to regularly communicate the project's mission and progress. And make sure everyone understands what the new system will—and won't—do.

- **Build the right project team.** Ensure that both functional and technical leaders participate in your project team. They bring different expertise, skills, and insights into how processes work in your organization. Also recruit team members who are open to change, who enjoy participating in long-term projects, and who have good attendance records. Consider arranging for substitutes to fill in for key team members who are sick or on vacation.

- **Foster team identity.** Your project team may comprise people who aren't used to working closely together—individuals from HR, IT, payroll, and other parts of your company. Encourage identification with the team by creating a logo, handing out T-shirts, and conducting team-building exercises. If team members will be spending much or all of their time on this project, publicize their accomplishments so they can maintain visibility in the rest of the organization.

- **Phase it in.** Guide your HRIS project through several phases. In phase one, build a system platform that takes over some simple processes your company previously handled in less efficient ways. Provide some features that make some processes—such as job application tracking—easier for end users. In phase two, install and test the major modules you've selected. In phase three, after your company has had experience with the system, refine it based on user feedback, and install some "nice to have" features.

- **Document, document, document.** Record each step you've taken to manage the project and how you've carried out each step. Also document all decisions your team has made. If you decide to customize the software you license from a vendor, keep in mind that when new releases of the software come out, your company will need to expend significant resources to update your customized version. Modify software only after careful thought, and thoroughly document all changes.[27]

See "HR in Action: Rescuing an HRIS Implementation at Cincinnati Children's Hospital Medical Center" for an example of how one HR practitioner applied his project management savvy to turn a failed HRIS implementation around.

HR in Action: Rescuing an HRIS Implementation at Cincinnati Children's Hospital Medical Center

When Ronald McKinley, Ph.D., SPHR, joined Cincinnati Children's Hospital Medical Center as vice president of HR, he inherited an HRIS implementation project that had been ill handled—with disastrous results. "The project lacked the internal and external talent it needed, as well as sufficient funding. And the company had made the mistake of customizing too much of the software," McKinley explains. "The approach wasn't working, and it was considered a failed implementation—despite the $2 million already invested."

Accountable for turning the project around, McKinley began by defining and executing a three-phase plan. In phase 1, he and his team stabilized the work that had already been accomplished. He explains, "We got rid of all the work-arounds—for example, correcting code so that processes such as payroll were no longer being done at the last minute." In phase 2, the team upgraded the system to the latest platform offered by a well-known vendor. In phase 3—which McKinley describes as "ongoing"—the team added new modules such as employee self-service.

Throughout the project, McKinley worked with a solid project team. Whereas the previous team had just one internal IT person handling all the work-arounds, McKinley's team comprised four such experts, in addition to three internal application specialists. He also ensured support from top management throughout the project: "We educated the CFO and CEO about what it really takes to have a successful implementation. We told them, 'You can't get a return on a share of stock unless you buy a share.' We also presented a lot of examples of successful cases where the HRIS worked well—and explained the resources those successes had required." Thanks to McKinley's careful case building, top management approved an additional $3 million in funding for the project.

McKinley's skillful management of the project has generated impressive results. For example, he hasn't had to add HR staff at the transactional level since the new system went live. Employees are now handling many of their own transactions, such as changing their addresses or enrolling in benefits programs online. And the job application process is now performed entirely online. Consequently, McKinley explains, "My staff can now focus on transformational, not transactional, work—including how they can better help the organization achieve its mission." The new speed and efficiency offered by the system has reduced costs and eased HR procedures. For instance, "We used to have a $1.4 million recruitment budget, and now it's $400,000," says McKinley. "In addition, in just four and a half years, we were able to hire four thousand employees, to bring our headcount up to eight thousand five hundred." Top management has been so appreciative of HR-related results that it has approved implementation of non-HR information system applications, such as supply chain management and grants management.

In summing up the practices that exerted the biggest impact on this successful implementation, McKinley cites the importance of keeping software customization to a minimum. "It's faster and cheaper if you don't customize," he says. "The previous team had customized one payroll process, and it cost us $250,000 each time the source software application was upgraded." He also advises being clear and up front with top management about the resources a successful implementation requires. And he advocates what he calls a "joint application definition session" at the outset of the project to define the effort's scope and objectives. He explains, "We held lengthy meetings with key decision makers from HR and internal client groups, facilitated by an outside specialist, to create the project plan. Based on the input from these sessions, we could easily present the project's needed resources, people, funding, and time line, as well as its expected return on investment."

SOURCE: Ronald McKinley, telephone interview by Lauren Keller Johnson, August 8, 2005.

Creating an Employee Expatriation Program

With the advent of globalization, more and more companies are sending employees on short-term and long-term international assignments. A company might ask one or more executives to travel abroad for various reasons:

- Develop assignees' careers by providing challenging tasks in an international setting

- Analyze a foreign market to see whether the firm's offerings will attract customers there

- Launch a new product or service in a new market

- Transfer technology or knowledge to the company's overseas worksite or to a key customer's worksite

- Manage a joint venture with another company

- Set up a new satellite office [28]

International assignments not only offer many valuable advantages for companies; they also benefit assignees in important ways. For example, expatriates may appreciate an opportunity to participate in a different culture, to take on stimulating and challenging assignments in a different work setting, to see their families broaden their cultural horizons, and to exercise their secondary languages and other skills.

As companies' use of international assignments increases, it's more vital than ever that HR professionals know how to create and manage an employee expatriation program. By applying your project management skills to this effort, you help ensure that your organization—and the assignees involved—extract maximum value from overseas stints.

To create and sustain an expatriation program, you'll need to take numerous considerations into account and establish a wide range of systems. Carefully thinking through matters such as the purpose of an assignment, ramifications for assignees' families and work teams, compensation structure, and so forth is critical to ensure proper planning of the project. Experts recommend asking the following questions as you work out the details of the program:

- **Context.** What is your company's structure in the overseas location: a start-up effort for a new product or service? An existing or new satellite office? A joint venture with a foreign company? A subsidiary of your firm? The context determines assignees' experience level. For example, you wouldn't want to send a relatively inexperienced individual to set up a new operation or office. On the other hand, sending a highly experienced person to work in an established business that presents few new challenges may result in boredom, dissatisfaction, and lukewarm performance on the assignee's part.

- **Purpose.** Why are you considering sending one or more of your people to the host location? Do you need to fill a vacancy in an existing operation? Transfer technology or knowledge to the worksite? Provide career development opportunities for assignees? Scope out a potential new market? Launch a new offering? Manage a specific project? Clarifying your company's purpose can help you figure out whether an expatriate or local employee might better fit the position. For instance, a local person—deeply familiar with the local culture and business climate—might be more effective at launching a new product.

    Your purpose can also help you determine whether a short- or long-term assignment is most appropriate. Many companies use short-term assignments (usually between three and twelve months) when the purpose of the arrangement is to manage or participate in a specific project. Short-term assignments differ from long-term assignments in several ways. For instance, assignees' family members usually stay at home, and an assignee will most likely remain on the home-based compensation and receive a per diem.

- **Temperament.** Do your potential assignees have the right temperament for the job? To perform successfully in a host country, expatriates must not only exhibit confidence, self-reliance, and perseverance; they need a strong work ethic, social sensitivity, adaptability, and good listening and communication skills. Other qualities such as a willingness to take risks and to initiate change also help. Therefore, as part of your project, you'll need to establish a way to assess potential assignees' temperament. You may also want to decide whether your company will send expatriates who already possess these personal qualities, as well as use training to help interested potential assignees strengthen any weak areas.

- **Skills.** Do your potential expatriates have the right skills for the job? Can they troubleshoot during a transfer of technology? Build relationships and work well with others? Master a new language? Deal with change in a positive, healthy way? Align your company's needs with local market needs? Again, it's vital to identify all the skills needed for overseas assignments and to set up a system for assessing possible assignees' capabilities along these dimensions.

- **Compensation, benefits, and assistance.** What pay and benefits structure would be most appropriate? Will assignees remain on the home-country payroll and benefits plans? Will the company reimburse them for any additional taxes incurred as a result of the assignment? Will it pay for a certain number of visits home or family visits abroad? Will the organization offer incentives and services such as needed training, insurance on personal belongings, shipment or storage of personal effects, per-assignment medical visits, and an orientation for the destination? What about security briefings, language and cross-cultural training, assistance for spouses seeking jobs overseas, and coverage of children's overseas education costs? And what about a supportive mentoring relationship established between the expatriate and someone back home? Mentors can provide the person with emotional support and help him or her maintain connections with the home office to ease repatriation when the assignment is over.

As always with compensation, benefits, and assistance programs, you may need to negotiate these with potential assignees. For example, if the company desperately needs someone to take a position in a host country that's undesirable in some respects, you might have to offer a more attractive incentive package to motivate an employee to take the job.

- **Other key parties.** Expatriation programs must take into account many more parties than just the assignees. Do you have a plan for including assignees' family members in discussions about the host location and culture, dual-career issues, concerns about aging parents left behind in the home country, or special needs for a child's education? What about the assignee's work team—will he or she supervise the team, be a peer, replace a local national? Has the team been briefed on expectations? Has the person's manager engaged in extensive conversations with him or her about the job, the manager's expectations, and the employee's expectations? Finally, what about the organization overall? If it's sending more and more employees abroad, can its existing administrative systems handle the associated complex tasks—such as currency exchanges and split payrolls? Be sure that your expatriation project takes these matters into account.

- **Assignment management.** Who will monitor expatriates' work performance and progress in settling into their new environment? What are the risks inherent in such assignments, and how will they be managed? Who will evaluate the relative success or failure of an assignment—and how? Finally, how will the company determine whether a particular assignment has generated the intended value and results? Who will conduct the cost-benefit analysis?[29]

Yes, creating an expatriation program entails a daunting array of considerations and challenges. But by asking the questions recommended, you can reduce the risk of omitting important tasks as you plan and implement the project.

Outsourcing HR Activities

Companies have long outsourced HR functions, but the trend is expected to see record growth in the United States alone.[30] One expert maintains that HR outsourcing will amount to about $38 billion by 2007—of an estimated $174 billion total in business process outsourcing.[31] Why such an interest in outsourcing HR functions? When handled skillfully, an outsourcing initiative can help your company reduce costs, provide higher-quality services to employees, free up HR staff to focus on strategic work, and gain access to outside HR expertise.[32]

Commonly outsourced HR functions include outplacement services, employee assistance programs, defined-contribution or 401(k) plans, COBRA administration, and defined-benefit pension plans—though some experts believe that companies will likely expand this arena to include such functions as leave management, learning and development, payroll, and recruiting.[33]

Companies decide to outsource one or more HR functions when it's clear that the benefits of doing so outweigh the risks and costs and that outsourcing will meet the organization's short- and long-term financial and strategic objectives. Another criterion some firms use is, "If you're touching the same piece of paper more than once, then it's a process you probably should eliminate or outsource."[34]

Once the decision has been made to pursue outsourcing, the HR practitioner managing the project faces numerous challenges. For one thing, how do you assemble the right project team? According to Melanie Young, SPHR, vice president of corporate HR and global services at Arrow Electronics in Melville, New York, you should assemble a team whose members understand how the outsourced functions work and have a company mind-set.[35] "Team members should also have a global mind-set," explains Young, "because outsourcing involves looking outside your current boundaries." The most effective large-scale outsourcing project teams comprise members from HR, as well as from the finance, contracts, IT, legal, and sourcing departments, says Scott Gildner, founder of international HR outsourcing firm Gildner & Associates.[36] (Gildner became partner and managing director of HR advisory services at Houston-based sourcing advisory firm TPI, Inc. after TPI and Gildner & Associates merged in 2005.)

Your project will stand a greater chance of succeeding if you also set up an oversight or steering committee, Gildner adds. "Business issues are going to crop up once you've signed a contract with a vendor," he explains. "Establish a regular, perhaps monthly, series of meetings between your company's project manager and the vendor's project manager. Set up mechanisms to resolve typical implementation problems, and alert the steering committee to conflicts such as misunderstandings about the scope of the project and significant delays."

What kind of time frame can you expect to deal with in managing your outsourcing project? Gildner maintains that it's difficult to generalize about expected time lines for implementing outsourcing projects. However, three months to twenty-four months seems a reliable rule of thumb. "A full-scale outsourcing of benefits administration," he says, "may take three to nine months, and transferring existing operations to your vendor can take one or two months." According to Mary Cook, president of Chicago-based HR consultancy Mary Cook & Associates, outsourcing a complex area such as defined-benefit pension plan administration or 401(k) pension plan administration—particularly if it involves a conversion to a vendor's proprietary systems platform—takes more time and deserves more care and due diligence than outsourcing a simpler function such as recruiting.[37] In considering how long it may take to realize the expected benefits of outsourcing, "It's reasonable to think in terms of five to seven years," adds Cook, "because outsourcing decisions represent significant changes in business strategy."

Beyond issues regarding time line, project team configuration, and so forth, the following aspects of managing an outsourcing project can prove particularly challenging:

- **Preparation.** "Outsourcing represents such a significant change in the way a company does business that it should come in stages that can be planned, implemented, and successfully managed over time," maintains Cook. Activities you may need to carry out during the preparation stage include developing and communicating a new HR strategy, laying the foundation for restructuring your HR function, and training HR staff to take on new responsibilities.[38]

- **Communication.** Gildner contends that outsourcing HR functions is more about change management than anything else. "There are lots of constituents," he says. "Outsourcing may mean that some jobs are lost and remaining roles redefined. It can also mean that managers throughout your company must do their work in new ways. If you don't deal with change management early, you'll be forced to react to problems after your vendor has started taking over processes for you." That's why achieving buy-in from employees and management is critical. You'll need to make a compelling case for the transition and explain why it's in the best long-term interest of your staff and the rest of the company.[39] In explaining the rationale behind the decision to outsource, treat employees as adults. Straight talk is far better than trying to deliver a sales pitch for outsourcing, getting defensive if the decision is challenged, and using corporate jargon or euphemisms for the painful aspects of the change.[40]

- **Vendor selection.** Create a vendor-selection team that includes various internal stakeholders—such as representatives from the IT, finance, and legal departments, as well as top executives. That way, when you ultimately offer a contract to a candidate vendor, you'll have your key constituents' backing. Use requests for information and requests for proposals (RFPs) to steadily narrow the field of candidates who meet your needs. To make comparisons as straightforward as possible, use as many yes-or-no questions as possible in your RFPs. When your selection team has narrowed the field to two or three finalists, conduct on-site visits to see product samples and gather additional information.[41] "Be very planful about your on-site visits," suggests Young. "Work out ahead of time what questions you'll ask—such as how the vendor would scan your health insurance claims, how their information systems work, and how they hire talent."

How can you recognize a promising candidate? Look for financial stability, an impressive service record, reasonable costs, technology leadership, the ability to safeguard your company's data, and training provided to help your people convert to an outsourced solution.[42] Additional criteria include demonstrated HR expertise, service-level agreements in contracts (such as transaction accuracy, data delivery, system availability, and employee satisfaction), and cost-saving guarantees in contracts.[43]

- **Contract negotiation.** While negotiating a contract with your selected provider, avoid treating the process as a "gotcha" game in which you try to trick concessions from the other party. Instead, negotiate deals as if you're looking for a collaborative relationship that benefits both sides over the long haul.[44] Young also advises "setting a minimum standard that must be met before a deal can be inked—such as 'no deal if we can't get costs savings of at least 20 percent.' In addition, be very clear about which functions and which processes you want to outsource and the level of service quality you expect to see."

- **Vendor relationship management.** Some experts liken an outsourcing partnership to a marriage: it takes time to establish, and it requires nurturing from both sides over the long term. For this reason, you'll need to ensure that once the outsourcing implementation gets under way, your company and your vendor continue to be on the same page regarding roles and responsibilities, as well as the scope of the arrangement. For instance, if you've outsourced benefits administration, discuss and resolve misunderstandings that arise over who handles claims appeals, reviews error reports, or makes corrections.[45] Also consider designating one or several people as vendor relationship managers. A thoughtfully negotiated contract should help you more productively manage your vendor relationship—but mutual trust and respect are even more important.

To gain a sense of the challenges involved in managing an HR outsourcing project—and ways to surmount them—see "HR in Action: Outsourcing HR Functions at Goodyear."

HR in Action: Outsourcing HR Functions at Goodyear

Charlie Edmisten, director of HR business process outsourcing and integration service for Goodyear Tire and Rubber Company, based in Akron, Ohio, found the contract negotiation and relationship management phases of managing an HR outsourcing project to be the most daunting. After initiating the outsourcing process in 2003, Goodyear and its provider had decided against hiring an external consultant to assist with the transition—something both parties now regret. "We had very little knowledge of HR outsourcing going into negotiating the contract with [our vendor]," says Edmisten. He believes that using an outside sourcing adviser would have helped Goodyear establish a solid relationship management model and smoother transition process.

Edmisten discovered that he needed to spend "plenty of time" defining his company's and the vendor's roles and responsibilities—what he terms "governance." "That's where having an adviser would have helped," he says. A consultant would have also been able to help his team and the vendor break down outsourced processes into their component parts.

The governance issue was not completely resolved before Goodyear and its provider signed their contract, and this led to some problems, acknowledges Edmisten. "Without governance, you can have finger pointing on both sides." But Edmisten and his team took other steps that helped create a positive relationship despite the rocky start. For example, he worked to build a strong bond between the vendor and the retained HR organization, so the company's remaining HR staff and those working for the provider felt as if they were on the same team. Goodyear also created an advisory committee comprising HR leaders from the company's various business divisions and the HR outsourcing operations team to meet monthly to identify and deal with problems. In addition, the firm established a governance board that met quarterly and that comprised senior-level HR leaders from Goodyear and its vendor. The governance board handled change-management issues and transition strategy.

Thanks to the ability of Edmisten and his project team to learn from the outsourcing process—in real time—"things [started] to come together" after nearly a year of hard work with Goodyear's vendor.

SOURCE: Adapted from Tom Starner, "Managing the Handoff," *Human Resource Executive,* March 2, 2005.

Winning Executive Support for Your HR Project

When your CEO or another member of your executive team sponsors an HR project that you lead, you'll have the confidence of maintaining their support as the project moves forward. But what about when *you're* advocating a particular project that you know is essential to your company's success? If the initiative is expensive, time-consuming, and risky, you may need to evoke your power of persuasion and your credibility to sell the idea to the rest of your executive team. In other words, you'll need to prepare and present a compelling business case for your idea. You can expect to encounter numerous roadblocks— among them competing initiatives, difficulty measuring the project's potential financial benefits, and lack of funds. The following practices can help you overcome these roadblocks:

- **Cite HR trends.** Study what analysts are saying about HR trends, and then use that information to persuade executives to support your initiative. For example, perhaps 90 percent of companies plan to increase spending on HR technology this year, or 70 percent are planning at least one major human capital management initiative. Such figures can prove persuasive to decision makers.

- **Show how your initiative supports other strategic projects.** Identify important business initiatives already under way, then work to place your project within those programs. For instance, if you work in a pharmaceutical company that's planning to introduce a new product, link your proposed recruitment of biochemists to the new-product effort.

- **Calculate ROI.** Explain how your project will cut costs, boost revenues, improve productivity, lower risk, and generate other forms of value important to your company and executive team. Express these gains in business terms used by executives: revenue, operating margin, fixed assets, shareholder value. Provide benchmark data, such as HR cost per employee.

- **Cite market research about HR's link to business performance.** Present market research showing the link between human capital practices and business performance. For instance, some studies show that superior HR practices are a leading indicator of financial performance—thus HR initiatives can help companies recover from an economic downturn.

- **Prepare responses to key questions.** In preparing to present your business case to other executives, ensure that you can answer these questions: (1) How will your project reduce the current company budget? For example, will an employee Web initiative reduce HR headcount, slash travel costs, or lower recruitment costs? (2) How will company costs increase or revenues decrease if your project is *not* implemented? For example, if the HRIS you're proposing does not receive approval, some IT costs may be duplicated. (3) How will your project make things easier for the workforce? For instance, will it help managers spend less time preparing reports? Will data be more accurate?[46]

If you'd like to know more about persuasion skills and business finance, see *The Essentials of Power, Influence, and Persuasion*; *The Essentials of Finance and Budgeting*; and *The Essentials of Negotiation*—all volumes in this series.

Summing Up

In this chapter, you learned about the unique challenges and strategies involved in managing the following HR projects:

- **Starting an HR department.** Clarifying the new department's purpose and taking stock of your company's existing payroll and personnel records are key steps in managing this type of project.

- **Conducting a legal compliance audit.** Determining the scope of the audit, developing your audit questionnaire, and deciding how you'll act on your findings constitute important activities.

- **Developing an employee handbook.** Assembling a cross-functional project team, getting managerial feedback on the handbook content, and striving for an engaging and welcoming tone are essential strategies for ensuring this project's success.

- **Designing an employee orientation and mentoring program.** Helpful practices for developing your orientation program include presenting information about your company in a variety of formats (visual components, lectures, quizzes) and finding opportunities to repeat the information; ensuring a well-managed mentoring program by using skills to match mentors with protégés; and persuading busy managers to serve as mentors through appealing to their responsibility to the company's welfare.

- **Implementing an HRIS.** Practices such as building on your company's existing IT platform, gathering input from end users on early versions of the HRIS, and arranging for training on the new system can help boost your chances of success.

- **Creating an employee expatriation program.** Clarifying the purpose of sending employees overseas and ensuring that potential expatriates have the required temperament and skills will help you manage this project effectively.

- **Outsourcing HR activities.** Managing the change associated with outsourcing and cultivating a positive partnership with your outsourcing vendor are two keys to successfully managing this project.

In addition, you learned tips for winning executive support for your HR project—including citing the measurable benefits the project will generate, ways in which the project fits with other important strategic initiatives, and citing market research showing the link between savvy human capital management and business performance.

Leveraging Chapter Insights: Critical Questions

- Of the seven HR projects described in this chapter, which are you preparing to manage?

- What key challenges do you expect to encounter for each of the projects you're readying yourself to manage?

- How might you best surmount those challenges?

- Do you have ideas for an HR initiative that may encounter resistance from other executives in your company? If so, what steps might you take to prepare a compelling business case for your idea? What information will you gather? How will you present your case to decision makers?

CHAPTER FIFTEEN

Supporting Critical High-Level Projects

HR's Vital Role

Key Topics Covered in This Chapter

- *Developing a crisis management or disaster recovery plan*

- *Assisting with mergers and acquisitions*

- *Managing a downsizing initiative, reduction in force, or restructuring*

- *Facilitating organization-wide cultural change*

- *Realigning an organizational performance appraisal system to meet your company's strategic goals*

I N CHAPTER 14, you read about strategies for managing numerous projects that you may initiate in the course of your career—from starting an HR department, conducting a legal compliance audit, and developing an employee handbook to designing an employee orientation and mentoring program, implementing an HRIS, creating an employee expatriation program, and outsourcing HR activities. In this chapter, we'll shift focus to your role in managing five types of projects that may be initiated by other executives—namely, developing a crisis management and recovery plan, assisting with mergers and acquisitions, managing a downsizing or restructuring initiative, facilitating cultural change in your company, and revising your company's performance appraisal system. Such projects, even when they're sponsored by non-HR executives, have important implications for your company's workforce and require your skills. You'll need to play a strong supportive role in planning and implementing these initiatives.

In the sections that follow, we'll examine each of these project types closely and explore ways in which you can make valuable contributions. By assisting effectively in such projects, you help ensure that the initiatives deliver their promised value.

Developing a Crisis Management and Recovery Plan

Workplace crises can take numerous forms—including terrorist attacks, natural disasters, and office shootings and other forms of violence. During such times, systems and processes can break down, and employees' intense emotional reactions can bring productivity to a halt. How your company treats employees during a crisis has crucial long-term implications for retention, productivity, and profitability. That's why it's essential that your company develop an effective crisis management and recovery plan. As an HR professional, you can play a central role in this project—creating much-needed value and mitigating risks to your organization and its employees.

To help your company develop an effective plan, apply these six steps:

1. **Assess the risks.** Consider the range of potential crises your company could face, such as natural events (floods, fires, earthquakes, hurricanes, tornadoes), environmental events (hazardous materials spills, chemical explosions), and criminal acts (workplace violence, terrorism, bomb threats, riots, hostage situations). Decide which crises are indigenous to your company's business environment and how likely they are to occur.

2. **Gauge the crises' potential impact.** Of the crises you've identified as most indigenous and most likely to occur, ask yourself, "What would be the impact on our organization if this type of event did occur?" In particular, consider the effect of a crisis on workers' emotional state and productivity.

3. **Identify resources.** Survey potential resources that would be essential for each type of crisis. For example, area businesses might be interested in forging mutual aid agreements in the event of a natural disaster. Also consider governmental agencies, hospitals, and other emergency service providers. In addition, identify vendors—grief counselors; workplace violence specialists; plumbing, electrical, and roofing contractors; security guards—with whom you could establish contractual relationships to guarantee their availability in the event of a crisis. List all such resources, and periodically update the list to reflect any changes in contact information.

4. **Prepare a written plan.** Outline step-by-step how various individuals in your organization will respond should a crisis occur. For instance, people in administration could take charge

of property security, utilities, and maintenance. Experts in finance could be responsible for cost control, insurance claims, and accounting. Those in marketing or public relations could handle customer and media relations.

5. **Review and test the plan.** Share the protocol with other senior managers to ensure that all possible crisis scenarios have been considered. Invite the managers to provide ideas for improving the plan. Also test the plan, developing and incorporating changes to address any shortfalls that are revealed during the test.

6. **Implement the plan.** Communicate the plan to all employees, and deliver drills and training exercises that simulate specific credible threats so as to test workers' ability to follow the plan. Immediately address any deficiencies in response. Incorporate communication of the plan into all new-employee orientation sessions. And make participation in training and drills by every employee a requirement.[1]

A key component in any crisis management plan is how your company will help employees work through and recover from the emotional impact of a crisis. How you handle this aspect of crisis management will strongly determine how quickly your workforce returns to productivity. The following practices—which you can apply yourself as well as train managers to apply—can help:

- Let people talk about the crisis. The more they talk, the healthier your organization will become.

- Meet with people at all levels to express grief and promote available services, such as your employee assistance program. Provide a place for people to watch or listen to news at the workplace.

- Let people know that it's OK to cry or to feel anger in response to a crisis, but don't allow people to direct their anger toward others. Provide a chaplain who can help those employees who may want to seek spiritual solace.

- Equip supervisors and middle managers with training, information, and authority to help their employees—including recognizing post-traumatic stress disorder, knowing how to communicate with people under stress, and knowing how to compartmentalize their own emotions in order to help their employees.

- Help employees feel some measure of control by identifying and giving them opportunities to contribute to a cause in which they feel they can make a difference. Examples include contributing time or money to a charity and donating blood.[2]

Preparation, planning, and practice are key elements in the effectiveness of your company's crisis management and recovery program. See "HR in Action: Crisis Preparation at Morgan Stanley" for an example of how one HR professional helped save lives at his company.

HR in Action: Crisis Preparation at Morgan Stanley

Rick Rescorla, former vice president for corporate security at Morgan Stanley, had long had an evacuation plan in place for his company. But he did far more than just develop the plan and communicate it to his company's workforce. Despite grumbling from busy employees who didn't want to be interrupted in their work, Rescorla insisted that people practice the evacuation process every few months. His motto? The "Seven Ps: proper prior planning and preparation prevent poor performance."

In 1993, when the World Trade Center was bombed, Rescorla's philosophy and planning enabled all employees to escape the building safely. On September 11, 2001, about twenty-seven hundred Morgan Stanley employees successfully evacuated the South Tower of the World Trade Center after the terrorists had struck, thanks to Rescorla's insistence on the Seven Ps. On a day when numerous companies headquartered in the twin towers lost huge numbers of employees, only six Morgan Stanley employees perished in the attack. One of those six was Rick Rescorla.

SOURCE: Adapted from Heather Collins, "It Pays for HR to Be Prepared for Disasters," *HR News,* June 2002.

Assisting with Mergers and Acquisitions

During any merger or acquisition (M&A), the management and transition of employees to the new entity strongly determines whether the deal succeeds or fails. How will workforce morale be maintained once the two companies have combined? Will the new entity have the right people with the right skills? How will the formerly separate groups of employees work together in the new organization? What cultural issues may crop up as two previously separate companies blend into one? Will the two organizations' HRISs be combined, or will one system be retained and the other retired? Or, will an entirely new HRIS be constructed? What about benefits—will the new entity offer the same benefits that one or both previously separate organizations offered?

Human resource professionals on both sides of a merger or acquisition play a critical role in answering all these questions—before, during, and after a merger or acquisition. This is particularly true in today's economy, where many companies' principal assets are their people. In a company that's acquiring another firm or merging with a smaller entity, HR practitioners participate in the due diligence process—evaluating the other company's employment practices before the merger or acquisition. This evaluation helps the organization to avoid unwanted legal, financial, and strategic consequences and to enable the best possible transition for its workforce.[3] In a company that's being acquired, HR professionals are key to providing the information needed in the due diligence process. They also help put a measurable value on their company's human capital so as to ensure the highest possible purchase price. All of these activities require top-notch project management skills.

For the sake of brevity in this already full chapter, let's assume that your company is considering acquiring another firm or merging with a smaller entity and that you'll be supporting the project. You can help ensure the project's success by carrying out the following activities:

- **Deepening your understanding of M&As.** Participate in all strategy planning sessions in which the role of acquisitions and

mergers is discussed. That way, you can deepen your understanding of the purpose of M&A strategies.

- **Facilitating data gathering.** Research due diligence models
relevant to your industry so that you know what to expect as
the due diligence process unfolds. Develop a list to guide the
gathering of data on the target company.

- **Clarifying an M&A's impact on human capital.** Educate
other members of the M&A team on the deal's potential implications for the new entity's human capital. For example,
what morale problems might arise, and how could your company address them during and after the merger or acquisition?

- **Creating a communications plan.** Develop a plan for communicating about the M&A (including possible staff reduc-
tions) with your company's workforce. To ensure that your plan
is consistent with rules on disclosure and insider trading, consult with your company's legal counsel.

- **Identifying valued employees.** Ask managers throughout your
company to help you identify high-potential people and assess
where they might fit in the new entity. Learn who the top
performers are in the target company as well, and reach out to
them early to secure their loyalty.

- **Retaining high-value employees.** Develop an incentive program (such as stay bonuses) to encourage key employees to
remain with your company through the transition and beyond.

- **Integrating two companies' structures, systems, and cultures.**
Form project teams to address integration initiatives such as
combining the two companies' HRISs, blending the two HR
departments, redesigning benefits and compensation programs,
and merging two different organizational cultures.

- **Developing a staffing plan.** Create a staffing plan to be implemented after the merger or acquisition has occurred. For example, which employees will be redundant after the M&A project
has been implemented? How will the new entity assist those

who lose their jobs? Which individuals will be needed for the transition only? Which people will the new company want to retain, and how will the organization win their loyalty?[4]

See "HR in Action: M&A Strategy at SYSCO" for an example of how one company ensures successful merger and acquisition projects.

HR in Action: M&A Strategy at SYSCO

At food-service marketing and distribution giant SYSCO, acquisitions constitute a major element in the company's competitive strategy. According to Chief Administration Officer Ken Carrig, the company has an M&A team comprising professionals from its HR, legal, finance, and operational groups, as well as from other functions. The team reviews potential acquisitions on a quarterly basis and meets with the CEO and CFO to discuss opportunities and explore their potential fit.

By taking into account a target company's culture, talent, and other characteristics, the M&A team arrives at a high-level assessment of how promising a particular acquisition might be. "We could identify a great company to acquire but end up deciding against doing so, because the implementation would prove too difficult," says Carrig, also the author of Building Profits Through People (Society for Human Resource Management, 2006).

During the due diligence phase of a potential acquisition, the M&A team assesses the target company's pay practices, safety record, and employee benefits, among other things. It also takes stock of the company's strengths, weaknesses, opportunities, and threats, and considers possible time lines for integrating the acquired company into SYSCO. Says Carrig, "We figure out how long the integration might take and which key practices should be implemented when during the first three months and the first year."

Carrig advocates several strategies for HR practitioners participating in the M&A process. In particular, he notes, "People issues are key in acquisitions. The HR and other members of the acquisition team need to talk with people in the target company who have direct insight into that company's leadership team. You want to know what their team's experience and education levels are and how the two companies' leadership teams might relate together. You also want to know about the target company's reward systems and staffing practices. For example, is there any evidence of nepotism?"

In addition, Carrig recommends thinking carefully about how quickly a particular acquisition should be implemented. "It's OK to go slowly," he says, if doing so would help ensure a successful transition. "If the target company's HR programs and benefits differ substantially from our company, we might let them maintain those differences for a while—say, the first year after the acquisition. Then we would gradually implement the transition."

SOURCE: Ken Carrig, telephone interview by Lauren Keller Johnson, August 10, 2005.

Managing a Downsizing Initiative

Sometimes a company has no choice but to lay off a portion of its workforce. Perhaps the organization desperately needs to cut costs in the short term, and other tactics (such as pay cuts or freezes, or divestitures of assets) haven't generated the depth of cost cutting needed for the company to survive. In such cases, a company may be forced to implement a downsizing initiative in order to avoid jeopardizing the survival of the overall organization and the jobs of all its remaining employees.

The way your company handles a downsizing can strongly determine its financial performance after the initiative has been implemented. For example, if employees perceive the downsizing process as unfair, those who are laid off will likely tell their friends and family about the experience—making it more difficult for your organization to recruit talent in the future. Employees who survive the layoff will probably lose trust in the organization, feel less motivated to give their best, and withhold personal commitment to your company. And of course, laying off workers means that those who survived the downsizing must shoulder the workloads of those who have left—which can further erode morale and heighten on-the-job stress. Add up all these consequences of a badly handled layoff, and it's not surprising that most downsizing initiatives fail to generate the intended improvements in the company's financial performance and productivity.

As an HR professional, you can play a central role in supporting a downsizing project so that it stands a better chance of yielding the desired results. How? Apply the following practices:

- **Clarify purpose.** Encourage other executives and managers throughout your organization to articulate the intended benefits of the layoff. Ask, "In what ways will the layoff help us better serve customers or reach our strategic goals? How might we orchestrate the downsizing to best ensure that it fulfills our purpose?"

- **Retain top performers.** Discourage managers from making across-the-board job cuts or cuts based on criteria such as who was hired most recently. Instead, help managers identify their top performers—the people who work well together and who are most difficult to replace. Devise strategies for retaining these individuals: your firm will need them to innovate, create new markets, and attract new customers as your company moves through this transition period.

- **Identify needed changes to work processes.** Remind management that layoffs require changes in the way work gets done. Instead of loading the work of laid-off employees onto the shoulders of those who survive the layoff, encourage managers to identify new ways of working that will ease the burden on survivors. For example, can several processes be combined for greater efficiency? Can some tasks be eliminated for a while? The payoff to this technique is that you'll help remaining workers avoid burnout and debilitating stress—and therefore preserve their productivity.

- **Communicate openly and honestly.** Work with other executives to develop a plan for providing regular, ongoing updates about the layoff to workers. Don't let employees hear about cutbacks only through the grapevine. In the absence of honest information, people's imaginations run amuck—and rumors abound that often prove far worse than the truth. Trust is critical to ensuring an effective downsizing—and communication cultivates trust. When employees trust that company leaders are telling them the truth, they become more willing to follow those leaders—even after a layoff. Thus, it's vital that you help management develop messages about the downsizing that include explanations of why the cutbacks are necessary, acknowledgment of the pain that downsizing causes, and commitment to help those who will lose their jobs. In addition, ensure that employees who will lose their jobs hear the news from the manager who selected their jobs for cutting—not from someone who wasn't involved in the decision.

- **Treat laid-off employees right.** Train supervisors to handle the emotions of employees who are losing their jobs. Develop programs to provide assistance to departing employees—such as outplacement services, counseling, financial advice, and other forms of help. As laid-off employees leave the office, treat them with dignity and respect. Discourage management from having security guards parade people off company property in full view of colleagues who still have jobs: victims of such treatment may retaliate with wrongful discharge and discrimination lawsuits, negative word of mouth about your company, sabotage, and even workplace violence.

- **Manage survivors effectively.** Remind managers of the emotional damage that layoff survivors suffer while watching their colleagues lose their jobs. Research shows that survivors often feel betrayed, suffer high levels of stress and burnout, and feel uncertain about their roles in the downsized organization. Develop strategies for addressing their concerns—such as describing the new opportunities that may become available to them in the restructured organization and explaining how the company's new business strategy will help it compete more effectively in the marketplace going forward.

- **Manage other stakeholders.** Talk with other managers to determine how the layoff will affect customers, suppliers, shareholders, and the local community. For example, could a key customer defect if his or her long-time contact person is being laid off from your firm? Will local newspapers publish inaccurate stories about the company's circumstances? How will analysts and investors perceive the downsizing project? Develop plans for addressing questions and concerns and for ensuring that your company's image and brand are protected.

- **Learn from the process.** Help your company learn from its downsizing approach so that it can correct mistakes during any future layoffs. Ask employees and managers at all levels what they thought worked well about the downsizing and what didn't work well. Ask customers whether the company has met their needs more effectively since the layoff and what suggestions they might offer for the future.[5]

No downsizing initiative is easy and painless. But such a project stands a better chance of fulfilling its intended purpose if HR professionals offer the forms of support just described. See "HR in Action: Successful Downsizing at Agilent Technologies" for an example of how one company effectively managed a massive layoff.

HR in Action: Successful Downsizing at Agilent Technologies

Spun off by Hewlett-Packard, Agilent Technologies was struggling financially. In an attempt to turn the company around, leaders imposed across-the-board pay cuts, froze hiring, and slashed travel expenses and equipment purchases. But these measures proved insufficient. To survive, the company was forced to initiate two rounds of layoffs in 2001—cutting a total of eight thousand full-time employees, which constituted a whopping 27 percent of its workforce. It also eliminated bonuses and imposed temporary 10 percent pay cuts on eighteen hundred senior managers.

Yet HR leaders and other executives managed the downsizing initiative so well that Agilent avoided the decline in productivity and morale that many companies suffer in the wake of a massive layoff. For example, employees who were losing their jobs had to be told by their direct managers. Moreover, across-the-board cuts were forbidden. Instead, leaders in each division carefully reviewed the strategic importance of each product line and the job performance of each employee. Regular communications from managers and the CEO kept employees informed.

Thanks to Agilent's savvy handling of the cutbacks, morale remained surprisingly high throughout the entire process. One employee even said, "It's like a family. Everyone knows we have to chip in to make sure that everyone else is okay." Owing to the pay cuts, employees felt that everyone at Agilent was "sharing the pain"—which contributed to the sense of community and mutual support during this very painful time. Because Agilent had earned its employees' trust, those who survived the layoff were able to maintain their commitment to the company and continue giving their best.

SOURCE: Adapted from Wayne F. Cascio and Peg Wynn, "Managing a Downsizing Process," *Human Resource Management,* Winter 2004.

Facilitating Cultural Change in Your Organization

Many executives have realized that a positive workplace culture directly affects their company's bottom line and gives the organization a substantial competitive advantage. How? A company that's viewed as having a positive culture finds it easier to attract and retain talented employees. Moreover, workers in such organizations tend to understand their company's strategic direction, are more productive, and feel strongly committed to their firm.[6]

But what exactly does a positive culture look like? It has several distinctive characteristics—including flexible work schedules, positive reinforcement of employee achievements, trust in workers to do the job well, and freedom for employees to be creative.[7] Companies with a positive culture take specific actions to foster that culture. They:

- Create a compelling vision that all employees share and to which everyone feels he or she can make a contribution

- Have senior leaders who commit their attention to fostering a positive culture and who model the right behaviors—such as challenging prevailing wisdom, persevering in the face of hardship, and continually assessing the business environment

- Audit their current culture to identify and address problems such as lack of motivation, negativity, and confusion about strategic direction

- Explain to the workforce how a positive culture directly affects the company's bottom line—and therefore everyone's job opportunities

- Win employees' hearts by including them in decision making and inviting their ideas for solving pressing business problems

- Use coaching and feedback to enable people to perform at their best

- Watch for and overcome resistance to change

- Align systems and processes—such as hiring practices, training programs, and reward and recognition—behind the desired culture

- Use two-way and up-and-down communication to address problems and encourage the sharing of knowledge and ideas

- Strive for a diverse workforce whose members value commonalities and differences[8]

If your company has conducted a culture audit and decided that it needs to take steps to craft a more positive culture, you can play a vital part in this project. Your key activities in providing this form of project support include the following:

- **Facilitate the selection and development of leaders who can establish and maintain a positive culture.** For example, some

HR practitioners establish succession-planning programs to identify gaps in their company's leadership—that is, places in the organization where leaders lack the attitudes and behaviors necessary to foster a positive work climate. These HR professionals then use the resulting information to develop training programs and other tools to develop leaders' cultural abilities, and to recruit talented managers and executives from outside if necessary.

- **Attract employees who support a positive culture.** Develop recruiting strategies to attract job candidates who embody positive cultural traits. For example, stress your company's vision, its flexible job opportunities, and its emphasis on autonomy and creativity. Search actively for candidates who want to work in a collaborative environment and who feel a strong sense of ownership of their job responsibilities. Look for people who yearn to contribute to something larger than themselves and who seek meaning in their work beyond just a paycheck.

- **Model positive cultural behaviors yourself.** By demonstrating the attitudes and behaviors necessary to support a positive culture, you gain credibility as an effective "change agent" and inspire similar behaviors in other executives and managers.

- **Align systems and processes.** Develop training programs and reward and recognition systems that encourage the behaviors and attitudes characteristic of a positive culture. For instance, workshops that help managers translate the company's vision and strategy into compelling terms for employees can be valuable. You can also assist managers throughout your company with developing recognition programs for employees who contribute to a positive workplace culture.

- **Recognize and address resistance to change.** Any effort to change a company's culture is likely to encounter resistance from people who prefer the status quo. You can help support a cultural change effort by encouraging managers to identify potential resistors and to develop strategies for addressing resistance. The company's culture won't change unless a critical number of individual managers and employees embraces the need for change and commits to changing their own behaviors and attitudes. By helping managers address resistance, you boost the odds that your company will achieve that needed critical mass.[9]

To learn more about facilitating organization-wide cultural change, see *The Essentials of Managing Change and Transition,* another volume in the Business Literacy for HR Professionals series. To gain additional insights into translating your company's strategy into accessible terms so that people throughout the organization can help execute it, see *The Essentials of Strategy,* in this same series.

And as with many high-level projects in which you can and must make an important contribution, it can be helpful to see how other HR executives have supported major cultural change in their organizations. See "HR in Action: Fostering Cultural Change at Henry Ford Health System" for one such example.

HR in Action: Fostering Cultural Change at Henry Ford Health System

Since 2002, John Hayden, vice president and chief learning officer at Henry Ford Health System (HFHS) in Detroit, has served as project manager for HFHS's cultural change initiative—called the Organizational Transformation and Renewal Project. Sponsored by HFHS's CEO and launched in 2000 to address low morale stemming from financial difficulties, the project had several goals—including improving workforce awareness of the organization's mission, vision, and values; encouraging employees to be accountable for their actions; and fostering high quality in people's work.

The project began with a cultural audit of senior managers. The HR staff then hired a consultancy to develop a framework for addressing cultural problems identified in the audit. During a three-day off-site attended by HFHS's CEO, senior management team, and medical department chairs, the project team developed a plan for implementing the initiative. According to Hayden, three project teams were formed to address major components of the initiative: clarifying HFHS's mission, vision, and values; educating leaders about change; and aligning systems and processes behind the needed change.

The mission, vision, and values team, for instance, set out to craft a vision statement that was short, clear, and easy to understand. The solution? "Each patient first." "We wanted to send the message that people should treat patients as they would want to be treated themselves and as they would want their families to be treated," says Hayden.

The leadership education team conducted multiday sessions initially for the CEO and his thirty-member executive team, and then for the next tier of leaders, to help them understand the qualities needed for leaders to foster positive cultural change. "We used insight-based learning," explains Hayden. "With facilitation, we asked participants to identify their problem behaviors and the reasons behind them. We laid out the reasons for the cultural change project. And we stressed the importance of modeling the right behaviors—since people emulate leaders." Through collaborative games, reflection on participants' behaviors during the games, and journaling, participants generated ideas for applying what they learned in the sessions to their workplace relationships and responsibilities. HFHS has since trained twenty-five in-house facilitators to lead these sessions and has rolled the sessions out to more than ten thousand individuals.

The alignment team examined HR programs and assessed how well they supported the cultural characteristics and behaviors the project was striving to encourage. For example, the team evaluated HFHS's hiring practices and performance management systems and developed exit strategies for individuals who could not or would not change their behaviors to support

continued

a more positive climate. This team also stressed the importance of coaching in fostering behavioral change. "Coaching is more powerful than an annual review," Hayden maintains.

The project is about halfway there. (Hayden contends that real cultural change is a five- to ten-year journey, and "we have ninety years of culture to impact.") Yet it has already begun generating measurable results. For example, Hayden notes that "we went from losing $20 million in 2002 to earning a net income of $90 million in 2004. People also have more insight into their own behavior and its impact on patients. Employee satisfaction has risen on all ten dimensions that we track. And patient satisfactions scores are up."

The keys to the project's success? Hayden cites several examples. For one thing, "We had support from the CEO and COO right from the beginning. They are still committed to the effort and know that the renewal project drove our turnaround. And we used a consistent, common language that resonated with employees." The toughest part, Hayden says, is keeping the cultural change effort at the forefront of people's minds. "We avoid a flavor-of-the-month approach," he says. "Instead, we provide regular refresher courses for leaders, and we bring up the notion of renewal at every key meeting. We constantly reinforce the language and remind people that the effort is ongoing."

SOURCE: John Hayden, telephone interview by Lauren Keller Johnson, July 20, 2005.

Realigning Your Company's Performance Appraisal System

Most companies have an organizational performance appraisal system (PAS)—a method for measuring the business results the company is generating.[10] An organizational PAS consists of objectives (e.g., "increasing shareholder value," "improving customer loyalty," and "reducing process errors"); performance metrics (e.g., "percentage increase in share price," "ratio of repeat to first-time buyers," and "number of process errors per month"); and performance targets or desired performance (e.g.,"10% increase in share price,""five to four ratio of repeat to first-time buyers," and "five or fewer process errors per month").

Organizational performance appraisal systems offer numerous benefits. Most important, they enable managers to define (and track performance on) metrics for every strategic objective set by their unit and company. By noting performance that falls short of targets (e.g., "Our goal was to reduce order-processing errors 10%, but we only reduced them 5%"), managers can address the causes of the shortfall and work to continually improve performance. Organizational performance appraisal systems also let managers see how performance in different parts of the company affects performance in other parts. For instance, a company may discover that when the logistics staff achieves the objective to "accelerate order-delivery time 10 percent," the customer service group meets the objective to "increase customer satisfaction 15 percent."

Companies can choose from among a variety of organizational performance appraisal systems. Just a few examples follow.

Dashboards or Cockpits

Possibly the simplest type of organizational PAS, a dashboard or cockpit, combines the company's numerous metrics, targets, and performance data into one online or printed document (such as a spreadsheet) that's prepared monthly, quarterly, or on some other schedule.

A dashboard enables executives and managers to easily digest the company's aggregated performance data. In addition, many dashboards use a "traffic light" coding system to evaluate performance on each metric, enabling leaders to spot and address problems promptly. For example, red indicates performance that's significantly below target; yellow, slightly below target; green, at or above target.

While dashboards have been used primarily by executives, many companies are now customizing their dashboards for managers at operational levels as well. For instance, at an airline, a manager in charge of stocking meals on board may see a different dashboard than the

manager who oversees fuel purchasing. But each manager's customized dashboard also shows which planes are flying where.

Quality Improvement Systems

Quality improvement systems come in many different forms—including the following:

- **Plan-Do-Check-Act.** Popularized by total quality management founder W. Edwards Deming, the Plan-Do-Check-Act
  framework helps managers establish a cycle of continuous
  improvement. The cycle comprises these four steps:
  1. **Plan.** Identify a performance problem and the processes
     affecting it.
  2. **Do.** Explore potential solutions and implement one.
  3. **Check.** Assess how well your solution worked.
  4. **Act.** If your solution worked well, institutionalize it and
     look for another improvement opportunity. If it didn't, re-
     turn to step 1.

- **Six Sigma.** With roots tracing back to the 1920s, Six Sigma is
  a data- and measurement-driven approach that helps managers
  continually improve business processes through reduction of
  errors. Many companies that use Six Sigma apply it to all their
  business processes—manufacturing, product development,
  order fulfillment, customer service, and so forth.

- **Baldrige National Quality Program.** Established in 1987 by
  a congressional act, the Baldrige National Quality Program
  was developed by the United States' National Institute of Standards and Technology. (The program is named after Malcolm
  Baldrige, who served as secretary of commerce from 1981
  until 1987.) The Baldrige program defines criteria for high-
  quality business performance in numerous areas—leadership,
  strategic planning, customer focus, knowledge management,
  and so forth.

Every year, companies can apply for the Malcolm Baldrige Award, which recognizes organizations for achievement in specific categories: manufacturing, small business, education, and health care.

Balanced Scorecard

Introduced in 1992 by professors Robert Kaplan and David Norton, the Balanced Scorecard (BSC) system holds that financial performance is just one part of the larger picture of organizational performance. The system seeks to balance a company's financial perspective with three nonfinancial perspectives: customer, internal processes, and workforce learning. Companies that implement the BSC methodology develop and use two powerful tools:

1. **Strategy map.** A one-page document called a "strategy map" graphically depicts the cause-and-effect relationships between the four scorecard perspectives—showing executives' theories about how achievement of objectives in one perspective will affect performance on objectives in other perspectives. Many companies develop a corporate-level strategy map as well as strategy maps for each division, unit, and department that contain objectives supporting the high-level map.

2. **Scorecard.** The scorecard contains the objectives shown on the strategy map, as well as metrics, targets, and actual performance data for each objective. As with the strategy map, many companies create a corporate-level scorecard in addition to unit-level scorecards linked to the high-level one. Organizations often automate scorecards so that when unit managers input data into their scorecards, the data is automatically aggregated into the high-level scorecard to show overall company performance.

Adopted by corporations, not-for-profit organizations, and public-sector entities (including government agencies, municipalities, and military forces), the BSC has become widely used for strategy execution.

. . .

A company may use a particular organizational PAS for some time and then decide to revise or replace the system. In some cases, executives may define a new high-level strategy that requires the company to begin measuring different aspects of performance than before. For example, if the new corporate strategy requires extensive collaboration across functions, the executive team may want to start appraising cross-functional teamwork more than individual performance—and develop reward and incentive programs to encourage collaborative work. In other cases, a company may decide that its current organizational PAS doesn't give it a comprehensive enough picture of organizational performance. So it adopts a new system entirely.

Whatever the reason for realigning an organizational PAS, the project won't likely succeed without support from the HR unit. As an HR professional, you can assist with the project in the following ways:

- **Suggest objectives, metrics, and targets.** Using your knowledge of how workforce quality affects your company's bottom line, suggest to your executive team the objectives that you believe will best build a workforce that can meet your company's strategic goals. For example, if your company's new strategy hinges on improving customer service, objectives such as "increase employee retention," "reduce order-processing errors," and "enhance workforce knowledge of company products and services" would likely be appropriate.

  Offer your ideas for metrics as well, based on your knowledge of how to measure aspects of corporate performance such as turnover, employee knowledge and skills, and work attitudes. Also suggest appropriate targets. For example, if you know that turnover rates in your industry are about 10 percent, then it may be unrealistic for your company to strive for a much lower turnover rate.

  In addition, share your understanding of how performance on one metric affects performance on other metrics. For instance, if the logistics team reduces order-processing errors by 5 percent, that achievement may enable the customer service group to reach its goal of increasing customer loyalty 15 percent.

Finally, alert other executives to ways in which appraising performance can generate unintended—and unwanted—consequences. In particular, a company's selection of metrics can sometimes lead managers to game the system so as to meet the targeted performance. For example, consider a car company that aims to be "the best rated customer service car company in the industry." This company will have metrics related to customer satisfaction, customer loyalty, and the number of customer complaints. New-car salespeople who work in this company know that their compensation depends on what customers write in the feedback forms that corporate headquarters sends customers after a sale. Immediately upon closing a deal, salespeople may coach customers on how to fill out the form. They may even appeal to the customers' compassion: "My income depends on what you say on the form. I hope you'll help me." The result? Annoyed customers who feel manipulated. The lesson? Organizational performance appraisal systems can change employees' behaviors—sometimes in ways a company never intended!

- **Design communication and training programs for the realigned organizational PAS.** When a company changes its organizational performance appraisal system, it often begins evaluating and rewarding employees' on-the-job results in new ways. People may be confused by the changes or feel upset about having to demonstrate new and more daunting levels of performance. Communication and training are keys to addressing these responses. Develop communication programs—companywide e-mails, articles in your organization's newsletter, presentations by the CEO—to explain why the organizational PAS is changing and what those changes mean for managers and employees in terms of performance expectations, compensation, and so forth. Design workshops and other training opportunities to educate people on how to use the new system.

- **Suggest new reward systems.** The right reward systems can further boost the chances that an organizational PAS realignment project will succeed. Share with the rest of the executive team your ideas for designing incentives, compensation, and reward and recognition programs to support the changes in your company's PAS. For example, suppose your company wants to improve and appraise the quality of team-based work, but the current bonus system calls for rewarding individual achievement. In this case, you'll want to suggest developing reward programs that motivate collaboration and teamwork.

Summing Up

In this chapter, you discovered ways in which you can support the following critical high-level projects in your company:

- **Developing a crisis management and recovery plan.** Keys to effective support include identifying potential risks and available resources, preparing and testing the plan, and developing strategies for managing the intense emotions that arise in a workforce during and after a crisis or disaster.

- **Assisting with mergers and acquisitions.** Important HR contributions include participating in the due diligence process (assessing a potential acquisition's HR practices, employee benefits programs, and possible liabilities, such as pension plan obligations); deciding how to integrate two formerly separate companies' HR departments; and determining whether to select one company's HRIS over another's or to create an entirely new HRIS.

- **Managing a downsizing initiative.** Key HR activities include designing communication programs to keep the workforce informed, helping managers identify and retain top performers, and assisting employees who are losing their jobs.

- **Facilitating cultural change in your organization.** Vital HR support consists of activities such as conducting a culture audit to determine needed change, adapting hiring and other practices to build a workforce that personifies a positive culture, and helping managers recognize and address resistance to cultural change initiatives.

- **Realigning your company's organizational performance appraisal system.** Important HR contributions include offering your ideas for new objectives, performance metrics, and targets, and designing communication and training programs to help managers and employees understand the purpose behind new ways of appraising performance.

Leveraging Chapter Insights: Critical Questions

- Of the five high-level projects described in this chapter, which are currently unfolding (or are about to be launched) in your organization?

- What contributions do you need to make to each of these projects to help ensure their success?

- What actions might you take now to ensure that you contribute sufficiently to these projects' success? Consider matters such as the composition of your project teams, the ways in which you're planning your participation in these projects, the methods you'll use to measure a project's progress, and so forth.

- Of the five high-level projects described in this chapter, which do you find most challenging to support? Why? How might you improve your skills in these areas?

CHAPTER SIXTEEN

Next Steps

Honing Your Project Management Skills

Key Topics Covered in This Chapter

- *Review of important project management principles*

- *Learning from your project management experiences*

- *Enhancing your project management skills*

CONGRATULATIONS! By reading the previous fifteen chapters in this book, you've vastly increased your knowledge of HR project management. But reading about project management isn't sufficient in itself to sharpen your skills. You also need to distill the key principles and practices required for successful project management. And you must be able to learn from your project management experiences and then apply your insights to future efforts. Finally, you need to look for additional opportunities to continually strengthen your project management talents and develop a plan for addressing any weak areas in your skill set. In this chapter, you'll find guidelines for all three of these activities.

Revisiting Key Principles and Practices

Managing HR projects isn't easy. You have to keep numerous principles and practices in mind, juggle many different tasks, coordinate one or more teams, and process enormous volumes of information. To help you get a handle on all of this, we've distilled key principles and practices presented in this book and highlighted them here:

- **Project management as a vital HR competency.** When you manage HR projects deftly, you help your company execute important strategies, you build your personal and professional credibility, and you deliver valuable HR services to your inter-

nal customers. Successful project management may also open
doors to promotions and raises, add variety to your work (since
every project is different), and give you a profound sense of on-
the-job achievement and satisfaction.

To gain these benefits, you need a complex blend of personal and professional abilities and traits—including a willingness to master project-planning tools and technologies, the
ability to manage team conflict, a flair for keeping the big
picture in mind despite the many details that crop up during a
project, and a high tolerance for ambiguity, complexity, and
uncertainty.

- **The many faces of project management.** Each project has
  numerous individuals associated with it—including the project
  sponsor, the project manager, the leaders of project teams and
  subteams, and the members of the project teams. The most
  effective project teams address interpersonal conflict productively, put the needs of the project ahead of their individual
  concerns, and have a clear, shared sense of purpose and commitment to a common goal.

- **Project management as a process.** Managing a project means
  shepherding it through four distinct major phases. These phases
  include defining and organizing the project, planning the project, managing execution of the project, and closing the project
  when the execution is finished. Each of these phases can be
  further broken down into crucial activities—which we've listed
  in subsequent bullet points.

- **The project charter.** At the outset of any project, it's important to craft a written charter that lays out the purpose of the
  project, defines its objectives, presents the overall time frame
  within which it must work, and clarifies the scope and available
  resources. The charter serves to keep the project team on track
  as the effort moves forward and to help the various players
  resolve disagreements about resources, schedule, and other
  matters.

- **Operational mechanisms.** You increase the odds of seeing your project move along more smoothly if you establish operational mechanisms early on. These mechanisms clarify how decisions will be made, how project participants will stay informed and in touch, how conflicts will be resolved, and what the budget for the project will look like.

- **Work breakdown.** HR projects vary in terms of their complexity. But all projects become more manageable if you break them into a set of tasks needed to accomplish the initiative's larger objectives. By breaking the work down in this way, you can estimate the time and other resources needed for each task, as well as assign tasks to project participants.

- **Scheduling.** To develop a detailed, informed schedule for your project, you need to determine the relationships between tasks—that is, which tasks must be performed in what sequence in order for the project to succeed? You draft a proposed schedule and revise it with project participants' input. Knowledge of scheduling software can prove valuable at this stage.

- **Adjustments and trade-offs.** All projects require adjustments and trade-offs, as some of the assumptions the participants made early on turn out to be inaccurate. For example, a team determines that it can't deliver the expected outcomes by the deadline requested by the project sponsor. Or the resources the project manager thought would be available won't be there after all. Savvy project managers acknowledge and respond to these challenges promptly—by revisiting the project plan and generating ideas for resolving the challenges. Solutions may include changing project specifications, bringing in new resources or reallocating existing ones, and streamlining tasks.

- **Risks.** All projects have inherent risks: a key member of the project team leaves the company. A supplier handling a crucial task for the project falls behind schedule. The subteam responsible for creating a prototype delivers a faulty device. Effective project managers identify and prioritize the risks inherent in their project, take steps to avoid or minimize the high-priority risks, and develop contingency plans to handle setbacks, should they occur.

- **Iterative project management.** Some risks simply can't be anticipated. These come from new and unfamiliar technologies that you and your team must master quickly, work that you've never done before but must perform, and the sheer magnitude of a first-of-its-kind, large-scale project. To protect your project against risks stemming from these circumstances, use an adaptive, iterative approach: handle small, incremental tasks—evaluating each in real time and making adjustments to the way you handle subsequent tasks. Ensure that your project team members are open to and capable of learning and adapting on the job. Deliver results in small pieces, after each stage of the project. That way, you can gather feedback and use it to handle subsequent deliverables.

- **Essential ingredients.** The most successful project managers incorporate three essential ingredients into their leadership of a project. These ingredients include an official launch meeting to clarify the project charter and introduce project participants to one another; regular communications, meetings, and social gatherings to keep players up to date and connected as a team; and behavioral norms (such as expectations about attendance and guidelines for discussing difficult issues) to which participants adhere.

- **Project control.** As projects move through the execution phase, their managers need to use budgets, quality checks, and milestones to regularly assess progress. These mechanisms can reveal problems early on—when they're much easier to fix than they would be if ignored until later. Controlling your project also involves addressing typical challenges that arise—such as conflicts between team members, unfair distribution of workloads and responsibilities, insufficient skills, delays, and poor quality work. Good communication practices, along with

creative problem solving, can help you keep your project from
derailing.

- **Closedown.** Every project offers valuable opportunities for its
manager and team members to improve their skills while handling subsequent projects. After completing a project, meet
with your team to evaluate what went well, what didn't, and
how you might do things differently next time around. Document lessons learned, decisions made during the project, and
the rationale behind decisions. Other project teams in your
company may find this documentation invaluable if they end
up tackling a similar effort or encounter similar challenges as
those you and your team have dealt with. And of course, don't
forget to celebrate completion of your project with your team:
you'll further strengthen the bonds and team spirit you culti-
vated while working on the project—making it even more
likely that you'll work well together on future efforts.

Learning from Your HR Project Management Experience

Every HR project—no matter how straightforward or manageable—
offers important lessons that you can apply not only to future projects
but also to many other aspects of your job. For example:

- **New software.** By familiarizing yourself with project management software (such as scheduling and budgeting tools), you
can use these applications more easily and effectively on subsequent projects. You may also become more comfortable with
mastering other types of software that make your job more
efficient.

- **Interpersonal skills.** On any project you manage or contribute
to, you work with a diverse group of people—often individuals
from many different functions and units within your company.
These experiences sharpen your interpersonal skills—helping

you negotiate conflict, sell your ideas, build collaboration, and strengthen team effectiveness while handling other aspects of your job.

- **Productive bonds.** When you manage a project, you cultivate productive bonds with others who are supporting or participating in the effort. These bonds have potential future value: perhaps you will work with some or many of these same individuals on future projects. Or maybe you'll report to one or more of these colleagues on subsequent projects they're leading.

- **Self-knowledge.** As you manage projects, you learn more about your strengths and weaknesses and generate ideas for addressing those weaknesses. Many HR practitioners, as a result of managing a particularly challenging project, decide to enroll in a course or get additional training in a particular subject area to strengthen their skills.

- **Company knowledge.** Because HR projects often require cross-functional participation, they expose you to new vistas on the way your company operates. For example, after managing or supporting a number of projects, you may learn that your company tends to operate in crisis mode: it sponsors projects only in response to impending problems rather than proactively defining and launching projects to meet long-term goals. If you discover something like this, you can take steps to help your company adopt a more proactive stance—and hence avoid the expense and chaos of responding only to crises.

    Managing projects also sheds light on how the different parts of your organization work together (e.g., how information flows through the company), how productively leaders from different units collaborate, and where bottlenecks and other problems occur in the company. Knowledge of these matters can help you anticipate potential difficulties you might encounter on future projects—and prepare contingency plans for them.[1]

To capture the lessons offered by the HR projects you're managing, you need to take a disciplined approach. The following practices can help:

- Maintain a notebook or computer file of key insights you gained while managing each project. When you prepare to take on a new project, review your file to see which insights can be applied to the upcoming initiative.

- List all participants in each project, and record their specific skills and capabilities. This information will help you assemble a talented project team for your next endeavor.

- Collect books, audio-visual materials, software, Web site addresses, and any other information resources that proved useful on projects. Some or all of these same resources may be helpful on subsequent projects.

- Cultivate relationships with vendors, consultants, and other outside individuals who played a valuable role in a project. These same individuals may prove useful on additional projects you undertake.

- Nurture your relationships with every project's key stakeholder groups—customers, employees, sponsors, team leaders, managers of related projects, and so forth. These connections will almost certainly help you manage additional projects in the future.[2]

Enhancing Your Project Management Abilities

To further strengthen your project management abilities, you can do more than learn from previous projects. You can also take courses in project management, establish mentoring relationships with colleagues who you know are excellent project managers, and read additional books that focus on specific aspects of project management that you find most challenging.

Of course, experience is always an able teacher. Thus, you can enhance your skills by carefully selecting the projects you get involved in. For example, if you know that you tend to have difficulty with ambiguous and highly complex initiatives, you might seek opportunities to manage more straightforward projects initially—and then take on more complex efforts as your skills and confidence grow. Serving on project teams or subteams can help you master new skills, acquire knowledge, and build confidence so that you can later lead a major initiative.

Everyone learns differently and has different learning needs. How might *you* best enhance your project management skills? Assessment tool 16-1 can help.

Assessment Tool 16-1
Enhancing Your Project Management Skills

Use this worksheet to record your ideas for strengthening your project management skills.

1. **What do you consider your greatest strengths as a project manager? Cite specific projects you've led or supported that reveal specific strengths.**

2. **What do you view as your greatest difficulties as a project manager? Cite specific projects you've led or supported that reveal specific weak areas.**

continued

3. What resources might you draw on to address the weak areas you've identified? Brainstorm as many ideas as possible—including mentors, colleagues, books and articles, courses, insights from past projects, and software tools.

4. For every resource you've identified in question 3, determine how you will use that resource. List your ideas below. For example, if you've identified a peer manager who could help you strengthen a particular project management difficulty you struggle with, write your ideas for how and when you will initiate a mentoring relationship with that person, and how you'll structure your meetings and feedback sessions so as to maximize your knowledge.

5. Based on your knowledge of your project management strengths and weaknesses, identify the types of future projects that you believe will best help you further enhance needed skills.

6. For each of the future projects you identified in question 5, write your ideas for taking on those projects. For example, will you approach the manager of a project you're interested in and ask to become a member of his project team? Will you describe your idea for a project to your CEO and propose that you serve as the project manager while she serves as the sponsor?

7. **What other steps—in addition to those discussed above—might you take to continually enhance your project management skills? List your ideas below.**

Summing Up

In this chapter, you read about the following:

- Highlights of the key principles and practices of project management—such as the overall process of managing projects, the players typically involved, the skills and attitudes needed to manage projects successfully, and so forth.

- Ideas for extracting lessons from your project management experiences and applying them to future projects—for example, identifying resources and individuals who may play a valuable role in subsequent initiatives and maximizing your use of project management software.

- An action-planning worksheet for further enhancing your project management skills.

Leveraging Chapter Insights: Critical Questions

- Think of several HR projects you've managed or supported recently. What do you see as the most important lessons that can be drawn from those experiences? How might you apply those lessons to future projects you manage or contribute to?

- Look again at your responses to assessment tool 16-1. Of the many ideas for enhancing your project management skills, which do you consider the most promising? Why? How might you make those actions a priority in your work?

- Identify a major HR project that you'll soon be leading. What are the one or two changes you could make to your approach to project management to best ensure the effort's success?

APPENDIX A

Implementation Tools

This appendix contains a number of tools that can help you be more effective in forming a team, managing its progress, and handling typical problems. All the forms are adapted from Harvard ManageMentor, an online product of Harvard Business School Publishing.

1. **Defining Your Project (figure A-1).** This form will help you uncover the issues and parameters at the core of your project.

2. **Work Breakdown Structure (figure A-2).** Use this form to develop a work breakdown structure to ensure that you do not overlook a significant part of a complex activity or underestimate the time and money needed to complete the work. Use multiple pages as needed.

3. **Project Progress Report (figure A-3).** Use this form to help assess progress, present information to others, and think through next steps. For the convenience of readers, a downloadable version of this tool can be found on the Harvard Business Essentials series Web site: http://elearning.hbsp.org/businesstools.

Defining your project

UNCOVER THE ISSUES AND PARAMETERS AT THE CORE OF YOUR PROJECT.

The "real" project
What is the perceived need or purpose for what we are trying to do?
What caused people to see this as a problem that needed to be solved?
What criteria are people going to use to judge this project a success?

The stakeholders
Who has a stake in the solution or outcome?
How do the various stakeholders' goals for the project differ?
What functions or people might the project's activities or outcomes affect?
Who is going to contribute resources (people, space, time, tools, money)?

Skills required for the project	
Skill needed	Possible team member
1.	1.
2.	2.
3.	3.
4.	4.
5.	5.
6.	6.

Source: Harvard ManageMentor on Project Management (Boston: Harvard Business School Publishing, 2002), 50. Used with permission.

FIGURE A-2

Work breakdown structure

Describe the overall project:			
Major task	**Level 1 subtasks**	**Level 2 subtasks**	**Level 2 subtask duration**
Total duration (hours/weeks/days)			
Major task	**Level 1 subtasks**	**Level 2 subtasks**	**Level 2 subtask duration**
Total duration (hours/weeks/days)			

Source: Harvard ManageMentor on Project Management (Boston: Harvard Business School Publishing, 2002), 51. Used with permission.

282   Appendix A

FIGURE A-3

Project progress report

Project: **Prepared by:**

For the period from: **To:**

Current status

Key milestones for this period:

Achieved (list)	Coming up next (list)

Key issues or problems:

Resolved (list)	Need to be resolved (list)

Key decisions:

Made (list)	Need to be made (list)	By whom	When

Budget status:

Implications

List changes in objectives, time line/delivery dates, project scope, and resource allocation (including people and financial).

Next steps

List the specific action steps that will be done to help move this project forward successfully. Put a name and date next to each step if possible.

Step	Person responsible	Date

Comments:

Source: Harvard ManageMentor on Project Management (Boston: Harvard Business School Publishing, 2002), 52. Used with permission.

A Guide to Effective Meetings

Meetings are a fact of life in most organizational work, and equally so with projects. Because they are so frequent and so important, it's in the project's interests to make those meetings as effective as possible. You can conduct effective meetings if you pay attention to these key aspects of meetings: preparation, the meeting process itself, and follow-up. This guide is adapted from Harvard ManageMentor, an online product of Harvard Business School Publishing.

Be Prepared

You've undoubtedly attended meetings for which there was little or no preparation. Did those meetings accomplish anything? Probably not. In some cases, the purpose of the meeting was unclear from the beginning. In others, one or more of the people needed to make a decision didn't receive an invitation. You can avoid such mistakes by following these commonsense rules:

- **Make sure that your meetings are necessary.** Meetings eat up time for everyone at the table. If you can accomplish your objective without calling a meeting, do so.

- **Clarify every meeting's objective.** Every attendee should be able to answer this question: why am I here? If the objective is to make a decision, be sure that everyone understands this in advance, and that team members have the time and materials needed to prepare.

- **Involve the right people.** Invite only those who have some-thing to contribute, whose participation is necessary, or who can learn from the discussion.

- **Provide an agenda in advance.** An agenda indirectly identifies the meeting's objective.

- **Sound out key participants in advance.** You'll be better prepared for a meeting if you know in advance what key par-ticipants think about important items on the agenda. What you learn may suggest an alteration in the agenda.

- **Insist that people be prepared.** This means being up to speed on the issues; bringing relevant documents, reports, or physical objects; and being ready to contribute to the discussion and a decision.

During the Meeting

Good preparation will set you up for this second stage. Here you should:

- **State the meeting's purpose.** Even though you said it already when you invited people to the meeting, it's always smart to reiterate the meeting's purpose.

- **Let everyone have a say.** If one or two individuals are domi-nating the conversation, or if certain attendees are shy about leaping in, say, "Thanks for those ideas, Phil. What are your thoughts about this problem, Charlotte?"

- **Keep the discussion from wandering.** Meetings that wander off the key issues quickly degenerate into time-wasting gab sessions.

- **End with confirmation and an action plan.** Your meeting should transition to some action. "OK, we've decided to hire DataWhack to install the new servers. And, as agreed, I will obtain the purchase order, Bill will phone the salesperson and set up the schedule, and Janet will begin looking for someone to take the old equipment off our hands."

Follow-Up

Once a meeting is over, we're all tempted to relax and say, "I'm glad that's over with." But it isn't over if you led the meeting or agreed to accept responsibility for actions resulting from it.

The meeting leader should rapidly follow up with a quick memo in the same spirit as this one:

From: Gayle

To: The HRIS Project Team

Thanks for your contributions to this morning's meeting. We have selected BizView as the provider for our new information system software platform. I view this as a good choice and a decision that moves us one step closer to the completion of our project. The action steps from this decision are as follows:

- *I will obtain the purchase order.*

- *Bill will contact BizView's salesperson about the schedule.*

- *Janet will begin looking for someone to conduct the training on the new system.*

Let's complete these chores within the next two weeks. Then we can get on to the next scheduled task.

This type of follow-up memo encourages people by saying that they are one step closer to their goal, and it reminds certain attendees about the action steps to which they have agreed.

Notes

Chapter 1

1. Wayne Brockbank and Dave Ulrich, *Competencies for the New HR* (Society for Human Resource Management [SHRM], Michigan Business School, and Global Consulting Alliance, 2003), 32–37, 47, 64.

2. Gary R. Heerkens, *Project Management* (New York: McGraw-Hill, 2002), 3.

3. Ibid., 36–43.

Chapter 2

1. Lynda M. Applegate, Robert D. Austin, and F. Warren McFarlan, *Corporate Information Strategy and Management*, 6th ed. (Burr Ridge, IL: McGraw-Hill/Irwin, 2002), 278.

2. *Managing Projects Large and Small* (Boston: Harvard Business School Press, 2004).

3. Gregory H. Watson, *Strategic Benchmarking* (New York: John Wiley & Sons, Inc., 1993), 114–115.

4. For a discussion of heavyweight and lightweight leaders and core teams, see Steven C. Wheelwright and Kim B. Clark, *Leading Product Development* (New York: Free Press, 1995), 81–85.

Chapter 3

1. Richard Leifer et al., *Radical Innovation* (Boston: Harvard Business School Press, 2000), 163.

2. Jeffrey T. Polzer, "Leading Teams," Class Note N9-403-094 (Boston: Harvard Business School Publishing, 2002), 7.

3. Jon R. Katzenbach and Douglas K. Smith, "The Discipline of Teams," *Harvard Business Review*, March–April 1993, 118.

4. The essential characteristics listed here are largely drawn from two important trains of thought on teams. Competence and commitment to a common goal reflect the work of Jon R. Katzenbach and Douglas K. Smith, whose popular book *The Wisdom of Teams* appeared in 1993, published by Harvard Business School Press (HBSP). J. Richard Hackman is the source for two other key characteristics of team success: an enabling structure and a supportive environment. Hackman's *Leading Teams*, also published by HBSP, was released in 2002. For other important ideas about teams and their management, see the list of books and articles in "For Further Reading" at the end of this book.

5. For a discussion of heavyweight teams and team leaders, see Steven C. Wheelwright and Kim B. Clark, *Leading Product Development* (New York: Free Press, 1995), 81–85.

Chapter 4

1. J. Richard Hackman, *Leading Teams* (Boston: Harvard Business School Press, 2002), 83.

2. Ibid., 74.

Chapter 5

1. Thomas J. Allen, "Communication Networks in R&D Labs," *R&D Management* 1, (1971): 14–21.

2. Marc H. Meyer and Alvin P. Lehnerd, *The Power of Product Platforms* (New York: Free Press, 1997), 137.

Chapter 10

1. Robert D. Austin, "Project Management and Discovery," *Science's* Next Wave, September 12, 2002, http://nextwave.sciencemag.org/cgi/content/full/2002/09/10/4.

2. See Robert D. Austin, "The Effects of Time Pressure on Quality in Software Development: An Agency Model," *Information Systems Research* 12, no. 2 (2001): 195–207.

3. Lynda M. Applegate, Robert D. Austin, and F. Warren McFarlan, *Corporate Information Strategy and Management,* 6th ed. (Burr Ridge, IL: McGraw-Hill/Irwin, 2002), 269–270.

4. Robert D. Austin, "Project Management and Discovery."

Chapter 11

1. Jon R. Katzenbach and Douglas K. Smith, "The Discipline of Teams," *Harvard Business Review*, March–April 1993, 118.

2. Ibid.

Chapter 12

1. Jeffrey T. Polzer, "Leading Teams," Class Note N9-403-094 (Boston: Harvard Business School Publishing, 2002), 15.

Chapter 13

1. Frank R. Gulliver, "Post-Project Appraisals Pay," *Harvard Business Review*, March–April 1987, 128–130.

Chapter 14

1. SHRM, "HR Department Start-Up Toolkit," http://www.shrm.org/ hrtools/toolkits_published/CMS_008099.asp.

2. Unless noted otherwise, content in this list was adapted from Nina Drake, "Setting Up an HR Department in a Small Company," SHRM White Paper, September 1996.

3. As suggested by William G. Bliss in Lin Grensing-Pophal, *Human Resource Essentials: Your Guide to Starting and Running the HR Function* (Alexandria, VA: SHRM, 2002), 16.

4. Ibid.

5. Ibid.

6. Ibid., 7–8.

7. This section draws extensively from Teresa A. Daniel, "HR Compliance Audits: 'Just Nice' or Really Necessary?" SHRM White Paper, November 2004.

8. This and other comments attributed to Ronald Adler come from a telephone interview by Lauren Keller Johnson, July 15, 2005.

9. Dale Scharinger, "Preparation of the Employee Handbook," SHRM White Paper, November 1996.

10. Maurice Baskin, "Is It Time to Revise Your Employee Handbook?" SHRM Legal Report, Summer 1998.

11. These and other comments attributed to Michael Lotito were obtained during a phone interview by Lauren Keller Johnson, August 9, 2005.

12. Scharinger, "Preparation of the Employee Handbook."

13. Ibid.

14. Ibid.

15. Ibid.

16. Baskin, "Is It Time to Revise Your Employee Handbook?"

17. Ibid.

18. Unless noted otherwise, content in this list was adapted from Rick Galbreath, "Profiting Through Employee Orientation," SHRM White Paper, March 2002.

19. Christina Morfeld, "Focus Remains on New Hires During Effective Employee Orientations," SHRM Employment Management Association Forum, http://www.shrm.org/hrtools/toolkits_published/CMS_010201.asp.

20. Ibid.

21. Ibid.

22. Nancy Nelson and Carolyn Sperl, "The Buddy System and New Hire Orientation," SHRM White Paper, July 2004.

23. Morfeld, "Focus Remains on New Hires During Effective Employee Orientations."

24. This section draws heavily from comments made by Donna Horkey in a telephone interview by Lauren Keller Johnson, July 18, 2005.

25. Steven J. Gara, "How an HRIS Can Impact HR: A Complete Paradigm Shift for the 21st Century," SHRM White Paper, November 2001.

26. Donna L. Keener, "Preparing a Business Case for a Human Resources Management System," SHRM White Paper, January 2002.

27. SHRM, "Good Planning, Realistic Scope, and Executive Sponsorship Important in HRIS Projects" SHRM HR Technology X-Change Forum, http://www.shrm.org/hrtx/library_published/nonIC/CMS_006631.asp.

28. Tricia A. Danielsen and Stephanie V. Stagnitta, "Questions to Ask Before Deploying Expatriates," SHRM Global Forum, http://www.shrm.org/global/library_published/subject/nonIC/CMS_009571.asp.

29. Ibid., and Siobhan Cummins and Meredith Lohbeck, "New Trends in Short-Term Assignments," SHRM Global Forum, http://www.shrm.org/global/library_published/subject/nonIC/CMS_008456.asp.

30. Kathy Gurchiek, "Record Growth Seen in Outsourcing of HR Functions," *HR News*, April 20, 2005.

31. Terence F. Shea, "Experts: Partnerships Pave Way to Outsourcing Success," SHRM Consultants Forum, http://www.shrm.org/consultants/library_published/nonIC/CMS_009921.asp.

32. Gurchiek, "Record Growth Seen in Outsourcing of HR Functions."

33. Ibid.

34. Stephen Miller, "Outsourcing: Start Off Right," SHRM HR Technology X-Change Forum, http://www.shrm.org/consultants/library_published/nonIC/CMS_008847.asp.

35. All comments attributed to Melanie Young come from a telephone interview by Lauren Keller Johnson, July 18, 2005.

36. All comments attributed to Scott Gildner come from a telephone interview by Lauren Keller Johnson, August 22, 2005.

37. All comments attributed to Mary F. Cook come from written notes prepared and submitted by Cook on July 20, 2005.

38. Gurchiek, "Record Growth Seen in Outsourcing of HR Functions."

39. Miller, "Outsourcing."

40. Shea, "Experts."

41. Miller, "Outsourcing."

42. Mikio Manuel, "How to Calculate and Maximize Outsourcing ROI," SHRM HR Technology X-Change Forum, http://www.shrm.org/hrtx/library_published/nonIC/CMS_006564.asp.

43. Gurchiek, "Record Growth Seen in Outsourcing of HR Functions."

44. Shea, "Experts."

45. Ibid.

46. Julie Britt, "How to Get Executive Approval for HR Projects," *HR News*, October 9, 2003.

Chapter 15

1. Philip S. Deming, "Crisis Management Planning: A Human Resource Challenge," SHRM White Paper, April 2002.

2. Gregory P. Smith, "Leading Employees in Times of Crisis," SHRM White Paper, October 2001.

3. Linda S. Johnson, "The Human Resource Perspective in Mergers and Acquisitions: Non-Benefits Issues," SHRM Legal Report, July 2000.

4. Dennis L. Roberts, "The Role of Human Resources in Mergers and Acquisitions," SHRM White Paper, January 2002.

5. Wayne F. Cascio, *Responsible Restructuring: Creative and Profitable Alternatives to Layoffs* (San Francisco: Berrett-Koehler Publishers, Inc. and Alexandria, VA: SHRM, 2002), 100–105.

6. Phyllis G. Hartman and John T. Hayden, "Creating a Positive Culture," SHRM White Paper, March 2005, 1.

7. Ibid., 2.

8. Ibid.

9. Ibid., 4.

10. This section draws substantially from the "Measuring Business Performance" topic of Harvard ManageMentor, available online at http://elearning.hbsp.org.

Chapter 16

1. Jeff Davidson, *10 Minute Guide to Project Management* (Indianapolis: Alpha Books, 2000), chap. 14.

2. Ibid.

Glossary

BOTTLENECK   Any task on the critical path that causes the work feeding it to pile up.

BUDGET   The translation of plans into measurable expenditures and anticipated returns over a certain period of time.

CHARTER   A concise written description of the project's intended work. The charter may contain the name of the sponsor, a timetable, a description of deliverables, the benefits to the company, and a budget.

COACHING   A two-way activity in which the parties share knowledge and experience in order to maximize a team member's potential and help him or her achieve agreed-upon goals. It is a shared effort in which the person being coached participates actively and willingly.

CONTINGENCY PLAN   A course of action prepared in advance of a potential problem; it answers this question: "If X happens, how can we respond in an effective way?"

CRITICAL PATH METHOD   A planning technique used for complex projects that consist of several individual activities. If one or more of the activities need to be completed before others can move forward, then those activities are called "critical"—and necessary for the on-time success of the project. The total duration of the project is defined by the critical path.

FINISH-TO-START   A task relationship in which one task must finish before the other can begin.

GANTT CHART   A bar chart with tasks listed in the left-hand column and fitted into appropriate time blocks. These blocks indicate when a task should begin, based on task relationships, and when it should end.

INTERPERSONAL SKILL   The ability to work effectively with others—a very important trait for team-based work.

LAGGING   A task relationship in which one task must await the start and partial completion of another.

NETWORK DIAGRAM   A scheduling chart that reveals all the dependent relationships between tasks. It also reveals the critical path. Generally synonymous with a PERT chart.

ORGANIZATIONAL SKILL   The ability to communicate with other units, knowledge of the political landscape of the company, and possession of a network.

PERFORMANCE EVALUATION AND REVIEW TECHNIQUE (PERT)   A scheduling method that, when charted, represents every task as a node that connects with other nodes required to complete the project. A PERT chart may have many parallel or interconnecting networks of tasks so that periodic reviews are encouraged for complex projects. Unlike the Gantt chart, it indicates all the important task relationships and project milestones.

PROBLEM-SOLVING SKILL   An individual's ability to analyze difficult situations or impasses and to craft solutions.

PROJECT   A set of activities that (1) aims to produce a unique deliverable (i.e., a new commercial airframe) and (2) is time bound within a clear beginning and ending point.

PROJECT MANAGEMENT   The allocation, tracking, and utilization of resources to achieve a particular objective within a specified period of time.

PROJECT MANAGER   The individual charged with planning and scheduling project tasks and with day-to-day management of project execution.

PROJECT STEERING COMMITTEE   A project entity that approves the project charter, secures resources, and adjudicates all requests to change key project elements, including deliverables, schedule, and budget.

PROJECT TEAM   A team organized around a nonroutine task of limited duration.

RISK MANAGEMENT   The part of the project planning process that identifies the key risks and develops plans to prevent them and/or mitigate the adverse effects of their occurrence.

SPONSOR   A manager or executive who has a stake in a team's outcome and the authority to define and approve its work.

STAKEHOLDER   Anyone who has a vested interest in the outcome of a project, who will judge a project's success or failure.

STEERING COMMITTEE   See *project steering committee.*

TEAM ROOM   A physical space dedicated to project team work. The team room is used for meetings, informal gatherings, and the display and storage of artifacts and documents that are central to the team's mission.

TECHNICAL SKILL   Specific expertise—in market research, finance, software programming, and so forth. Usually acquired through special training or education.

VARIANCE   The difference between actual results and expected results in the budget. Variance can be favorable or unfavorable. Managers use variance to spot sources of trouble and exceptional performance.

WORK BREAKDOWN STRUCTURE (WBS)   A planning routine that decomposes a project's goal into the many tasks required to achieve it. The time and money needed to complete those tasks are then estimated.

For Further Reading

Notes and Articles

Britt, Julie. "How to Get Executive Approval for HR Projects." *HR News*, October 9, 2003. Britt explains how to build a compelling case for an HR project you want to sponsor or manage. She defines typical roadblocks to winning approval for your project—such as lack of clear financial benefits, competing initiatives, and insufficient funds—and describes ways to surmount them.

Daniel, Teresa A. "HR Compliance Audits: 'Just Nice' or Really Necessary?" SHRM White Paper, November 2004. This comprehensive document defines HR compliance audits and explains how to manage an audit project—including determining the project scope, developing the audit questionnaire, collecting data, and benchmarking your findings. Daniel offers additional suggestions for saving money on an audit project, safeguarding audit results, and achieving other successful outcomes.

Danielsen, Tricia A. and Stephanie V. Stagnitta. "Questions to Ask Before Deploying Expatriates." SHRM Global Forum Library. Managing an expatriation project requires careful attention to numerous factors. The authors provide suggestions for clarifying the purpose of the project, analyzing the situation into which overseas assignees will be entering, assessing assignees' skills and attitudes to match the right individuals with the right assignments, and conducting cost-benefit analysis of overseas assignments.

Deming, Philip S. "Crisis Management Planning: A Human Resource Challenge." SHRM White Paper, April 2002. Deming describes steps for orchestrating development of a crisis management plan—including conducting a risk assessment, identifying valuable resources that could be available on short notice (such as plumbing contractors), preparing a written protocol, reviewing your plan, and communicating the plan to your workforce.

Drake, Nina. "Setting Up an HR Department in a Small Company." SHRM White Paper, September 1996. This concise guide lists the considerations to keep in mind while establishing a new HR department—a project that you may well find yourself managing at some point in your career. Drake describes numerous essential project tasks you and your project team will need to coordinate—such as reviewing existing personnel files, creating an employee handbook, deciding how payroll and benefits will be processed, designing a compensation system, and ensuring legal compliance.

Gara, Steven. J. "How an HRIS Can Impact HR: A Complete Paradigm Shift for the 21st Century." SHRM White Paper, November 2001. Gara explains what an HRIS is, what it comprises, and how HR professionals can most effectively help their companies develop and implement an HRIS that suits the organization's needs. Project management strategies include educating management and staff on the benefits of an HRIS, conducting a needs analysis, selecting and testing system modules, selecting vendors, and managing costs.

Gulliver, Frank R. "Post-Project Appraisals Pay." *Harvard Business Review,* March–April 1987. BP began operating a postproject appraisal unit—a team of inside analysts and investigators who scrutinized projects several years after they had been completed to learn why they succeeded or misfired. The author explains how the appraisal process has helped managers be more accurate in developing project proposals and more efficient in implementing them. He also indicates that every BP project generated a return on investment at least as high as that in the project's forecast.

Hartman, Phyllis G., and John T. Hayden. "Creating a Positive Culture." SHRM White Paper, March 2005. As an HR professional, you will likely need to manage projects aimed at improving your organization's culture to meet strategic objectives. Hartman and Hayden explain how to handle a cultural change initiative effectively. Their suggestions include understanding the defining characteristics of a positive culture, facilitating the selection and development of leaders and employees who personify the desired culture, and designing reward and training systems to support the behaviors and attitudes necessary for a more productive culture.

Harvard Business School Publishing. *Project Management Manual.* Boston: Harvard Business School Publishing, 2002. A brief primer on getting a project organized and managing it to completion.

Keener, Donna L., Diane Heard, and Michelle Morgan. "Implementing a Human Resources System: Lessons Learned." SHRM White Paper, February 2000. This paper offers additional suggestions for successfully managing implementation of an HRIS—including how to assemble your project teams, how to avoid scope creep, and how to bring the project to completion on time and within budget. Additional suggestions cover maintaining team spirit, managing internal customers' expectations, and deciding how much to customize technology provided by software vendors.

Manuel, Mikio. "How to Calculate and Maximize Outsourcing ROI," SHRM HR Technology X-Change Forum Library. This handy resource shows you step-by-step how to calculate the return on outsourcing one or more HR processes. By demonstrating a healthy return on a proposed outsourcing project, you stand a good chance of winning support for the project from the rest of the executive team.

Nelson, Nancy, and Carolyn Sperl. "The Buddy System and New Hire Orientation." SHRM White Paper, July 2004. Setting up a mentoring program is a demanding project. Nelson and Sperl explain how to boost your odds of success—including matching mentors to protégés and clarifying the mentoring role.

Pinto, Jeffrey K., and Om P. Kharbanda. "How to Fail in Project Management (Without Really Trying)." *Business Horizons*, July–August 1996, 45–53. Project management techniques are widely accepted as a means of expediting product development, making efficient use of resources, and stimulating cross-functional communication. Not only manufacturing firms but also legal offices, hospitals, and local governments have accepted project management as an indispensable part of their operations. Yet failures and outright disasters abound. A study of these unsuccessful attempts by these authors indicates a dozen surefire methods for dooming a project.

Roberts, Dennis L. "The Role of Human Resources in Mergers and Acquisitions." SHRM White Paper, January 2002. You can be fairly confident that you'll need to support a merger or acquisition (M&A) project at some point in your career—whether your company is acquiring another or is being acquired. In both situations, you can help ensure the project's success in numerous ways. Roberts explains how—by laying out the stages of an M&A project and describing HR's unique contributions at each stage.

Scharinger, Dale. "Preparation of the Employee Handbook." SHRM White Paper, November 1996. Successfully managing development of your company's employee handbook can generate important benefits for your organization—such as orienting new hires to your firm's culture, mission, and strategy; clarifying employer and employee responsibilities; and ensuring that workers understand company policies and procedures. Scharinger explains how to manage preparation and use of this vital document—including guidelines for achieving the appropriate writing style, deciding how much detail to include, and handling disclaimers.

Smith, Gregory P. "Leading Employees in Times of Crisis." SHRM White Paper, October 2001. As part of leading the development of a crisis management plan, you'll need to define principles and practices for managing employees' emotions after a crisis. Smith provides helpful advice—such as keeping lines of communication open, letting people know it's OK to cry, conveying calm, and helping people regain a sense of control.

"What You Can Learn from Professional Project Managers," *Harvard Management Update,* February 2001. Companies that manage large-capital projects or a multitude of simultaneous projects have long recognized the need for expertise in the techniques of planning, scheduling, and controlling work. But over the past decade, non-project-driven firms— especially those that see themselves as selling solutions rather than products—have seen the light too. As a result, project management has become increasingly important and complex. This article outlines how companies can benefit from the professionalism of the field.

Books

Crisis Management: Master the Skills to Prevent Disasters. Harvard Business Essentials. Boston: Harvard Business School Press, 2004. This volume offers help for dealing with numerous project management challenges associated with developing crisis management programs. Such challenges include preparing your company for crises, enabling people to recognize crises when they occur, developing contingency plans, and applying lessons learned from past crises to future crises.

Frame, J. Davidson. *The Project Management Competence: Building Key Skills for Individual, Teams, and Organizations.* San Francisco: Jossey-Bass, 1999. Like other management arts, effective project management requires skill at the individual, team, and organizational levels. This book shows how project management skill at those levels dovetails to achieve successful outcomes. It explains the competencies needed by project managers and how they must be supported by the larger organization.

Grensing-Pophal, Lin. *Human Resource Essentials: Your Guide to Starting and Running the HR Function.* Alexandria, VA: SHRM, 2002. Establishing a new HR department and getting it up to speed may be one of the more challenging HR projects you'll encounter during your career. This book guides you through the process—offering advice for handling start-up, staffing plans, recruiting, hiring, training and development, and many other HR responsibilities. The author provides a wealth of sample forms and reports, a summary of federal laws, and other helpful tools. This resource includes contributions from HR and management experts such as Wendy Bliss, John Drake, Sharon Jordan-Evans, and Beverly Kaye.

Harvard ManageMentor on Project Management. Boston: Harvard Business School Press, 2002. Project management is the ultimate juggling act, involving the use of sometimes scarce resources like people, time, and money to meet a goal or solve a problem. This essential guide shows you how to scope out a project, develop schedules, set deadlines, manage and monitor progress, and overcome some typical project snags, such as mission creep and schedule slippage. It also covers the four phases—planning, buildup, implementation, and phaseout—and the tasks associated with each. Written in an engaging style designed for easy scanning, the guide is packed with advice, tips, worksheets, and more to help you become a more efficient and effective multitasker.

Huselid, Mark A., Brian E. Becker, and Richard W. Beatty. *The Workforce Scorecard: Managing Human Capital to Execute Strategy.* Boston: Harvard Business School Press, 2005. Realigning your company's performance management system can be a particularly daunting project. The authors provide help in the form of suggestions for selecting performance metrics, translating metrics into specific actions and accountabilities, clarifying performance expectations, and designing compensation and incentive systems. As the book makes clear, when your company's performance management system aligns behind your company's strategy, employees at all levels know precisely what they must do to excel and generate value.

Kerzner, Harold. *Applied Project Management: Best Practices on Implementation.* New York: John Wiley & Sons, Inc., 2000. This book offers commentaries from managers on their decision-making processes, including their successes and failures, in project management implementation. Twenty-five case studies highlight important project management issues, problems, and their solutions. Also included are commentaries on benchmarked best practices.

Mingus, Nancy. *Alpha Teach Yourself Project Management in 24 Hours.* Indianapolis: Alpha Books, 2002. A step-by-step guide of twenty-four lessons for building and managing a project.

Schmaltz, David A. *The Blind Man and the Elephant.* San Francisco: Berrett-Koehler Publishers, Inc., 2003. Using the familiar metaphor of six blind men who fail to describe an elephant to each other, this author seeks out the cause of difficulties in project work. That cause, in his finding, is the inability of a group of coworkers to create common meaning from their common project experience.

Schmidt, Jeffrey A. *Making Mergers Work: The Strategic Importance of People.* Stamford: Towers Perrin and Alexandria: SHRM, 2002. This book contains the detailed results of a survey of more than 450 HR executives on the challenges inherent in a merger and acquisition project—and an array of suggestions for surmounting those challenges. You'll read about the stages of the M&A life cycle—such as pre-deal, due diligence, integration planning, and implementation—and ways in which you can support those stages to ensure that the merger or acquisition delivers on its promise.

Additional Titles from the Society for Human Resource Management (SHRM)®

Carrig, Ken, and Patrick M. Wright. *Building Profit through Building People: Making Your Workforce the Strongest Link in the Value-Profit Chain*

Collier, T. O., Jr. *Supervisor's Guide to Labor Relations*

Cook, Mary, and Scott Gildner. *Outsourcing Human Resources Functions: How, Why, When, and When Not to Contract for HR Services*

Gardenswartz, Lee, and Anita Rowe. *Diverse Teams at Work*

Grensing-Pophal, Lin, SPHR. *Human Resource Essentials: Your Guide to Starting and Running the HR Function*

Landry, R.J. *The Comprehensive, All-in-One HR Operating Guide.* 539 ready-to-adapt human resources policies, practices, letters, memos, forms . . . and more.

HR Source Book Series

Bliss, Wendy, JD, SPHR, and Gene Thornton, Esq., PHR. *Employment Termination Source Book*

Deblieux, Mike. *Performance Appraisal Source Book*

Fyock, Cathy, CSP, SPHR. *Hiring Source Book*

Hubbartt, William S., SPHR, CCP. *HIPAA Privacy Source Book*

Lambert, Jonamay, MA, and Selma Myers, MA. *Trainer's Diversity Source Book*

Practical HR Series

Bliss, Wendy, JD, SPHR. *Legal, Effective References: How to Give and Get Them*

Oppenheimer, Amy, JD, and Craig Pratt, MSW, SPHR. *Investigating Workplace Harassment: How to Be Fair, Thorough, and Legal*

Phillips, Jack J., PhD, and Patricia Pulliam Phillips, PhD. *Proving the Value of HR: How and Why to Measure ROI*

Shaw, Seyfarth, LLP. *Understanding the Federal Wage & Hour Laws: What Employers Must Know about FLSA and Its Overtime Regulations*

How to Order from SHRM

SHRM offers a member discount on all books that it publishes or sells. To order this or any other book published by the Society, contact the SHRM-Store.®

Online: www.shrm.org/shrmstore

Phone: 1-800-444-5006 (option #1); or 770-442-8633 (ext. 362); or tdd 703-548-6999

Fax: 770-442-9742

Mail: SHRM Distribution Center, P.O. Box 930132, Atlanta, GA 31193-0132, USA

Index

accountability
  of project managers, 43
  of team members, 60
action orientation, 165
adaptation. *See* changes to projects
adaptive management approach,
    151–157
adjustments and trade-offs,
    123–132, 270
  challenging assumptions and,
    126–129
  with deliverables, 128–129
  to tasks and times, 129–131
Adler, Ronald, 208–209, 210
agendas, for meetings, 284
Agilent Technologies, 252–253
agility, 95
alignment, 43, 63–66
  cultural change and, 255
  performance appraisal and,
    258–264
Allen, Tom, 92
ambiguity. *See also* risk manage-
    ment
  over objectives, 72
Anderson, Barbara, 220
Applegate, Lynda, 30, 152
Arrow Electronics, 232
assessment tools, for project
    managers, 13–24

assumptions, 103, 126–129, 195
attendance policies, 89–90, 164
attitude, 49, 165
audits
  culture, 254
  legal compliance, 6, 208–211
  risk, 136–137
Austin, Robert, 30, 32, 95, 149,
    152
  on the adaptive approach,
    153–155
authority
  in charters, 71
  decision making, 81–82
  of project managers, 43–44, 45
  of project sponsors, 40
  responsibility vs., 11
  of steering committees, 41
automakers' vehicle platform
    project, 150–151

Balanced Scorecard system,
    261–264
Baldrige National Quality Pro-
    gram, 260–261
behavior
  modeling, 46–47, 255
  norms for, 163–168, 180–181
benchmarking, 209

About the Series Adviser

WENDY BLISS, J.D., SPHR, has experience as a human resource executive, attorney, senior editor, and professional speaker. Since 1994, she has provided human resource consulting, corporate training, and coaching services nationally through her Colorado Springs–based consulting firm, Bliss & Associates.

Ms. Bliss is the author of *Legal, Effective References: How to Give and Get Them*, the coauthor of *The Employment Termination Source Book: A Collection of Practical Samples*, and a contributor to *Human Resource Essentials*, all published by the Society for Human Resource Management. She has published numerous articles in magazines and periodicals, including *HR Magazine, Employment Management Today, HR Matters,* and the *Denver University Law Review.*

Ms. Bliss received a B.A. degree 'With Highest Distinction' from the University of Kansas and a J.D. degree from the University of Denver College of Law. She is certified as a Senior Professional in Human Resources by the Human Resource Certification Institute. Since 1999, she has conducted human resource certificate programs for the Society for Human Resource Management. Previously, she was an adjunct faculty member at the University of Colorado at Colorado Springs and at the University of Phoenix, where she taught graduate and undergraduate courses in human resource management, employment law, organizational behavior, and business communications. Additionally, Ms. Bliss has served on the board of directors for several professional associations and nonprofit organizations and was a President of the National

Board of Governors for the Society for Human Resource Management's Consultants Forum.

National media, including *ABC News, Time* magazine, the *New York Times,* the Associated Press, the *Washington Post,* USAToday .com, and *HR Magazine,* have looked to Ms. Bliss for expert opinions on workplace issues.

About the Subject Adviser

ROBERT D. AUSTIN is a member of the technology and operations management faculty at the Harvard Business School. His extensive experience managing real projects came as an executive in a new business that was created by a prominent technology firm and also during ten years at the Ford Motor Company.

Professor Austin's research focuses on management of nonrepetitive, knowledge-intensive activities and on information technology management. He is the author of four books: *Artful Making: What Managers Need to Know About How Artists Work* (coauthored with Lee Devin, 2003), *Corporate Information Strategy and Management* (coauthored with Lynda M. Applegate and F. Warren McFarlan, 2002), *Creating Business Advantage in the Information Age* (also coauthored with Applegate and McFarlan, 2002), and *Measuring and Managing Performance in Organizations* (1996).

About the Writers

LAUREN KELLER JOHNSON has contributed to numerous volumes in the Business Literacy for HR Professionals series. Based in Harvard, Massachusetts, Keller Johnson writes for a variety of business publications, including the *Harvard Business Review* OnPoint Series, *Harvard Management Update, Contingent Workforce Strategies, Sloan Management Review,* the *Balanced Scorecard Report,* and *Supply Chain Strategy.* She has written numerous modules for Harvard Business School Publishing's online instructional series Harvard ManageMentor, Case in Point, and Stepping Up to Management, as well as online training modules for the Balanced Scorecard Collaborative. She has a master's degree in technical and professional writing from Northeastern University.

RICHARD LUECKE is the writer of several books in the Harvard Business Essentials series. Based in Salem, Massachusetts, Luecke has authored or developed more than thirty books and dozens of articles on a wide range of business subjects. He has an M.B.A. from the University of St. Thomas.

About the Society for Human Resource Management

THE SOCIETY FOR HUMAN RESOURCE MANAGEMENT (SHRM) is the world's largest association devoted to human resource management. Representing more than 170,000 individual members, the Society has a mission to serve the needs of HR professionals by providing the most essential and comprehensive resources available. As an influential voice, the Society has also defined a mission to advance the human resource profession to ensure that HR is recognized as an essential partner in developing and executing organizational strategy. Visit SHRM Online at www.shrm.org.

Acknowledgments

The writers and adviser would like to thank the talented HR professionals and experts in a wide range of fields who agreed to share their expertise and offer insights and recommendations from their experiences. Their contributions have helped make this book particularly valuable. They are:

- Ronald Adler, president and CEO, Laurdan Associates, Inc., Potomac, Maryland

- Kenneth Carrig, chief administrative officer, SYSCO, Houston, Texas

- Wayne F. Cascio, professor of management, University of Colorado, Denver, Colorado

- Mary F. Cook, president, Mary Cook & Associates, Chicago, Illinois

- Scott Gildner, founder, Gildner & Associates; partner and managing director of HR advisory services at TPI, Inc., Houston, Texas

- John Hayden, vice president and chief learning officer, Henry Ford Health System, Detroit, Michigan

- Donna L. Horkey, PHR, founder, Missing Link Consultants, Inc., Plantation, Florida

- Michael Lotito, Esq., partner, Jackson Lewis, San Francisco, California

- Ronald McKinley, Ph.D., SPHR, vice president, human resources, Cincinnati Children's Hospital Medical Center, Cincinnati, Ohio

- Lorraine Mixon-Paige, manager, human resources, Missouri Consolidated Health Care Plan, Jefferson City, Missouri

- Melanie Young, SPHR, vice president, corporate HR and global services, Arrow Electronics, Melville, New York

The Results-Driven Manager

The Results-Driven Manager series collects timely articles from Harvard Management Update and Harvard Management Communication Letter to help senior to middle managers sharpen their skills, increase their effectiveness, and gain a competitive edge. Presented in a concise, accessible format to save managers valuable time, these books offer authoritative insights and techniques for improving job performance and achieving immediate results.

These books are priced at $14.95 U.S.
Price subject to change.

How to Order

Harvard Business School Press publications are available worldwide from your local bookseller or online retailer.
You can also call

1-800-668-6780

Our product consultants are available to help you
8:00 a.m.–6:00 p.m., Monday–Friday, Eastern Time.
Outside the U.S. and Canada, call: 617-783-7450
Please call about special discounts for quantities greater than ten.

You can order online at

www.HBSPress.org